C000051592

Suffolk
County Council

Please return/renew this item
by the last date shown.

Suffolk Libraries
01473 584563
www.suffolk.gov.uk/libraries/

Through the Barrier

To my dearest wife Terry, without whom
none of this could have been.

Through the Barrier

Flying Fast Jets in the RAF and USAF

Clive Evans

Pen & Sword
AVIATION

First published in Great Britain in 2012 by
Pen & Sword Aviation
an imprint of
Pen & Sword Books Ltd
47 Church Street
Barnsley
South Yorkshire
S70 2AS

Hardback 978-1-84884-754-5

Typeset in 11pt Ehrhardt by
Mac Style, Beverley, E. Yorkshire

Printed and bound in the UK by CPI Group (UK) Ltd, Croydon, CRO 4YY

Pen & Sword Books Ltd incorporates the Imprints of Pen & Sword
Aviation, Pen & Sword Family History, Pen & Sword Maritime, Pen &
Sword Military, Pen & Sword Discovery, Wharncliffe Local History,
Wharncliffe True Crime, Wharncliffe Transport, Pen & Sword Select, Pen
& Sword Military Classics, Leo Cooper, The Praetorian Press, Remember
When, Seaforth Publishing and Frontline Publishing.

For a complete list of Pen & Sword titles please contact

PEN & SWORD BOOKS LIMITED
47 Church Street, Barnsley, South Yorkshire S70 2AS, England
E-mail: enquiries@pen-and-sword.co.uk
Website: www.pen-and-sword.co.uk

Contents

Introduction

My history is an everlasting possession, not a prize composition which is heard and forgotten

Thucydides, 404

My friends have asked me why I have chosen to write an autobiography. The easy answer is that I think that I have something of interest to record but the true reason is much more complex and goes back to the time of my parents' death. As I cleared their personal effects I came across some boxes filled with every letter that I had written to them during my time in the Royal Air Force. The total was surprisingly large because I had written at least once per week and I quickly became lost in reminiscence as I opened some at random and became transported in time as I read of my feelings at flying solo for the first time and then joining my first squadron.

Discussing my find with my wife she remarked that it was a real treasure for her because it would enable her to learn so much more about me in the years before we met. Whilst agreeing with her I reflected that I was now denied that opportunity with my own mother and father and I suddenly realised just how much I wanted to know about their early lives. I had loved them so much and had seemed to know so much about them, but now that they were gone there was no way to fill the gaps that I had identified. It was at that moment that I determined to use my letters to write some sort of script so that my children would have an easily digestible record of their parents' lives.

Needless to say my good intentions were put to one side throughout the remainder of my RAF career but with my retirement the time became available and it seemed a wholly appropriate moment to look back and reflect on my life in uniform. Once started the recollections fell into a definite pattern, with a catastrophic car accident in the USA, in which my wife and I suffered major injuries, becoming a turning point in our lives. We were both asked to overcome physical and mental barriers of an order that we had not met before and as a result we both went through a complete re-evaluation of our values and priorities in life. Our lives were changed in a way that we could never have guessed and, despite the losses and pain that we endured, we were enriched and blessed in so many ways. For all these reasons it is appropriate that any attempt to tell my story should start with this, the turning point in our lives.

Part I

Chapter One

The Turning Point

There is no road of flowers leading to glory
Jean de la Fontaine, 1668

The world was pain and the world was colour. And the sharp jolting of the pain and the pulsing red of the colour fused and excluded all other senses. Nothing mattered to me except the pain and the colour; as a repetitive experience I began to fear and savour them as their impact gained in intensity and each pulse of colour seemed to bring with it its own excruciatingly exquisite torment.

How long I lay there in the wreckage of the car before other feelings intruded I have no idea but it seemed an eternity and it was with a strange feeling of almost reluctance that I allowed them to register. There seemed to be an odd comfort in having my world reduced to such a simple state and I became angry with the distraction of having to acknowledge the existence of stars overhead and someone moaning at my feet. Why were the stars there, for they had no part in my life? And who was making these anguished cries, because it was I who was hurting and they had no right to claim any part of my experience?

Slowly, however, my brain began to function and the sounds, feelings and memory started to build a mosaic which developed haphazardly into a partial realisation of who I was and what was happening. Voices began to make an impact and torches illuminated my surroundings. These were all now identifiable and it was clear to me that I was in some way the focus of the activity that was gathering momentum around me. But I now had a fresh complication in that I suddenly realized that I could not move; not that I was restrained in any way but I could not translate thoughts into action. I began to panic and struggle, although this latter aspect was as much mental as physical, because nothing moved.

Panic began to turn to real anger and was directed at whoever was moaning near me, particularly as they had been joined by someone who was crying in a shrill and unrelenting fashion. I felt the need to lash out, and must have been near to a personal breaking point when a voice that I knew well suddenly intruded: 'Well now, you are in a fine mess, but nothing I guess that a Limey can't handle.' Into my restricted line of sight, obscuring the stars, and lit by a flashlight came the friendly face of Senior Master Sergeant Gerry Garrison, a colleague of mine with whom I had spent many hours in the F-111 simulator. As I know now, Gerry was the person who truly saved my life but at that moment he was the friend who saved my reason and started my fight for survival.

Like the true professional that he was he began to plan the operation to save me and my family. He calmed me and briefed me. He answered my questions and told me what was expected of me. That I had been involved in an automobile accident had registered but to my eternal shame it was only as he spoke that it came to me that the noises that had so irritated me had been the sounds of anguish and suffering of my heavily pregnant wife and our two-year-old son.

That evening in January 1969 had started well enough, with a party at my commanding officer's home to say 'Goodbye' to us as a family before our return to the United Kingdom the next day following a two year tour of duty with the United States Air Force (USAF). Colonel 'Bart' Bartholomew and I had developed a close personal relationship during my tour as we worked together on introducing the swing-wing F-111 fighter-bomber into service with the USAF, and his gesture in throwing a party for us was wholly in keeping with the nature of this warm and generous man. Enjoyable though the party had been, therefore, there had been considerable sadness and a great sense of nostalgia as we made our final round of farewells in the belief that we would be unlikely to ever meet again. How wrong we were to be in this, as we strapped ourselves into our borrowed VW Beetle and started our short drive back to the Visiting Officers' Quarters at Nellis Air Force Base, Las Vegas, Nevada. As usual, a cloudless sky and unlimited visibility gave us unrivalled views of the surrounding mountains and the panoply of stars overhead, and my wife Terry turned from tucking our son Guy more firmly under his coverlet on the back seat to remark on the beauty of the night and to comment on just how much we would miss Nellis upon our return to England in the grip of winter. Completely in agreement with her I grunted in assent and concentrated on turning onto the six-lane divided highway running from Las Vegas alongside our base at Nellis. Little did I know that by so doing I was passing up the opportunity to speak to her for nearly a month and that our lives would never be the same again.

Of the impact and crash I remember nothing and Terry's memory is blanked off from the time that we strapped into the car. The facts of the accident I therefore have to draw solely from the USAF and Highway Patrol's report and discussion with Gerry Garrison, who was attracted to the crash after seeing what he described as 'an immense Catherine Wheel of lights on the northbound highway as a car clearly rolled over into the desert following an impact.'

First on the scene, however, was Sergeant Wilburn Baker who was also attracted by a 'Roman Candle of lights coming blazing down the street and a Chevrolet skidding and fish-tailing to a halt near the median strip.' What he and Patrolman Eric Hatch found in the desert approximately 100 feet from the highway was an extensively damaged Volkswagon Beetle standing on its wheels with a body hanging from its rear window. The shattered left rear of the vehicle showed where the impact had occurred but their immediate concern was for the motionless body at the rear and for the trapped occupants who, from their cries, were in considerable distress. With the doors hanging from their hinges there was little difficulty in extracting the injured occupants, who turned out to be a small boy suffering from bruises and shock, and an unconscious woman who was heavily pregnant and in a great deal of pain. Help by this time had arrived from the nearby air base, and once the woman and boy had been removed to the base hospital, the trickier operation to move the man began. Although he was by now conscious he was unable to move and from the extreme angle that his head made with his body it was clear that his neck was broken. It was at this moment that Gerry Garrison made his decisive move; with considerable experience in dealing with crash casualties he realised that any movement of the victim's head could result in the spinal cord being severed. To try and prevent this he crawled into the wrecked car and, lying alongside his friend's body, acted as a human splint during the extraction of the pair of them from the Beetle. Just how successful he had been in preventing further injury he did not at that moment know, but he did know that his friend was still alive because he had thanked him just before he slipped into drug-induced unconsciousness in the base ambulance. As the ambulance accelerated away towards the base, Gerry Garrison crossed his fingers and thanked God that Nellis was blessed with an up-to-date hospital and first-class flight surgeons. He had done his bit and it was now up to them.

My memory of events from the time of Gerry Garrison's arrival is fragmented and incomplete but in the years that have passed I have tried to reconstruct and record them because of their importance to me.

I began to fight the pain that was beginning to threaten my reason once Gerry had established my link with reality: his presence and calm reassuring voice quietened my panic and brought into focus what had, until then, been the nightmare qualities of my situation. My wife and son were, he stressed, safe and well and had been removed to the hospital for observation. With their departure I no longer had the distraction of their cries and was able to concentrate on my own problems, all of which diminished as they were identified and made understandable. Pain was the immediate enemy, but once isolated and confronted could, I found, be taken on and brought under control; not that I achieved this satisfactory state of affairs easily or quickly but I did at least start the fight – and I was damned if I was going to lose.

The Faustian qualities of the pulsing red surroundings were translated instantly into warmth and comfort as I realised that they came from the posse of Highway Patrol cars that now surrounded the accident, and the stars which had so bothered me by their presence now became companions on which I could focus in my personal fight. It was explained that we had been struck from behind by a Chevrolet being driven by an airman from my own base; the overtaking speed was considerable and this in conjunction with the much greater mass of the Chevrolet had resulted in our little Beetle being slammed off the highway and, after dropping down the verge, rolling over at least once before coming to rest on its wheels. The impact had been sufficiently severe for both our seats to be torn out of the floor mountings and for me, after my neck had snapped between cervical vertebrae four and five, to separate from my seat and continue backwards through the rear window, which I had smashed out with my head. Terry had remained strapped in her seat but had taken the full impact on her stomach with catastrophic effects on the little baby boy that she was carrying. Miraculously for Guy he was shunted forward by the impact and must have passed under us because our seats came to rest in the rear of the car exactly where he had been lying asleep; shaken and bruised he ended up entangled in the car's pedals, frightened but otherwise unhurt.

The arrival of the ambulance and medical orderlies brought immediate relief with their administration of drugs, but at the same time induced a strange time warp into my memory of events. Gerry's face seemed to disappear backwards down a long tunnel but the warmth and reassurance of his grip strangely remained with me long after he had gone. The velvety blackness of the night with its myriad puncturing of the stars was suddenly and shockingly replaced by the blindingly, brilliantly lit interior of the ambulance. Voices came and went, merged and separated, boomed and softened. Meaningless images remain with me to this day but out of them coalesce some vivid fragments from the first surgical experience of what was to be a long series of such encounters with my doctors.

Pain was no longer a problem as the drugs had taken effect but a subsidiary result that was to occur repeatedly in the next few days was an odd sensation of separation of mind from body. Not that it seemed strange at the time, despite the fact that I seemed somehow to have become a bystander rather than a participant. It was in this detached environment that I was asked, in the politest manner possible, by one of the medical attendants if I would object to them cutting me out of my clothing. I can recall that I considered the matter but, having decided that the effort involved was too great, did not bother to respond but turned instead to observing the activity going on around me.

My lack of response prompted my helpers to proceed and also, presumably because they assumed me to be beyond comprehension, to discuss me and my condition in muted tones. I listened without much interest, but one exchange not only caught my attention but possibly affected my whole attitude to coping with injuries: 'Do you think he's going to recover?' asked my first interrogator. 'With the injuries he's got I shouldn't think he's got a chance,' came the response.

I can recall so very clearly that this response really bothered me, not because it frightened me but because it affronted me. It affronted me because I was an Englishman being discussed by Americans and, having successfully proved myself as an 'alien' in the USAF flying environment it seemed that I was going to have to do it all over again in the medical world. Looking back on it, it was an extraordinary reaction, but it started a hardening in the process of my resolve to recover and was perhaps the foundation stone of my determination to show my American colleagues that a 'Brit' could do what a 'Yank' could not!

My memories of the next few days are extremely fragmented but they remain as incredibly clear snapshots and mark for me my progress along the path to recovery.

The operating theatre provided only one image but that was a dramatic one and, although I was not to know it, it gave a clue as to how operations were to be conducted on me in the days ahead. The clue was that I was conscious during surgery because for the type of surgery that I was to undergo no general anaesthetic would be used. The drama was that the surgeon was referring to x-rays and talking to a surgeon in Los Angeles on a phone-patch before starting to operate.

With no ability to move, my field of view was limited but I took in the brilliantly lit interior of the theatre with almost academic interest, although the reassuring voice of the surgeon relaxed me wonderfully well. He talked me through the insertion of the Crutchfield tongs into my skull and the whole process seemed strangely familiar and not at all painful or frightening.

Quite suddenly it was over and I was lying in a darkened room strapped into a rotational Striker frame with 10 pounds of traction stabilizing my spine. I lapsed in and out of consciousness and pain established itself as a constant companion, concentrating itself in my neck and peaking every time the nurses rotated me. No matter how carefully they performed this task there was no escape from the pain and I came to fear their ministrations: on the positive side, however, I began to be able to move my limbs, even though they responded weakly and sluggishly to my commands.

I have vague memories of my surgeon reassuring me that my wife and son were physically unharmed by the crash and were making a strong recovery from their ordeal. He wanted me to understand this because he stressed that the emergency surgery that he had carried out was 'life-saving' only and that I had to be moved urgently to a neurosurgical facility if I was to survive. To this end a DC-9 Nightingale aero-evacuation aircraft was being re-routed to transport me to Fitzsimons General Hospital in Denver, Colorado: an army hospital with one of the largest and best neurosurgical teams in the country. Despite the most careful handling my transfer to Fitzsimons remains as a nightmare experience, as every movement translated into knife-like pains which seemed designed to test my ability to retain my sanity. Of the flight I remember little except that the landing, which I am sure was as smooth as satin, appeared to have achieved what the accident had failed to do, namely the severance of my neck! Every jolt experienced during the lengthy taxi to the terminal remains with me to this day, as does the extraordinary sensation of snowflakes falling gently onto my upturned face as I was transferred to an ambulance. Denver was, of course, in the grip of severe winter weather, something that I had not experienced during my two years of flying out of the Southern States and which now came as a further shock to my system.

I remember flinching as the ambulance started moving and set its siren and red light in operation; a perfect recreation of the accident scene in Nevada which I had until then managed to suppress. It was a long ride and it not only enabled me to regain control of my emotions but also, for the first time since the accident, to start taking an interest in something other than my own condition.

The falling snow with the red reflections from the ambulance beacon was eerily beautiful and the passing buildings, partially obscured by the screen of snow, seemed to belong to a world of which I would now never be a part. As we swept along the deserted roads it was a surrealistic scene in which I seemed to have become incorporated into one of those films featuring a dramatic accident, rescue, and hospital sequence; the difference was that I had no way of stepping out of it and

I was becoming increasingly bothered about what was going to happen to me.

I was beginning to hurt again and I started to become more and more agitated as I began to worry about what had happened to Terry and Guy. My concerns suddenly became entirely personal as the ambulance braked to a halt and I was unloaded and wheeled into the hospital. Although I did not realize it I was no longer a special case but just another unit being processed by this huge 4,000-bed hospital, which was a main returning medical centre for casualties from the war in Vietnam.

Taking my place in the queue for processing I became acutely aware of the presence of the battle casualties from the sounds of pain that they made as they lay with me in the dimly lit corridor. Bonded to me in their pain their presence was strangely comforting and, although I had no idea of their identity, they became companions from whom I had no wish to be separated. This unwelcome separation came all too soon as, with wrist-tag attached, I was moved to an empty room, injected and left alone. The darkness and loneliness made time stretch into an eternity but I must have slept because the sound of a door opening dragged me back to consciousness. Although the room was in darkness, light came through the open door from the corridor and against this was the silhouette of a giant of a man. Completely filling the doorway, he waited for a moment before turning on the lights and moving over to my side.

Tall, heavily built, crew-cut, and wearing a standard issue white hospital coat, he was an impressive new arrival in my life. He was clearly in no hurry to introduce himself, however, as he gazed down at me for some considerable time before speaking.

'Well you're a sorry looking son of a bitch,' he said.

'I can't say that you are any oil painting yourself,' was my immediate response.

A huge grin greeted this, followed by: 'You sound like my kind of guy.'

Thus started one of the most significant relationships in my life, which has endured to this day and continues to develop and enrich me. At that moment, however, all I knew was that he appeared to be offering me hope of recovery.

Part II

Chapter 2

Early Days

Whose bosom beats not in his country's cause?
Alexander Pope, 1713

The mouse danced, pirouetted, and then pressed its tiny forepaws against the glass of the cage and pleaded with us for its release. This, my earliest memory, occurred in the summer of 1940 at our home in Green Street Green, Kent, when I was just over three years old.

The incident has stuck with me as it was both heartbreaking and instructive. My father and I had discovered the fieldmouse in a box in the garden shed and nothing would do for me but that I should keep it as a pet. My protestations finally overcame my father's objections and with great reluctance he built a cage for the little creature. The inevitable occurred and the poor animal died a few days later, despite the continuous attention that I lavished upon it.

Very wisely my parents used the tragic event to impress upon me the undesirability of trying to influence the natural order of life. Through my tears I took their message to heart and many of my actions since have been influenced by my desire not to distort normal relationships and naturally occurring courses of action.

We had moved into our home a few months after my birth in April 1937. Until then we had lived with my mother's parents at their home in Woodcote Road, Bickley, with my mother working in a department store in Bromley. My father was a bank clerk with Banque Belge pour L'Etranger, the London-based branch of the main Banque de la Société Générale de Belgique. He had started work with them from school in July 1923 and I can recall him telling me how lucky he felt to have a job when so many well-qualified people were unemployed during the Depression. This sense of gratitude and good fortune affected his career decisions adversely in later life and in a very direct sense led to the failure of his marriage.

None of this was apparent in 1940, however, and my childhood was happy and my memories of my parents then are of loving and caring individuals. Despite the fact that there was little spare cash in the family – indeed restrictions imposed by my father's bank prevented his marriage until July 1934 when his salary reached the mandatory minimum of £250 per annum – we took part in the full range of family activities, with seaside holidays, picnics, and family outings. The start of the Second World War affected me little except to add interest to my life when a Bofors gun was installed in the field alongside our house. Its dramatic firing without warning did nothing for my mother's nerves but was all that a boy of my age could desire and I became firm friends with the crew, who adopted me as their mascot. This happy turn of events came to an abrupt halt when I fell into the guncrew's cesspit and was forbidden by my mother from taking part in any army-associated activity!

The house was small, bright and with a long garden bordered by fields – a perfect home in which to play and develop. Protected by Mosey, the family's black spaniel, I was allowed a considerable amount of freedom and the garden and countryside became my playgrounds and founded and fostered my lifelong love of the outdoors and of animals. Long hours spent in the company of the dog, roaming and exploring, instilled a sense of self-sufficiency and a happiness with my own company that were to stand me in good stead in my future life and career.

As the clouds of war gathered and the aerial combat of the Battle of Britain commenced, my life changed. Situated as we were in the proximity of the Royal Air Force fighter station of Biggin Hill, we became inexorably drawn into the conflict as bombs fell nearby and the Bofors gun fired repeatedly, deafeningly, and often unexpectedly. Although I may have revelled in the excitement my mother did not and, as her nerves became more ragged, it was decided that we would move back to her parents. This move to Bickley was short-lived, however, because my Grandfather Butcher, who was an engineer, was installed as manager of a factory in College Road, Epsom, that was responsible for producing aircraft components.

Initially he commuted on a daily basis and as a special privilege I would be allowed to accompany him. The journey in his Morris 8 was always exciting as our route took us through Croydon and skirted the airport, which was the home of Spitfire and Hurricane squadrons. How thrilled I was to see them landing and taking off, and there was a special magic for me when we returned after dark and I could see the great beam of light sweeping round and round from the control tower.

I cannot say for certain that it was this experience that planted the seed of interest in aviation in my soul but I do know that my fascination with aircraft seems to have been extant since that time. Exulting as I did in the exploits of our RAF pilots I was plunged into despair, however, when news reached us that my beloved Uncle Bill had been shot down over Holland and was a prisoner of war.

Bill Butcher was a big man in every way. Tall and well built, with a larger-than-life personality, he was a trial to his sister, my mother, as he blazed through our lives with a succession of attractive girlfriends and a bewildering array of sports cars. I can recall so very clearly being swept into the bosoms of the former and hurtled around the countryside in the latter, to the alarm of my mother. It was almost inevitable that he would join the RAF Volunteer Reserve as a pilot and, although he was a Blenheim pilot rather than one of my role-model fighter pilots, he became my firmly established favourite and hero from then on.

I must confess that the concept of him as a POW somehow eluded me but the fact that I was made to contribute all my sweet coupons to buy chocolate to send to him in the POW camp kept him firmly in my mind! And his demise as a pilot resulted in a two-fold legacy for me; first, my enforced abstinence from sweets has left me with a permanent lack of desire for sweets of any kind and secondly, and most importantly, I vowed that I would become a pilot like him, to do what he could no longer do.

It is perhaps fanciful to think that events such as these shape one's later life but they may have been the small bricks that needed to be in place in order to influence decisions on matters that were otherwise finely balanced.

My father had by now received his warning order that he would be called into the RAF in the near future and, as the daily commuting was becoming too much for my grandfather, a decision was made to move to Epsom so that he would be close to the factory. Apart from my parents, the most important person for me was my father's sister Norah, who developed into an auntie that I would have laid down my life for. Kindness personified, she exuded warmth and love and I was never happier than being in her home playing with my cousin Grahame, who was four years older than me.

With no apparent reason or rhythm I seemed to rotate between all the family homes, except that during term time I was always with Mum and her parents. The large house in Epsom with its vast grounds was a wonderful environment for a child to grow up in. My grandmother became our Air Raid Precautions (ARP) Warden and conducted her watch periods in a brick building very close to the house, which meant that I could go 'on duty' with her: I even had the important task of inspecting the white-painted board near the building which was meant to change colour if mustard gas was present. I am not at all sure that I understood how heartless my grandmother would have been to subject her grandson to such sacrificial duties if she really had believed that such an attack had taken place. I do remember just how important I felt performing my role.

Air raids were part-and-parcel of our lives and frequent use was made of the Anderson and Morrison shelters that were erected. To this day the smell of damp canvas and wet earth bring back the vivid memory of being put to bed in the Morrison shelter in the garden, with its interior metal walls glistening with condensation and the entrance protected by a wall of sandbags. Flasks of hot drinks and sandwiches were consumed by torchlight once the blanket had been pulled across the doorway to prevent the egress of light. When the raids were imminent but not yet signalled by the siren we spent time in the specially converted hidey-hole under the grand staircase of the house, where I would have stories read to me or would help my grandmother do jigsaw puzzles on a specially made board.

My father applied to join the armed forces in 1940 but because of his poor eyesight he could not be considered for his preferred choice of aircrew. In the event he received his call-up in 1941 and joined the RAF for administrative duties in the specialization of Pay Accounts on 18 November at RAF Penarth, Wales but, as I rarely saw him, I had few memories of him until he returned from Africa in 1945 when I was eight years old.

My life changed in the winter of 1942 when on 29 November my sister was born in Epsom hospital (a five-minute walk down the road from our house). I do remember being dressed very carefully and told to behave myself extra well as we inspected Carole Mary.

In 1943 the random nature of air raids and some heavy loss of life in the vicinity resulted in my family deciding that it would be safer if we moved away from London, so we moved into a little white cottage in the village of Alcombe, near Minehead in Somerset. With no running water or electricity, and gas for providing lighting downstairs only, conditions were primitive and, as the front and rear doors were of the half stable variety, it was cold and draughty. We washed outside the back door in a stone trough protected by overhead sheeting with the privy at the end of the garden; every night I went up the stairs to bed carrying my own light in the form of a candle. All the privations were more than compensated for by the immediate proximity of the countryside and combes which became perfect Cowboy and Indian, or Tommy and Hun, adventure landscapes.

We had access to a beach hut on the seafront at Minehead close to where the Butlins resort now exists; it was the site then of the town's open-air swimming pool. Every day I would walk over the fields after school, across the railway line and make my way to the beach hut where Mum would be waiting with Carole and our newly acquired smooth-haired fox terrier, Rufus. Although there were beach defences embedded in the sands I was made to change into swimming trunks and run into the sea. Mum insisted that I underwent this daily total immersion and give some impression of trying to swim before I was allowed back into the beach hut where I would be towelled dry and served delicious hot tea with cakes or scones. Carole would watch my torture with smiling equanimity whilst Mum firmly resisted my pleas that it was unfair that my sister should not have to undergo the same treatment.

The years passed very quickly and I have only the happiest of memories as I made great friends with the boys in the village, loved the outdoor life in which Rufus became my constant companion, and had no trouble with school work. I suppose that I did become rather wild because I know that I spent nearly all my time outside and the social graces were not considered a necessary part of village life. What was required, however, was a respect for elders as well as politeness, and transgressions were dealt with summarily.

Then in 1945 two very memorable events occurred because my father returned from Africa and my Uncle Bill was repatriated from POW camp. Strangely, Uncle Bill's return occurred first just at the beginning of May 1945, when I was confined to bed in the cottage with mumps and I was petrified that I would not be allowed to see him. Typically for him this was no problem and, after hearing his very noisy arrival downstairs, there was a crash of boots on the stairwell and the door nearly came off its hinges as he threw it open and hurled millions of Reichmarks into the air and, whilst they came fluttering down like confetti, scooped me out of bed and danced round and round and round. It was all so exciting and, even though he was thin, he seemed enormous and glamorous to me in his pilot's uniform with medal ribbons. He then pinned German medals and insignia onto my pyjamas and made me salute with the Nazi salute whilst he blew raspberries at me and Mum tried with no avail to restrain him. Much to my annoyance she refused to let him take me downstairs, as he was determined to take me out in his red sports car, so my contact with him was confined to his regular visits to my room.

On 15 June 1945 I was scrubbed and dressed in my best clothes whilst Carole was put in a pretty white summer dress with new sandals and we waited at Minehead railway station for our first glimpse of our father, without any idea of what he would look like. A huge crowd of people poured out of the train's doors but I suddenly saw him in his RAF uniform and he ran to us and, after kissing and hugging Mum, knelt down and put his arms round Carole and me at the same time.

By referring to the detailed diaries kept by my father we clearly had a wonderful homecoming with him, spending nearly every day at the beach because, as he noted, 'the kiddies love the beach and beach hut better than anywhere else and seem to be very happy playing together, building sandcastles, playing cricket and going in the sea'. I helped Dad when he spent a day in the hayfield assisting the farmers and we all had days out at Dunster, as well as having picnics in the combes and picking wortle berries. On 2 July Dad's leave was over and he reported for duty at his new appointment at RAF Innsworth, little knowing that 40 years later I would serve at the same station as the Deputy Air Secretary with the rank of Air Commodore.

At the beginning of September we packed up the cottage and went back to Epsom prior to moving over to Eden Park near West Wickham in Kent where we moved in to 'Chinsurah', South Eden Park Road – a large detached house with a substantial garden. Dad was still in uniform as an LAC (Leading Aircraftman) with a daily rate of pay of 7 shillings and 3 pence (30p in current money) and was posted to RAF Stapleford Tawney in October, which made travelling much easier for him as well as being closer to his parents in Bromley.

By this time I was the proud possessor of a bicycle and able to travel large distances to see my friends. Unfortunately, on 20 November I was the victim of a hit-and-run driver 200m from our house. I remember nothing about it as I was hit from behind at some speed and taken to Beckenham Hospital in a state of concussion. I remained either asleep or unconscious all day (from Dad's diaries) on 21 November but reverted to a normal sleep condition the next day. I was kept in hospital because my skull was cracked but after ten days I was released and moved back into my own bedroom where I made a gentle recovery in a state of permanent semi-darkness because I developed blinding headaches if the curtains were open. The strangest aspect was that the skull became spongy along the line of the crack and I recall being drawn irresistibly to gently touching it so as to experience the odd sensations that resulted. Eventually the skull hardened and mended and I have never suffered any adverse effects from the crash.

I had started school in an establishment just up the road and continued there for a year before moving to Pickhurst School in Pickhurst Lane. Mum also made me join the Cubs and when Dad was demobilized in July 1946, we worked together on improving my field skills. It was at this time that I became aware of the growing differences between Mum and Dad. They were very different personalities and whereas Dad was quiet, enjoyed the home life and family, and was steady and unambitious, Mum was very ambitious and, whilst being devoted to Carole and myself, was restless and ever keen to be involved in activities outside the home. Our relative lack of money frustrated Mum and I can recall arguments developing over finances with comparisons being made to other families. I later found out that Banque Belge, whilst keeping Dad's job available for him whilst he was in uniform, stopped paying him a salary and he had to support himself and us as a family during the war on his very small RAF pay. He returned home, therefore, to an exhausted bank balance and I can recall how in 1948 there was a minor celebration when he breached the £10 per week salary scale after having worked at the bank for 25 years.

My parents kept on stressing to me the importance of good schooling and at their direction I sat, and passed, the entrance exams to the City of London School and also to St Dunstan's College, Catford. Dad was very impressed with the playing fields surrounding St Dunstan's and unimpressed by the fact that City of London had to travel to their grounds, and this, rather than any academic reason, resulted in my starting at St Dunstan's in September 1947 aged ten years and five months. I settled in very quickly and thrived in the demanding environment, keeping easily in the top ten places for all subjects, out of classes of 30, during my year.

Money was causing a real problem at home because the decision had been made to purchase a large house in Grosvenor Road in West Wickham so that my mother's parents could live with us. I was told explicitly that Mum and Dad would be unable to pay for my schooling and that I had been entered for the Kent County Council Free Place Scholarship examination in March 1948 and that if I did not pass it I would be withdrawn and go to a state school: St Dunstan's had agreed to offer me a free education place if I did pass. Most fortunately I succeeded and on 12 April my parents were advised that free education would start for me as from September. I have often pondered on what turn my adult life would have taken if I had failed this one exam and not had the advantages of being educated at St Dunstan's.

Grosvenor Road had a large garden with mature trees, a vegetable patch, conservatories and sheds. Carole and I were able to play together outside and she was always willing to go along with my games and suggestions, even when it meant climbing hazardously along the boughs of the largest tree. We also used to take Rufus on long walks into the nearby fields and woods, which on one occasion led to my first protective brotherly act when we were waylaid by four youths with an air pistol. I have no idea now what their real intention was but I made Carole run for home as I tackled them to stop them getting at her: as a result I suffered a mauling and had two air gun pellets fired into my bottom which had to be prised out by Mum en route to the doctor.

As differences between my parents became apparent so did the closeness between myself and Carole intensify. It was a particular cruelty, therefore, when the time came and my parents divorced, that the court's decision was to separate us so that Carole would be brought up by Mum and I would remain with Dad. I can recall the bewilderment I felt at being separated from Mum and Carole and how I directed my anger at my colleagues at school. My reports reflect the deterioration in my performance and from winning a form prize in the Second Form in 1950 I had to be cautioned for fighting and low academic standards in the year following. With the break-up of the family Dad was pushed to the limit financially and he and I moved to his parents' at 63 Crown Lane, Bromley and the house in West Wickham was sold. From then until I joined the RAF I was constrained by the Court Order to seeing Mum once per month and Carole likewise to seeing Dad.

That I returned to an even keel and even prospered was due in large part to the love and care of my father's parents and to my beloved Auntie Nor who became almost a surrogate mother. The interest they showed in me and my achievements was as great as if I was their own child and even my rather severe grandfather played his part in taking me on visits to all the London museums and to cricket matches. School did absorb a lot of my energy and time because I joined the army section of the Combined Cadet Force (CCF) when I was 13 and immediately discovered a liking for the disciplined yet adventurous aspects on offer. The CCF also came up trumps during holidays because it gave me the chance to get away on activity holidays (camps) which would not have been possible in a family sense because of Dad's precarious financial state. This enabled me to go on both Easter and Summer Camps and also to take advantage of the wider CCF activities to go for inter-Service courses at Royal Naval Air Stations (RNAS). The first of these was in 1952 when I went to HMS Daedalus.

HMS Daedalus was the RNAS station at Lee-on-Solent (which I was to visit later in 1962 to undertake decompression training) and was home to Sea Fury and Attacker aircraft: the latter was the first jet-powered Royal Navy aircraft to operate from aircraft carriers. Apart from the normal range of cadet activities the big attraction of these courses was that they provided flying experience for cadets. And it was here at the age of 15 that I undertook my first flight in an Avro Anson that was used by the RN as a communications aircraft. I can still recall vividly the sense of anticipation as well as the unique smell that is associated with aircraft of that generation. I had a good seat with a perfect window view and as the ground fell away and the aircraft banked so that we had a view of the coast, I can remember a feeling of exhilaration such as I had never had before. We were allowed to unstrap and make our careful yet unsteady way to the cockpit where we gazed uncomprehendingly at the vast array of gauges on the panel and, for the first time, experienced that wonderful view from the front of an aircraft looking ahead at the horizon and at the towering cumulus clouds: I was hooked. I also managed to get two more flights and these were in de Havilland Dominies (Dragon Rapides) which reinforced my belief that flying was something that I had to become involved in.

I applied immediately on my return to school to go on the next available RNAS course, which turned out to be to HMS Gamecock at RNAS Bramcote, near Nuneaton, in 1953. The course there was in some ways even better as it was tuned to attracting us to possible future service in the RNAS and we spent most of our time flying or in flying-related activities. I had three flights in an Anson, but best of all I flew in a two-seat Firefly Trainer which meant that I could handle the controls and we did aerobatics and some low-level flying. I can rarely have been so excited and on my return I did discuss with Dad how I might start flying. Nothing occurred, however, because there was no money available and Dad was determined that I should proceed to university.

As money was a continuing problem I only went on two proper holidays with Dad. The first in 1951 was to Weymouth where we stayed in a small hotel and did everything that epitomized an English seaside holiday, with beach activities, boat trips to Lulworth Cove and evening shows. It was good to have Dad all to myself and as we got to know each other so much better he opened up about the difficulties that he and Mum had had. The second holiday was in 1953 to Scotland by coach where we stayed near St Andrews with his friend from the RAF called Jim Weir, who owned a lovely farmhouse near the town. We toured Scotland in Jim's car, going right the way across to the Mull of Kintyre and going to the Tattoo at Edinburgh Castle as well as to the Highland Games at Braemar. I was treated in a very adult way and was fascinated to listen to Jim and Dad swapping wartime stories about their service in Africa and Egypt: they seemed to have had much more enjoyment and fun than I had assumed servicemen were entitled to in wartime.

It was not only Dad's stories, however, that conspired to focus my attention on the RAF. The newspapers and radio were full of the exploits of test pilots such as Neville Duke, John Derry, Geoffrey de Havilland, and Mike Lithgow as they established new world air-speed records and tested aircraft that could break the sound barrier. There was even a marvellous film made called The Sound Barrier which fired my imagination and which I went to see four times in one week. It featured the real prototype Supermarine Swift as it became the 'first' British aircraft to break 'The Barrier' and I just could not stop thinking about how much I wanted to dress and act like the glamorous pilots in the film. I became absolutely convinced that I had to be part of this exciting, dangerous company of supersonic fighter pilots, and I swore to myself that I would do anything to go through 'The Barrier'.

By the time 1954 arrived I was beginning to get really itchy feet about flying and school became more tedious and constraining. I found that I was going through the motions in class without the enthusiasm that I knew that I would need if I was going to progress satisfactorily to university. The catalyst for my decision making occurred in September when an ex-Dunstonian called Rogers, who had been a year ahead of me, returned to the school in RAF officer's uniform to tell us all about what had happened to him since leaving school. He went into raptures about flying and told us that even if we did not join full time the RAF was the perfect way to do your National Service because you would become an officer and be paid as such, and if you qualified for your 'wings' you could convert your qualification into a civil private pilot's licence at no cost. His talk was so exciting that, building on my existing experience and feelings, I went straight off with my friend Mick Ball to the recruiting office in Blackheath and told the surprised sergeant on duty that we wanted to train as pilots in the RAF. After convincing him that we were serious we completed a battery of tests and on 12 October I received a letter from Flight Lieutenant Robinson, OC No. 58 Recruiting Centre Blackheath, telling me to report to the Aircrew Selection Centre, RAF Hornchurch on Monday, 25 October.

The four days of testing at RAF Hornchurch were demanding but terrific fun because I felt increasingly confident as the events went by. The first day of medical tests were worrying because I had the feeling that they were probing into areas that I knew nothing about and they did seem particularly concerned about my bicycle accident and the fact that I had been unconscious with a cracked skull. At least half our cohort failed the medical and our reduced numbers went on to the aptitude testing, written exams, hangar tests, discussions and interviews. I made sure that I always contributed and without being pushy always tried to bring myself to the attention of the testing staff. At the end I had a very good feeling about things and on the way home treated myself to a concert at the Festival Hall featuring Johnny Dankworth and his big band with his new singer Cleo Laine. I was at this stage developing my fondness for modern jazz which seemed somehow to capture the mood of the age as it was fresh, invigorating and inventive. One week later came the letter informing me that I had been accepted for pilot training and requiring my confirmation that I could join the RAF in January 1955. What a discussion this caused because Dad wanted me to complete my A-level course and my degree before joining up for either National Service or a Short Service Commission, whereas all I could think about was starting to fly. At long last he agreed and I set about the formal disengagement from school.

Christmas came and went in a flash as I said all my 'goodbyes' to friends at school and received some very encouraging words from all my masters, in particular my Sixth Form and mathematics master, Geoffrey Matthews. The only sour note came from the headmaster, Hecker, who had never once spoken to me at school but chose to interview me in order to let me know how he disapproved of my leaving early and entering the RAF through the back door instead of going through the RAF College at Cranwell. He ended by saying: 'No good will come of this sort of behaviour.'

Only time would now tell.

Chapter 3

Into the Unknown

Being mad, I take to arms, even though there is little reason in arms
Virgil, The Aeneid, 19 BC

I stood with my father on a bustling platform at Liverpool Street station on a freezing cold day in January 1955 clutching my suitcase in one hand and a one way ticket to Bedford in the other. My father's bank, Banque Belge, was only a quarter of a mile away at No. 6 Bishopsgate and he would be going there to work as usual after having said goodbye to me, but for me the day would mark the severing of the last very close links with my family and the beginning of standing alone as an individual in an adult world.

Smoke and steam swirled and billowed from the many engines whilst the blowing of whistles brought the moment of parting into sharp focus and I know that I did, quite suddenly, feel very lonely and emotional, particularly as Dad pulled me close and hugged me tight. I scrambled on board and all that I can remember from what we said to each other was that he and my mother loved me very much and they were so proud of what I was doing – and then he was disappearing into the gloom; a small figure waving and waving until I could see him no more; I closed the window and watched the snow covered countryside unfold beside me. I had never travelled by train north of London and the countryside fascinated me as it was so very different from our native Kent; it was truly a journey into the unknown.

Bedford arrived and with it my introduction to the RAF, as there were uniformed corporals on the platform screaming for new arrivals to double up and make their way to the coaches outside. Suddenly we were bumping through the town and onwards to RAF Cardington where all new arrivals for the RAF were processed. Out of the coach, formed into squads and marched to a barrack hut, we were met by our corporal who allocated us a bed, showed us where the fuel for the coke stove was and where the ablutions and latrines were located, and then marched us to the cookhouse. The next three days passed in a blur as we were issued with equipment, clothing, uniforms, boots and personal documentation. We were shorn like lambs, photographed and, after swearing the oath of loyalty to the Queen at our induction, were given our Service Number; mine was 4163201 indicating, it was explained to me, that I had been a member of the Combined Cadet Force. The one thing that no serviceman will ever forget is his Service Number as it is the only constant that never changes no matter what else may happen to you. My memories of RAF Cardington are slight apart from the overpowering presence of the huge airship hangars, the shouting corporals and the freezing cold, with huge snow banks, and our desperate efforts to keep the coke stove alight to give us some comfort. I was also castigated by our corporal for not shaving properly (I was only used to scraping my chin about three times per week) and made to shave in cold water in the latrines until my face bled.

We formed no friendships at RAF Cardington and once the induction process had been completed we were despatched separately to our receiving units: in my case this was for RAF Kirton-in-Lindsey in Lincolnshire, just south of Scunthorpe, which was home to the massive Appleby Frodingham steel works. It was on the train to Scunthorpe that we did start to get to know our travelling companions who would become our friends and comrades for the next two years as the RAF turned us from raw unproven material into fully qualified pilots. The ubiquitous RAF blue-coloured coaches with roundels on their wings were waiting for us as we descended from the train and after a relatively short journey we drove through the gates of Kirton to be greeted by jeering and yelling figures at the windows of each barrack we passed, with the universal blandishment of 'You'll be sorry'.

The weather was becoming even colder and we could not wait to get inside the H Block that was to be our home for the next three months. Flight Sergeant Skelding, a sergeant and two corporals met us and told us that we were now Number Two Squadron of Blue Wing, Number 1 Initial Training School of the RAF and were reclassified from airmen to officer cadets for the purpose of our training. This would, however, bring us no privileges at all except that we would wear a white disc behind our cap badge and blue-and-white georgettes on our lapels. We would spend all our time in uniform and would not be allowed off camp for the next four weeks nor allowed to wear civilian clothes until we had graduated.

There was very little in the way of entertainment locally and on the rare occasions that we were allowed off camp we used to walk down to the village of Kirton-in-Lindsey and frequent the Queen's Head where the landlord encouraged us to sing service songs, providing we kept them clean. We also used to see the odd film that was shown under makeshift arrangements in the village hall on a screen made from sheets that billowed every time anyone opened the door from the street and pushed aside the blanket that hung across the doorway to stop light coming in.

Pay parades became a highlight of the week when all the cadets were paraded in a hangar and a young officer would call out your name and initials and you would march forward, salute, give the last three digits of your Service Number, and sign for whatever he gave you. I received £2 in cash every week whilst 10 shillings was kept back and paid into my Post Office Savings Account so that upon graduation I would have enough to buy a suit to wear in the Officers' Mess. The system worked because upon graduation I purchased a blue suit for £10 from Burtons as well as a pair of Cotton Oxford rugby boots for £3.9s.6d.

Friendships also started to develop and my closest friends became Jack Cupples, who had the bed space next to me in the dormitory, and Johnny Duckworth, who seemed very grown-up as he owned a BSA Bantam motorcycle. All of us were given the chance to lead exercises, work out solutions to practical problems, and act in support of others: imperceptibly, I now realize, we were not only building our own confidence but developing our critical assessment mechanisms for gauging the value and worth of others – by the end of the course I knew exactly who I would follow and trust and who I would avoid.

The days became a regimented process of breaking us down as individuals and forcing us to accept discipline and become a functioning unit in which the needs of the whole always came before the needs of the individual. We were fed well, exercised into the ground, taught drill, and run ragged, but we were always given the opportunity to make sacrifices in order that others might survive and beat the system, and this became our mantra. You learnt never to let anyone down and those that did were shunned and had to redeem themselves before they were allowed back into the family. Looking back on those months and re-reading the daily diary we were forced to write (and which was marked) it is remarkably clear how the training programme was designed to develop one's confidence, the ability to perform and speak in public, to encourage one to make decisions, and to defend one's position and attitude by logic and rational argument. I know that we were treated harshly and there was a coarseness in our handling, but I never recall any bullying or brutality and I emerged at my graduation one-and-a-half stone heavier than when I joined, in terrific physical condition, and very confident about coping with the next stage of my training.

The excitement about that next stage was intense because half of the cadets on the course would remain in England to undertake basic flying training on Piston Provosts, but the other half would go to Canada and learn to fly on Harvards, which seemed unbelievably glamorous. The implications of doing one or the other were lost on us because all we could think of was a glorious transatlantic liner passage followed by a year in the land of the Mounties, which, for someone who had only been abroad to the continent travelling by bicycle and staying at Youth Hostels, seemed to be the stuff of dreams. Preceding the decision about who would go where was the fitting of officers' uniforms, greatcoats and caps – it really was kids-in-the-candy-store time as we strutted up and down in our new plumage demanding salutes from whoever was silly enough to be impressed. We were also taken to the Officers' Mess, by the Padre of all people, and given a thorough introduction to the mysteries of this forbidden building. The function of each room was described and we were given a run through of a mock Dining In night, including precise directions as to which sherry should be drunk before the meal, the correct usage of all the complicated tableware and glasses, as well as the directions for passing the port and the order of the toasts.

At last on 18 April 1955 came the day of graduation on which we paraded as Premier Squadron, were inspected by an air vice-marshal and marched past him feeling on top of the world. We were then marched to the side and all the supporting squadrons marched past us and off the square before we were dismissed and allowed to throw our airmen's caps into the air and into oblivion – we were now classified as officers in the exalted rank of Acting Pilot Officer. Mum and Dad could not attend the ceremony so I linked up with some close friends to hear the news of where we would be going which, to my great disappointment, was not to Canada but to No. 6 Flying Training School at RAF Tern Hill, near Market Drayton in Shropshire.

As we did not have to report until 14 May it meant that I had ample time to gather all my new officer's kit together and, using my leave railway warrant, to bid Kirton goodbye. I travelled south to Bromley to be with my father and grandparents and to celebrate my eighteenth birthday on 21 April.

On 4 May 1955 I made the journey from Bromley via Shrewsbury to Market Drayton, where coaches were waiting to take us to RAF Tern Hill. I introduced myself to the half dozen members of the group that I did not know and we all made our way very nervously through the front doors of the magnificent old style Officers' Mess. We 'warned in' and were given information folders detailing our rooms, dress codes, meal times and the first week's programme. To my disappointment I was accommodated in a hut to the east of the main Mess, but the room and its facilities were adequate and I spent the afternoon walking round the camp and, after locating the flight line, entered a hangar and climbed into the cockpit of a Provost. What a wonderland of gauges, instruments, levers and wheels, and all of it accompanied by that most evocative aroma of aviation gasoline, oil and leather. Only a few of the items made any sense to me and, as I wrote in my first letter to Mum:

'I do not know how I shall remember them all or what they do, but I am going to have to learn quickly or they will never let me go solo.'

Once we had had our evening meal we all had to report to the ante room in our flying clothing to meet our instructors and to be introduced to our fellow course members. We then paraded outside the front door for our course photograph, with our instructors standing in the back row. I still have this photograph and it shows our instructors all giving the V sign because they were in fact all impostors: they were actually members of the graduating senior course masquerading with the connivance of the staff and did they ever take us in. They treated us to the most hair-raising flying stories and demanded in return a continuous and unlimited supply of beer. The pièce de résistance, however, was the first item on the next day's programme, when we were made to appear in PT kit outside the Mess at 0630 hours for sixty minutes' PT prior to breakfast. The PT instructors were brutal and it was only when we were dismissed at 0730 and all the impostors emerged from the Mess dressed in their correct uniforms and killing themselves with laughter that we realized just how we had been taken in. We vowed to take our revenge in turn once we became the senior course.

And so started our flying training as members of 117 Course. The first event was a visit to the No. 1 Squadron Crew Room where we met our real instructors and where I was put in the tender care of Flight Sergeant Stan Stannard. We were allocated lockers and, after putting on our flying clothing, were instructed how to move the aircraft into and out of the hangar by hand and then given a cockpit familiarization. Later that day we were issued with parachutes, shown how to fit them, and given instructions on how to abandon the aircraft if the situation demanded it. The next day was occupied completely with the issue of equipment and publications before we reported to the squadron on 9 May for our first Familiarization Flight. I do not think that I have ever been so excited and that evening in the bar was just not long enough for us all to swap our experiences.

The Provost T1 was an all-metal low-wing monoplane powered by a 550bhp Leonides 126 engine with a fixed undercarriage. Side-by-side seating for the pupil and instructor was provided in an enclosed cockpit which gave a good view when airborne but which suffered on the ground because of the big radial engine.

Having been carefully strapped into the left-hand seat by Stan, he then performed his cockpit checks at a speed which left me bewildered and, before I was ready for it, there was a big bang as he fired the starter cartridge and, with a magic that I recall to this day, the big three-bladed propeller started to turn before quickly becoming an incandescent disc.

He showed me how to weave from side-to-side when taxiing and then, after more incomprehensible checks, we were suddenly bumping down the runway and I felt the tail come off the ground before we lifted gently into the air. It was an unbelievable feeling as we rose effortlessly into the sky with the Welsh mountains taking shape on the horizon and the ground receding whilst the buildings on the airfield shrank to the size of matchboxes. The woods became green blots on a patterned quilt with wheat fields shining like yellow postage stamps. Villages and town were evident but I could no longer make out individual people and I was suddenly startled as shreds of cloud sliced past the canopy before I experienced for the first time the odd sensation of being hurled at a seemingly solid wall of cloud. I remember that I flinched just before contact and then gasped as we plunged through it without harm.

My instructor did most of the flying whilst showing me the local countryside as far south as Shrewsbury with that essential visual navigation aid in the area, the Wrekin, a large cone-shaped hill just south of the town. He demonstrated the effects of the controls and made me follow him through on the control column and rudder pedals as he showed me how to fly straight and level, dive, climb and perform turns. And then, gloriously, he put both his hands on the coaming of the cockpit and allowed me to handle the aircraft all by myself. At the age of just 18, before I had driven a car or a motorcycle, the feeling of being allowed to fly an aircraft was the most amazing event of my life and, from the conversation in the bar that night, my feelings were replicated by all my colleagues.

My letters home reveal how excited I was and although the general handling of the aeroplane proved no difficulty for me, trying to land the aircraft was a different matter. I could not synchronize the levelling off, throttling back and obtaining the correct three-point attitude at the correct speed. Most of my friends had gone solo at about ten hours but when I reached eleven hours and was still not getting it right every time, I was given an instructor change and Flight Lieutenant McNeill quickly located my problem, explained matters in a different way and at thirteen hours he hopped out of the aircraft at our relief landing ground of Chetwynd, buckled his aircraft harness together, and in time-honoured fashion informed me that he couldn't take any more punishment, so I had better go off by myself.

As my instructor strolled away from the aircraft I realized that I had better get on with it without any guidance from the empty right-hand seat. I taxied carefully to the take-off point, did my take-off checks twice and, having been given permission by air traffic control, opened the throttle, moved the stick forward to get the tail up and was airborne at 65 knots. I reached 1,000 feet and 100 knots before I was ready for it and, despite reducing the rpm to 2,600 was up to 120 knots and 1,200 feet before I relaxed and settled down. Easing the aircraft down to 1,000 feet I turned downwind, completed my checks and turned to the right-hand seat before I remembered that there was no-one there to criticize me. With a grin as big as a Cheshire cat, I turned onto finals, reduced speed to 80 knots, rolled level, crossed the hedge, eased back on the stick, reduced power and touched down gently in a perfect three-point landing. I taxied slowly back to where my instructor was squatting on the grass and waited with trepidation as he climbed back into the cockpit, strapped in and said, 'Not bad, but do watch your height in the circuit!'

How on earth could he have noticed that, I wondered, before giving in to a feeling of sheer exultation that on 10 June 1955, I had flown an aircraft all by myself at the age of 18 years and six weeks. So, no matter what happened now, I was a pilot.

That solo trip on 10 June was the happiest moment of my life and it was with huge reluctance that I shut down the engine after our return to RAF Tern Hill as I just did not want that very special flight to finish.

We worked and played hard, completing thirty-four trips in June as well as a full programme of ground school and Link trainer exercises to accustom us to instrument flying and blind SBA (Standard Beam Approach) instrument approaches. We also discovered the delights of girls at the Trentham Gardens Ballroom but, feeling handicapped by having to beg for lifts, I purchased a BSA 250cc motorcycle and persuaded Jack Cupples to teach me how to ride it. The purchase was facilitated by the opening of bank accounts for us all and the payment into mine of £32 for six weeks' salary: however, at a cost of £60 I had to buy it on a year's hire purchase.

The flying was becoming interesting and demanding with the introduction of the full range of aerobatics and instrument flying and this had led to the suspension of the first of my friends, Martin Brown, who was sent to the Aircrew Disposal Unit at RAF Booker: a unit responsible for determining the fate of suspended trainee aircrew. His departure caused us a lot of unease as we all suddenly felt vulnerable and redoubled our efforts to reach the standards required. We were also starting to stretch our legs as we had started our navigation training and made flights to Burton-on-Trent, Chester and the estuary of the Dee. One student on the course managed to confuse matters, however, by setting red on blue on his 'P' type compass (180° out) and merrily flew off in exactly the wrong direction. He quickly became completely disorientated and when transmissions became so faint that he could no longer hear Tern Hill and his fuel began to run low, he made a landing at an RAF airfield, which to his horror was RAF Feltwell in East Anglia: a very chastened pupil was retrieved by an instructor on the day following his landing.

I flew a very successful Mid Course Test on 8 August with a total of 53 hours logged, passed my Instrument Rating Test on 13 September with 77 hours and then started formation flying and low level navigation: the latter was to bring me instant fame and my first reprimand.

Formation flying, however, was something in which I excelled and which gave me a real thrill from the start. There always seemed to be something deliciously naughty about being allowed to manoeuvre one's aircraft right up to another aircraft in a manner which would bring an instant fine if one did it in a car on a public highway. The sight of another aircraft so close that you could almost touch it and to know that it was only your skill that was keeping them from colliding but yet to be able to turn, climb and even roll and loop whilst keeping the aircraft in perfect position is scary, frightening and thrilling all at the same time, and brings one the most wonderful adrenalin rush. The moment I started I knew with a certainty that I wanted to be a fighter pilot and go on doing it again and again. I can also remember the almost heart-stopping fright that I had the very first time that the leader banked and suddenly disappeared into the fireball of the sun and I froze on the controls until, by narrowing my eyes and squinting, I was just able to determine his shape: an immediate lesson learned – always wear your tinted goggles when formation flying! Diagrams of Vic, Echelon, Line Astern and Abreast littered my letters home and many were the sessions in the pubs with arms and hands waving all over the place to impress each other and the locals on how terrific we were.

And then on 4 October came my moment of truth. I had experienced a little difficulty with my navigation at low level as the different perspectives bothered me and I kept seeking to find landmarks rather than latching on to basic time and distance for locating my position. On a lovely sunny day I was, however, cleared to do a solo navigation exercise in WV498 and let down into the low flying area but soon became uncertain of my position. I decided to align the 'P' type compass and reset my DI (Direction Indicator) and after fiddling with this for some little time looked out of the cockpit to find that I had not only descended to about 50ft above the ground but that there was a line of high tension cables right in front of me. I had never been so frightened in my life, but I reacted instinctively by slamming the throttle wide open and pulling up as hard as I could to climb over them. No such luck. There was an enormous bang and the aircraft rolled uncontrollably with a ploughed field appearing above my head where the sky should have been. I rolled and ruddered the aircraft into some sort of controlled level flight and, when my heart had slowed down, took stock of my situation. The aircraft wanted to roll hard to port and wouldn't climb higher than 200 feet but the worst thing was that I could see a great hole in the left wing. Using two hands on the control column I turned the aircraft towards Tern Hill, told them what had happened, and soon had a shepherd aircraft flying in formation beside me. He took me past the control tower for an undercarriage check and then led me round a wide circuit for a landing. I was told to shut down the engine once I came to rest and was horrified to see the propeller blades had chunks out of them. When I climbed out of the cockpit I could see that the fairing had come off the left undercarriage, there were scratch marks over the canopy and upper fuselage and there was wire stuffed into the engine cowling; in short it was a miracle that the aircraft was still flyable. I was immediately taken up for a flight by Stan Stannard after giving an initial statement, and then allowed to continue flying until Air-Officer-Commanding No. 23 Group summoned me for an interview at Group Headquarters at Leighton Buzzard on 27 October.

The memories of the interview are sharp as I can remember wading through a thick carpet towards a man who seemed to be weighed down with medal ribbons behind a vast desk: I was not invited to sit down. He asked me if I drove a motorcycle or car and, when I replied in the affirmative, he asked me in a very civil voice if when travelling at 100mph I would fix my gaze on the petrol tank and not look up for five minutes. When I answered in the negative he suddenly roared at me that didn't I think the same principle applied when flying. Before I could answer he told me that one more incident would spell the end of my fledgling career and I was to remove myself forthwith and was lucky to just receive a reprimand. Severely chastened I returned to Tern Hill where to my surprise and delight I was welcomed home by the course and became the recipient of an impromptu drinks party to celebrate my escape both from the flying accident and the AOC's interview.

The pace of the course accelerated with night flying, repeat low-level navigation practice, final Navigation Test, my first Instrument Rating Test and a huge 'Course Party' to celebrate our passing the 100 hours flying mark. We also were able to do what we had promised ourselves, by passing ourselves off as instructors when welcoming the new course. I masqueraded as an ex-43 Squadron (The Fighting Cocks) Hunter pilot and spun no end of yarns about supersonic flight to open-mouthed new students: it was clear that I knew where I wished my future to be. On 16 December I took and passed my Final Handling Test with Squadron Leader McKay and also received news that I had passed my Ground School exams with an overall average of 70 per cent for the six subjects of Aerodynamics, Airmanship, Navigation, Meteorology, Engines and Signals.

With 132 hours under my belt I felt on top of the world and, with the rest of the course, really went to town on our Dining Out night. Too much so in fact because it had become the tradition for the passing out course to do something outrageous and we decided to cap previous efforts. We removed some red lanterns from nearby roadworks and set these up in the main road by the Officers' Mess, manned the diversion with two members of the course in uniform, and directed all main road traffic into the camp past the front of the Officers' Mess; a fact which gradually dawned on the senior officers present as large trucks rumbled past and over the Mess flowerbeds! Worse than this, however, was the arrival of the police as a result of two cars ending up in the trenches of the roadworks from which we had removed the lights. We were all summoned to the presence of the Station Commander who informed us that after the next day's passing out parade we would not go on leave as planned but remain behind 'in detention' and not depart until we had been interviewed by the police and also completed a 3,000 word essay on a subject of his choice. Our final parade was a very subdued affair and although I cannot remember any action resulting from the police interviews, I know that I didn't get away for Christmas leave until Christmas Eve. I then drove down to spend Christmas Day with my Dad before going across to see Mum on Boxing Day and reporting back to Tern Hill on 29 December for a last couple of flights on the Provost before indulging in an absolutely wild fancy dress party to see in the New Year.

It started well with a trouble-free train journey on 23 January 1956 to No. 5 Flying Training School at RAF Oakington, near Cambridge, where I was to undertake my advanced training on Vampires. Reunited with several friends on the train we were disappointed, at first, to be accommodated in the No. 2 Officers' Mess – a utilitarian building but one I came to love because of the terrific atmosphere generated by its inhabitants.

The excitement about going on to jets was palpable because, of course, in 1956 the only jets flying (except for the Comet) were military so one felt very much 'the elite'. We also traded in our sheepskin boots for black leather 'jet' boots and were issued with that defining item, 'the bone dome'. We started ground school and flying immediately and I had the immense good fortune to be allocated to Flight Sergeant George Smith who was one of the best instructors and the kindest man you could ever hope to meet. He had been a Royal Navy Lieutenant

Commander pilot during the war but on demobilization had not been happy in civilian life and asked to return to the services. The Royal Navy had no vacancies and the Royal Air Force would only accept him as an NCO, so that is what he became. I fell in love with the Vampire and my letters home bubble with the excitement and thrill of flying jets.

The Vampire was a twin-boom jet fighter built by de Havilland and powered by a de Havilland Goblin turbo-jet engine developing 3,200lbs thrust. A side-by-side two-seater had been developed for dual instruction with a performance almost identical to that of the single-seat fighter version and this would be the type of aircraft that we would fly until we had gone solo. With a nose wheel instead of a tail wheel the aircraft was much easier to taxi, land, and take-off, particularly as there was no torque to take account of: this being a feature of piston engines. Although the cockpit was superficially much more complicated than that of the Provost, the aircraft was simple and its systems easy to understand. Its handling was light, pleasant and effective right down to the stall at 95 knots. The higher speeds did take a little getting used to with a take-off at about 110 knots and approach at about 125 knots. The landing occurred at about 100 knots but I had no problems with this and went solo in Vampire T11 XD520 on 1 March 1956.

Everything was much more adult and relaxed and the instructors from the very first flight not only instructed us but tried to imbue fun into our flying which led to unofficial formation flying, tail chasing and aerobatics: on my third flight we spotted a B29 tanker refuelling a couple of Republic F-84 Thunder Jets and George immediately took control and we rolled down and made a couple of quarter attacks on these, which made my hair stand on end because we came so close to them.

Socially, life was also developing as the Mess held regular dances to which local hospitals chartered coaches to bring nurses along. We made regular forays into Cambridge where we investigated exciting foreign foods which were beginning to become available in English restaurants, as well as joining in many student parties: we were always welcome providing we took a bottle. I also discovered that a friend on the course called Mike Melville had a sister called Maureen who was in the Tiller Girls dancing troupe and together with another friend called Derek Eden we used to go off at weekends to party with the girls. There was also a much more relaxed atmosphere with the instructors and we would all go off as a group to pubs where we would become rowdy, sing, swap flying stories and listen avidly to what life was like on an operational squadron. What a change it made from the formal educational style of school and even basic flying training, and how we all enjoyed it.

We were also given much more latitude with our flying and on one cloudless day I climbed to about 30,000 feet and navigated my way to overhead RAF Biggin Hill so that I could fly over my home at 63 Crown Lane, Bromley; then after locating Croydon Airport I did the same at 163 Carshalton Park Road where my mum and sister lived, all the while streaming a beautiful condensation trail. The T11s that we flew were an early model that were not fitted with ejection seats and the solo flying was in Vampire Mk 5s or 9s which were all ex-squadron aircraft and it gave me a real thrill to see the old squadron markings under the camouflage, as well as the gun ports: I felt nearly operational.

On my nineteenth birthday I celebrated by taking Mk5 VV212 and performing a series of illegal and, most probably, highly dangerous low level aerobatics along a local feature called the Twin Canals, which led up towards the Wash. We then had an impromptu party in the Mess at which I bought the drinks and played the box bass in a skiffle group that we had formed. I also sold the motorcycle for £30 because a friend called Jack Lewarne had asked me to go in with him and buy a 1930s MG PB sports car and it seemed to be an offer that I could not refuse. I also went on my first proper overseas holiday as the course was given leave as from 23 May and a Swiss friend of my mother's (Elsi Scheidegger), who lived between Basle and Bern, had offered to look after me. I went by boat and train from Harwich to the Hook of Holland where I caught the Rheingold Express to Basle. The train ran down the length of the Rhine and I was entranced by my first sighting of the beautiful river and its fairy tale villages, castles and vineyards. Elsi lived in a classic chalet above the village of Huttwil with her husband, running a leather factory in the village. They took me all over Switzerland and even managed to take in an air show at Zurich airport where the highlight was the Swiss aerobatic team flying Vampires and was I envious when, as they taxied round the perimeter track with their cockpits open, they were thrown garlands of flowers by stunningly pretty girls. I told Elsi that it was not quite like that at Oakington!

Upon our return I was sent solo in formation flying and passed my Instrument Rating Test before starting Night Flying on 29 June. The weather was perfect but I was unprepared for the sheer beauty of my first flight solo out of the circuit. The Mk5 cockpit is very small and cosy and as I climbed higher with the lights of London becoming immediately visible it seemed as if I was the only person in the world. Every town or city was so clear and distinct with an extraordinary variety of colours for street lighting and little caterpillars of trains snaking their way between them. With the engine humming and the cockpit dials glowing greenish-white and a big fat moon shining down it was unbelievably beautiful and I just did not want it to end. Quite illegally, and dangerously, I rolled and looped the aircraft before very reluctantly identifying Oakington by its red flashing coded beacon and letting down into the circuit and landing: a magic flight.

Now we'd become proficient in all the basic handling our instructors, who were all ex-fighter pilots, entered into the formation flying phase with particular gusto and each sortie ended in a tail chase. This was in essence a 'dog fight' with the leader trailing you behind him by about 50yds and telling you to stay there no matter what he did. Invariably in the early trips you failed to hang on and got out of position or, to your shame, lost the leader altogether.

On 24 August, however, I had a defining trip which made such an impression on me that I wrote a long letter to Dad describing it in detail. I was flying Mk 5 WA808 as Blue 2 and, after climbing to 20,000 feet, the leader put us into line astern, told us to hang on, and pulled round in a hard, right turn. As I followed him I felt the G-forces pulling me down into my seat but I kept him square and centred in my windscreen. He suddenly rolled and turned hard in the other direction with the G-forces increasing and my vision beginning to go grey as the blood drained down into my lower torso and legs. Completing a perfectly circular turn we hit our own slipstream and the aircraft bucked and kicked in my hands before the leader slackened his turn and began climbing rapidly with the speed falling off before returning to a turn which brought us to the edge of the stall and the aircraft beginning to shake and buffet. Everything was now happening in slow motion as the controls began to feel sloppy: the Vampire became reluctant to respond to my commands and we were drawn inexorably together. Suddenly the leader's aircraft tipped over and vanished from my sight with my heart starting to pound as I feared for a collision until I could see him again. As my nose fell below the horizon with the aircraft still shaking I saw him again as he plunged earthwards and my aircraft became alive as the airspeed began to build again and the controls became responsive. The altimeter began to unwind from the 20,000ft that we had reached and we burst through small patches of cloud before I saw his wings rotate against the background as he rolled and climbed in a barrel roll. Back in full control of my aircraft I had no trouble in manoeuvring to place him in the centre of my windscreen and by increasing power to close up behind him: it came as something of a shock as I saw his wings emerge from a cloudy background at right angles to the horizon for me to realize that we had just been inverted, but by concentrating on him and not on the outside world I had no idea that we had been upside down. It all seemed so wonderfully easy and exhilarating and I almost shouted with frustration when he levelled his aircraft and called me into close formation so that we could return to base.

As I eased up into position and started to relax I could feel the tension draining from me as I also felt the hot sweat which covered my body start to cool and dribble to the base of my spine. We slipped into the landing pattern at Oakington after executing a hard fan break into the circuit. I selected the undercarriage down and dropped the aircraft onto its main wheels before lowering the nose, braking gently to a slow speed and turning off the runway.

I wound the canopy open, undid my oxygen mask and took in great gulps of fresh air as we taxied back to our dispersal: the air tasted like nectar and I felt like a god as I climbed from the cockpit and lowered myself to the ground – how could anything in the world be better than my tail-chase experience? I could not wait to get onto fighters!

But from the highs to the lows can be very sudden, as on 3 September one of my best friends, Dick Cooper, was killed during a high altitude formation flight. He, Paul Houselander and I went down to London for the weekend and had very little sleep because the parties went on until the early hours. We were using Dick's car and on the way home very late on the Sunday his driving was erratic and he kept dozing off. He was obviously tired when he took off on the Monday and at high altitude the aircraft rolled over, ended up in a spin and, although it partially recovered when he baled out at low level, his parachute did not have time to open. The funeral was my first for a friend and was held in the Oakington village church with the interment in the subsidiary graveyard some distance from the church. Dark sky, low clouds, growling thunder and the crash of the volley from the firing squad combined with the crying of his girlfriend and parents, conspired to make an indelible impression on me. It was to be repeated too many times in the future but as always was coped with by his flying friends having a tremendous party in the Mess, at which his memory was toasted again and again.

The final month passed in a flurry of formation flying, navigation trips and instrument handling prior to my final flying exams, which culminated in a 70 per cent pass in my Final Handling Test on 11 October with Squadron Leader Smith; my logbook showed 247 hours and Wing Commander Hoare authorized the award of my coveted pilot's brevet: my Wings. These were awarded at a very emotional parade on 24 September by the legendary Sir Geoffrey de Havilland who was flown in to the base in a de Havilland Vampire T11. My day was made complete when my family agreed to come together and attend the ceremony as a complete unit. As far as I can recall there was no animosity and my pride in getting my Wings was amplified so many times over by seeing my mother and father sitting side by side and the feeling that I had justified their faith in me. I was just so happy to be with them both at the drinks party and lunch that followed and then to be able to show them the aircraft and all the airfield elements needed to support the flying.

The icing on the cake was that I was one of a handful of graduating officers to be selected to go on to day-fighters. In the 1950s the cream of the RAF was still considered to be Fighter Command as it had the most glamorous role with its new supersonic fighters. The Soviet Union and Warsaw Pact were proving to be aggressive and seen as a real threat to the West with their vast fleet of jet bombers and fighters. Against this threat was ranged the RAF's fighter force, much as it had been when it faced the Germans in 1940: indeed there was still very much a 'Battle of Britain' feel about being an elite member of the Command.

On 9 January I had made the tedious journey by rail from Paddington with my friends Paul Houselander and Kiwi Macgill to Llanelli, where transport took us to RAF Pembrey which was home to the Hunter Conversion Unit. My letters reflect my shock at arriving at what I termed 'the most tumbledown camp in Britain'. It was in fact a completely wooden-hutted camp and our crew room appeared to be a farmer's converted barn. It was indeed a rabbit warren of a place but there on the ramp stood a line of shiny sleek Hawker Hunter Mk1s, the sight of which set the blood racing.

The first part of the course, which lasted until 15 February, was on Vampires where we were taught how to fly in battle formation (the tactical as opposed to close formation) conduct aerial attacks (so called quarter attacks) and then introduced to gun firing on target banners towed by Meteor aircraft. Nothing untoward occurred in this first phase except for my letting a wheel go off the narrow taxi way when moving out to take off one morning: it became stuck inextricably in the mud and my aircraft completely blocked the taxi way, resulting in a dozen aircraft behind me having to shut down their engines and be towed back to the ramp. I was not popular and after a one-sided interview with my squadron commander was left in no doubt as to my future behaviour. One interesting feature of the base was a big concrete ramp that led down to the Pendine Sands, a seven-mile long beach of perfect, flat hard sand on which the world land speed record had been attempted between the wars. So good was it that we were told that if the engine failed after take-off we should not attempt to turn back to the airfield but make a 90° turn left or right and land on the beach from which we would be retrieved by a tractor using this ramp.

The Hawker Hunter was a single-seat mid-wing fighter aircraft with swept-back wings and tail, full power ailerons, power assisted elevators, and a Rolls Royce Avon Mk113 engine developing nearly 8,000lbs of thrust. It was also armed with four Aden 30mm guns in a detachable package in the fuselage underside. The aircraft looked incredibly large to me and at 18,000lbs in weight and 13ft in height it dwarfed the squat Vampires that were lined up alongside it on the apron.

The great day came on 20 February when I was scheduled for my first flight in a Hunter at the age of 19 years and 10 months. As there were no two-seat Hunters and no Hunter simulator this check out was done in the very old fashioned way of answering written and verbal questions based on the Pilot's Notes and sitting in an actual aircraft going through the checks and instrumentation. Once he was satisfied my instructor went off to the Air Traffic Control tower to watch my take-off and landing and a flight sergeant supervised my start up. I taxied WT592 (an ex-43 Squadron aircraft) out to the runway and executed a standard Hunter learner pilot take-off: that is one in which one over-controlled because of the very light power assisted ailerons which led to a rapid left/right twitching until you learned to relax on the controls. The climb to height was exhilarating, as were the acceleration and beautiful handling characteristics, and all too soon I had to bring her back for a dummy approach followed by a final landing. The touchdown was perfect but my sense of well-being was shattered when I found that I had no braking and the short runway was rapidly coming to an end (we had no brake chutes on the Hunter Mk1). I careered off the end of the runway not daring to pull the undercarriage up (we had been told that swept wing aircraft would cartwheel if one leg came up before the other and the wing tip caught in the ground) but my stopping problems were solved when I went into a deep ditch, which tore my port leg off. I switched everything off and then couldn't open the canopy so I sat there like a lemon until the Wing Commander Flying arrived and told me very sharply to get out. This involved quite a jump from the cockpit and I stumbled, careered into him and we both ended up in a puddle with the rain falling on us and the fire crews laughing. He stormed off and I was taken to sick quarters for a sedative with images of my micro career finishing as my wrecked Hunter receded from sight in the falling rain. Much to my surprise my next summons to the Wing Commander Flying's office was for a pat on the back for my handling of the emergency as it had been caused by a faulty brake mechanism and, upon inspection, it was found that half the squadron were about to suffer the same fault: corrective action was rapidly taken.

Back on to flying and we were allowed to taste supersonic flight which was possible by rolling into a dive from high altitude with full power and aiming at whatever poor individual on the ground you wanted to give the shock of the week. And thus it was on 12 March I achieved my boyhood ambition of going through the 'sound barrier'.

Close and battle formation became the staple diet, spiced with cine camera tracking as we were not allowed to fire the guns. My accident had caused me to slip behind my friends' training programme and it was decided to make a concentrated effort on my behalf which resulted in the most intensive flying that I've ever done. On Monday 8 April I did four trips, another four on Tuesday, four on Wednesday, four on Thursday and the final two on Friday morning followed by clearance from the station that afternoon. I was drunk with my chums in the Brevet Club in Great Chesterfield Street in London by midnight on that same day! Eighteen hard trips in four-and-a-half days was really pushing it but I felt on top of the world and ready to become the world's greatest fighter pilot on my operational squadron, No. 111, based at RAF North Weald, to which I had to report on 23 April.

Chapter 4

The Formative Years: Hunters to Chipmunks

Learn to obey before you command
Solon of Athens, 638-559 BC

My arrival at RAF North Weald could hardly have been less propitious because I was running a temperature of 102°F and feeling very ill, and the Secretary of State for Defence, Duncan Sandys, had issued his White Paper detailing, inter alia, that the day of the manned fighter was over and that the future would rest with missile defence. The results were immediate. My name was one amongst 450 Hunter pilots detailed on a huge telex who were taken off fighter flying overnight as well as the list of Hunter squadrons that were to be disbanded and the disbandment of all the Royal Auxiliary Air Force squadrons flying Vampires and Meteors. The Station Doctor put me straight to bed and confined me to my room and the Station Adjutant informed me that my posting to No. 111 Squadron was cancelled as a result of the Duncan Sandys' edict and that I would be held as a Station Supernumerary with duties in Flying Wing as Station Navigation Officer: my flying would be confined to aircraft held on the Station Flight.

Initially I was housed in the main building of the Officers' Mess which itself was a gem of 1920s construction looking very much like a country mansion. My view from the window tormented me because I could see the black-painted Hunters of the Squadron practising their low-level aerobatic sequences for use in their routines as the Royal Air Force's Black Arrows aerobatic team. These views were soon denied me when I was told that I was far too junior to occupy a substantial room in the main Mess and I was packed off to a wooden hut at the south end of the Mess. In a way this was fortunate because Mum asked me if I would like a dog as a friend of hers had bought a pedigree

Saluki puppy but found that he was completely unsuitable for her flat in Streatham and had offered it to Mum. My recovery to good health coincided with a weekend off and I used it to go down to Sevenoaks to collect my 6-month-old dog called Hassan. He really was a handsome animal with a very individual character and a determination to get his own way: he did, however, immediately develop a 'one-man' animal bonding which was a delight in some ways but later on was to become a real problem during courtship and early married days.

Life was looking up a little as I started flying the Station Flight Anson and visiting airfields all over the UK. I also made a friend who was to remain close to me for the next 50-odd years and who currently lives only three miles away from me. It all came about because I heard the sound of a guitar playing in a room down the corridor in the Mess hut to which I had been moved. Intrigued by this I knocked on the door which was opened by an officer in short sleeves who introduced himself as John Downs, a fighter controller from the nearby Sector Headquarters at Kelvedon Hatch. It is strange how immediate friendships can be and we very soon became good chums. He was about to get married and I was bowled over when I met his fiancée Edwina, as she was absolutely lovely and reminded me so much of Ava Gardner (with whom I was in love at that time). Looking back on it I can sense that we both felt very much in the same boat because John was in love with flying but kept on the edge of things by directing fighter pilots but not actually being one of them whilst I was one, but was being denied the chance to actually fly the fighters.

My Anson flying was cut short when I was detailed to go to Bisley to act as a Range Safety Officer for the RAF's annual shooting meet at the end of May. We were accommodated in tents which was no hardship as the weather was beautiful and it made it easy for me to have Hassan with me as he was able to have freedom to roam once the day's shooting was finished. The most exciting thing that occurred was my purchase of my first wholly owned motor car. A group of us wandered down to the village of Brookwood (little did I know that I would buy my first house there 15 years later) and saw a Triumph Roadster for sale for £245 in the Brookwood Garage by the canal bridge. I just couldn't take my eyes off it and, goaded by my friends, I took it for a test drive, paid a deposit, and after entering into a two-year Hire Purchase agreement I drove it proudly back to the camp with Hassan sitting beside me on the spacious front seat. All of a sudden the world was my oyster and once the detachment finished I drove quite blithely through Woking and the centre of London back to North Weald, caring not a jot that I had no licence and had never had a driving lesson in my life: who cared, I was, after all, a Hunter fighter pilot!

Once again tragedy struck out of the blue with two Hunter crashes that involved officers that I knew. My next-door companion in the Mess hut, Dave Garrat, collided with another Hunter flown by 'Straw' Hall whilst practising formation aerobatics over the airfield. The team led by Squadron Leader Roger Topp went over a loop and then changed formation when pulling out with the two of them touching wings and Dave tipping straight into the ground from very low level in a high speed/high G-force condition. The crash scene was horrific with the aircraft fragmenting and parts even hitting the railway engine that pulled the trains on the little single-track line between Epping and Ongar. We had hardly got over this when Squadron Leader Les Mersham ran out of fuel in the Station Flight Hunter and crashed and was killed when attempting to force land on the emergency runway. A further crash occurred when one of the formation team went out of control during landing down slope and the pilot was involuntarily ejected at ground level after leaving the end of the runway but miraculously survived, with the aircraft breaking up completely. Flying was suddenly becoming a darker pursuit than that to which I had become accustomed.

It was with a sense of relief that I departed for RAF Thorney Island (near Chichester) from 17 July to 7 August to do the long RAF Survival Course so that I could fill the appointment of Station Survival Officer. The course at Thorney Island was excellent as the Officers' Mess was very large and beautifully decorated with wonderful food, and the dozen chaps on the course were all highly operational types and very keen to have a fun time. We spent every morning in lectures and every afternoon going out to sea on the High Speed launches from which we jumped into the sea to practise our dinghy drills and helicopter lifts. The course was also geared to the practical aspects of survival so we were made to live for three days and two nights in a wood on the island sleeping in shelters that we had to construct from natural sources and cooking recently killed rabbits and chickens. We then had a one-day supervised escape-and-evasion exercise; so that we could learn the current techniques (this was to come in very handy on my return to North Weald).

The evenings were spent partying and we quickly discovered the delights of the Pomme D'Or night club in Southsea which was noisy, played the latest tunes (Oh Diana) and had a wonderful collection of unattached young ladies. So good was my life that when the course ended I stayed on in the Mess for three extra weeks, which I took as leave to continue my 'lotus eaters' existence.

Flying took a turn for the better as I started to receive flying instruction on the twin-engined Gloster Meteor Mk7 (WA599) and was also checked out for solo flying in the de Havilland Chipmunk T10

(WK514). As a result I was able to take my friend John Downs up for a flight and overflew his home where his new bride Edwina was able to wave to us. The flight was quite significant for John because it was his first since crashing in a USAF C-119 Packet during his navigator training in Canada. He was one of the few survivors and acted heroically by going back into the blazing inferno to drag several survivors out before the fire rendered further help impossible. He was hospitalized and later awarded the highest award for bravery that America can grant to a non-American but, following a further aircraft emergency, he transferred to the non-flying branch of Fighter Controller in the RAF and had not flown since. I persuaded him to put this all behind him and to my great delight he agreed to come up with me and we had a successful and enjoyable flight.

My escape and evasion techniques were quickly put to the test as I was nominated as the station representative on the No. 11 Group team to take part in the annual Fighter Command Escape and Evasion exercise. We were all taken to RAF West Malling near Maidstone in Kent and formed into teams of two, my partner being Tony Aldridge, one of the pilots on No. 111 Squadron. We were taken out in a closed truck on Friday 1 November and dropped at five-minute intervals just west of Tunbridge Wells at Groombridge at 2100 hours. We had to make our way to a rendezvous at Polegate near Eastbourne and we had police, military, RAF Regiment and school cadet forces ranged against ourselves, with the public being alerted to the exercise and told to contact the authorities if they saw us. Tony and I decided that we would push as hard as we could all night and go off in a south-west direction, rather than due south, in an effort to outflank the cordons that we knew they were putting up. At daybreak we would find a hiding place and then lie low throughout the day and then continue to loop round until we hit the coast before coming into the rendezvous from the rear. We had several narrow escapes, including one where we had to force our way through a hedge to evade an army patrol with flashlights: unfortunately there was barbed wire in the hedge which ripped the bridge of my nose open and left me with a scar that I bear to this day. Everything worked as planned and we ended up as the second pair home (the first pair was from the USAF) with only 56 of 122 pairs evading capture. Our efforts were noted and my ACR (Annual Confidential Report) for the year commented 'He showed much initiative in the Escape and Evasion exercise and a stamina which wholly belied his rather weedy physique'.

I was settling in well, doing a fair amount of flying and making some good friends, so it came as a real shock when on 15 November I was called in to see the Station Commander (Wing Commander Barry Sutton) who informed me that all the surplus Hunter pilots were being posted to ground duties and that I was to report in ten days to HQ Home Command in the cadet branch. I started to protest that I was a trained fighter pilot and not at all happy about this, at which he got up and tapped me in the chest and said: 'It's not up to you to be happy in the Service, it's up to you to do what you are told.'

And that was the end of my first career talk!

I arrived at HQ Home Command in a despondent mood but was very pleasantly surprised by the Mess which was a delightfully converted set of cottages and which served marvellous food. My mood changed considerably when I ran into Brian Butterworth and Keith Webster who were both from my flying training course and had also been posted to the unit: we held an immediate and very drunken No. 117 Course reunion. HQ Home Command dealt with all the RAF elements that did not fit neatly into operational or technical Commands such as the Women's RAF, Cadet Forces, medical services and so on and we three youngsters were placed in the Cadet organization: I say youngsters because I noted that the average age was well over 40 with many retired officers doing staff jobs and that I was the youngest officer there. What I was impressed about was that the Air Officer Commanding-in-Chief, Air Marshal Sir Douglas Macfadyn, interviewed us on the day after our arrival and told us that he felt for us and that, subject to the office requirements, we were to get in as much flying as we could on the Command Communications Flight. This actually turned out to be easier then I imagined because the Flight operated Chipmunks, Ansons and Balliols, and during the previous month the AOC-in-C's pilot and navigator had been killed in a Balliol T2 when the aircraft's Merlin engine failed and they crashed into a wood (the Balliol glided like a brick): the elderly aircrew on the Flight were only too happy to let us fly the Balliol for them. After a quick conversion on WN521 I managed to do trips all over England. The funniest incident I had was when Brian Butterworth and I took a Balliol up to his home at Halifax and he inadvertently touched the canopy opening switch: the suction resulting from the opening canopy pulled our map out of the cockpit and we were left with nothing to navigate by. The weather suddenly worsened with rain and a lowering cloud base and as we realized that we didn't have all that much fuel to play with our hilarity suddenly ceased. All we could think of was to fly due south until we hit the Thames and then turn east and creep along it to Reading, from whence we could locate the airfield: much to our relief it worked and nobody found out about our predicament.

This was not so with a major goof of mine which earned me a severe telling off. On one of my first solo flights a mental aberration caused me to put the rudder trim in the ten o'clock position (as per the Piston Provost) rather than the fully over position required to counteract the enormous torque of the Balliol's Merlin engine. This mistake only became apparent at the point I became committed to the take-off and could not hold it with rudder alone. I swung wildly to the left, as I tried to control the aircraft and activate the rudder trim to help me, and flew at very low height right between the two canvas hangars on the south west edge of the airfield. Thank heavens for it being a grass airfield with no runways, but the Squadron Leader Operations was not impressed. Another life used up!

At long last I passed my driving test at the third attempt, which bolstered my morale. The first and second attempts undertaken when I was at North Weald were disasters and during the former I was summonsed for careless driving and not stopping after an accident when I scraped a bus and demolished my right side trafficator and then continued, hoping that the tester had not noticed. He had, of course, and after stopping me, told me that I had failed and to return him to the centre, from where he contacted the police. On my second test I failed my emergency stop and for driving too fast, so I took Dad's advice and went to the British School of Motoring and had two lessons from them before taking the test in one of their cars (an A35) rather than my own Triumph. It worked and I was at long last a legal driver with a valid licence.

A little variety came into my life when I was detached to RAF St Eval in Cornwall for a week to fly ATC (Air Training Corps) cadets and then wangled a flight out to Gibraltar on a 202 Squadron (Meteorological Flight) Hastings to act as escorting officer for twenty ATC cadets. On the flight out I met an army nurse who was based in Gibraltar so I really fell on my feet as she looked after me out there and took me to see all the sights in Gibraltar and the Algeciras area of Spain in her MG sports car. I was very reluctant to return and even more so when the co-pilot of the Hastings became ill and the Captain asked me to fly the aircraft manually to help him because the automatic pilot was unserviceable. Little did I realize that the whole experience of flying from RAF Lyneham with Transport Command in unserviceable aircraft was a foretaste of what would happen to me sixteen years later.

I celebrated my twenty-first, coming of age, in the Mess in company with Keith Webster and Brian Butterworth but the real events were the following weekend when I spent the first part with Dad and family and the second with Mum and family. Hassan rather spoilt things, however, by getting into the chicken run of the Beehive pub between the Mess and our huts and killing a load of chickens, for which I then had to pay: the annoying thing was how ridiculously pleased he looked with himself. I did, however, discover the joys of motor racing and took Dad with me to both Goodwood and Silverstone where Stirling Moss and Mike Hawthorn treated us to some spectacular racing and there were enough crashes to keep you on the edge of your seat.

Life then gave me another surprise when I was selected to do the Cryptographic and Cypher Course at RAF Compton Bassett, near Calne in Wiltshire. When I arrived I met a dozen other ex-Hunter pilots and it became obvious that the pool of grounded pilots was being used to fill all the odd jobs that were required and for which no proper complement was established. It was a hutted camp and a real problem arose because the President of the Mess Committee would not allow dogs in the rooms so I had to return Hassan to Mum who put him into kennels at Carshalton. We all graduated on what was quite a tricky six-week course in which the hardest part was to get up to twenty words per minute, error free, on the typewriter so that we could transmit and decode un-garbled secret messages. Typically, by the time we graduated the emergency was over and we were all returned to our units.

My Group Captain was delighted to get me back because he had just been asked to provide an officer to become the adjutant of a newly formed Air Experience Flight (AEF) at Exeter Airport in just one week's time. I had been involved in selecting the Reserve officers who would do the flying on these AEFs which were being formed to give air experience to ATC and CCF cadets. A flight had been formed in the south west of England at Bristol but it was then decided to base two Chipmunks at Exeter to cater for the cadets in Devon, Somerset, and Cornwall and a regular officer was needed to look after the unit as its adjutant. As the Group Captain explained:

'After all you do know all about the scheme and as you are single you can be down there in a couple of days because you don't have any ties here.'

There was just one problem – the RAF had no unit to base me at, as Exeter Airport was completely civilian, but this suddenly became no problem because he had a chum in the army and they could put me up on a temporary basis at the Regimental HQ of the Devon & Dorset Regiment at Topsham Barracks in Exeter. On 15 October, with yet another carefully planned career move, I got into my car with Hassan and all my worldly goods and drove off into the setting sun. Topsham Barracks turned out to be an old Victorian garrison and once again I was accommodated in a hut. The Mess, however, was wonderfully comfortable with dogs (of which there were many, mostly black Labradors) being allowed in every room of the Mess except the dining room. Every day I drove out to the airport where I was allocated an empty disused building and started to construct my little organization from scratch including decorating the building, furnishing it, devising a filing system and contacting the three ATC Wings and various schools that would fly in my aircraft as well as the Reserve pilots who would fly them. The army provided me with a thermos of coffee and a packed lunch and every day was my own. After examining my two aircraft, WK570 and WP872, I then checked out each of my pilots, who were all very experienced Second World War pilots. The Flight was established for four pilots per aircraft plus one to act as Flight Commander with the Reserve rank of Flight Lieutenant. He was Roy Crook and was the Senior Air Traffic Control Officer in the Exeter Airport Tower and his deputy, Eddie Edlund, was also one of my pilots. He was fascinating as he was Norwegian by birth and had seen his whole family killed by the Germans before escaping to England, joining the RAF and completing three tours of bomber operations – as he said to me: 'My only desire was to kill as many Germans as I could.'

Bas Pring owned a chicken-and-turkey farm nearby and Ron Christmas had a hotel in Paignton: he was completely hairless, having lost all of it, head hair, eyebrows and so on as a result of shock after being trapped in a flaming Spitfire shot down by an ME109 in the Battle of Britain. File, Greenaway, Hooper, Cumber and Horton made up my team and during the next eighteen months we flew more cadets per aircraft then any other Air Experience Flight in the UK. We made a very good team and not only got on very well together but also socialized, which engendered a great spirit and made my time at Exeter a very happy one.

Exeter Airport was proving to be more interesting than I had first thought as it housed the CAACU (Civilian Anti-Aircraft Cooperation Unit) flying Vampires and Mosquitos as targets for the army anti-aircraft artillery units based in Wales and the south west of England: the Vampires acting as high-speed targets for tracking-only practice but the Mosquitos towing banners for actual gunfire. I quickly became firm friends with all the pilots and was devastated when at the end of January 1959 I saw a Vampire flick whilst on finals straight into the ground. I was first to the scene as I was actually in my car but the pilot, Ken Munson, was dead, having been flung from the wreckage, which was burning fiercely. He was only 36 and had been a Lancaster pilot in the war, which made it seem so ironic to me that he could die in such benign circumstances. I took full advantage of the Mosquitos and the RAF check pilot Flight Lieutenant 'Curly' Curtis not only started giving me instruction in the T3 (TV959) but arranged for me to act as his co-pilot on a trip at the end of May to Benbecula in the Hebrides, where we acted as the high speed calibrating target for the newly built rocket range and tracking station. We stayed in the Benbecula Arms but were hosted by the army and I fell in love with the fast, agile, beautiful handling Mosquito and flew it whenever I could. We were also spreading our wings on the Flight as we regularly detached the aircraft to St Mawgan for a few days to fly the cadets from Cornwall.

I was left very much on my own during my whole time at Exeter with a really disgraceful lack of interest in myself, my well-being or my future career by those who were supposed to have responsibility for me. I can only assume that because the AEF was giving no problems and more than achieving its targets, the staff at HQ Home Command just could not be bothered to make the long journey to Exeter. The comments from my ACR for 1958 reveal the way that they evaded this responsibility as the Group Captain Cadets wrote: 'I have not met this officer but from my knowledge of the assessing officer accept his marking'. The marking he accepted was: 'This is a tall, weedy, rather lackadaisical young man who appears to have little spirit or drive although he appears to have organised his small unit of two aircraft at a civilian airfield very well indeed, earning high praise from civilian and service people alike. I do not consider that he will ever be worthy of a Permanent Commission.' My ACR for 1959 was almost a facsimile of this and with a complete lack of guidance from anyone in authority it was truly fortunate for me that I got on so well with the HQ Home Command check pilot ('Curly' Curtis) who visited to give me my Instrument Rating exam and my annual General Handling check, and who also flew me in the Mosquito. He became my mentor, took me under his wing and started mapping out a plan of action to get me back into the mainstream RAF which involved taking my 'B' promotion exam for advancement to Flight Lieutenant and an application to attend the Central Flying School (CFS) in order to become a Qualified Flying Instructor (QFI). I had no books or any other documentation and Curly arranged for everything I required and in due course I sat and passed the 'B' exam and was successful in my application to CFS. I did, however, still have another six months to serve at Exeter before I could start the CFS Course.

The lack of interest by my superiors in my welfare surfaced again when in July the Army asked me to move out because they required all the accommodation at Topsham Barracks for a new intake of subalterns. I was left to find somewhere to live and ended up by converting a parachute room in the Exeter Airport terminal, where my AEF was based, into a bedroom. I did arrange for some bedroom furniture and bedding to be delivered from RAF Mount Batten in Plymouth but from then on fed myself and did all my own washing and ironing until I left the unit. For the whole of this time I had no offer of help or indication of interest from anyone and there is no doubt that this experience played a large part in how I tried to treat people later on in my career. I became determined that others should not suffer in the way that I had.

On 18 July I was detached to RAF Waterbeach near Cambridge for one month to fly cadets at the ATC Summer Camp that was being held there. I was reunited with my friend Paul Houselander and it became an idyllic summer with more flying then we could handle and all conducted under cloudless skies and hot sun. We revisited our old drinking and partying haunts in Cambridge and extended our repertoire by dating a couple of girls in a truly novel manner. Whilst flying cadets during the morning I noticed a classy motorboat cruising on the River Ouse from Cambridge to Ely with two lovely girls in bikinis sunbathing on its deck: I buzzed the boat and did some low-level aerobatics and they responded by waving. When I landed and handed over to Paul for his stint we devised an emergency contact method by emptying a bottle of lemonade, putting a piece of paper inside with 'Ring Fred for a Good Time + the Officers' Mess telephone number' on it and replacing the stopper. Paul then did his flight, dive-bombed the boat with his cockpit open and dropped the bottle into the river: later that night in the bar the telephone went and, after answering it, the barman asked innocently:

'Is there anyone called Fred here?' – and the rest was history!

The other incident to stand out from this marvellous detachment was my conversion onto Meteors. I did three trips in the Meteor Mk7 (WA639) and was sent solo by Flight Lieutenant Ray Leask, the OC Station Flight. One week later during a Fighter Command exercise the Station Commander needed to send a package graded Secret to his fellow Station Commander at RAF Horsham St Faith, near Norwich. There were no other Meteor qualified pilots available so I volunteered and, having taken the package, was alarmed to find that the Meteor Mk7 was not available and the ground crew were preparing the single seat Meteor Mk8 (WL106), which was a completely different variant which I did not even know how to start. The ground crew flight sergeant was unperturbed by my admission and supervised the cockpit start for me and, with a pat on my shoulder, sent me off with the warning:

'For God's sake don't stop the bugger as there is no one at Horsham to help you start it again.'

My logbook records a fifty-five minute return flight instead of the usual two separate entries because I sat petrified in the cockpit in front of the Horsham ATC Tower waiting for someone to collect the package and refusing orders to shut down and deliver it by hand whilst watching the fuel gauges move towards 'Empty'. On my return to Waterbeach I had less than 10gall in each tank and had learned yet another valuable lesson!

My last few months at Exeter went quickly and quite suddenly I was handing over the Flight on 21 February 1960 and reflecting on a very formative couple of years. Largely unsupervised, the tour had made me stand on my own feet, organize myself and a group of disparate very mature individuals, and cope with a host of unexpected problems and demands that a pilot on his first squadron tour would have been unlikely to face. And, above all, despite the difficulties I had enjoyed myself immensely and flown aircraft such as the Balliol, Meteor and the incomparable Mosquito. I knew that I had matured and felt well prepared for the next demanding phase of becoming a QFI (Qualified Flying Instructor) and teaching others to fly.

Chapter 5

A Shock to the System

To be prepared for war is one of the most effectual means of preserving peace
George Washington, 1790

My move to the Central Flying School (CFS) at RAF Little
Rissington near Bourton-on-the-Water in Gloucestershire
went smoothly and I moved, for the first time in my life, into
a large room in a magnificent Officers' Mess: a real change from my
usual hutted accommodation.

Only QFIs are allowed to conduct flying instruction within the
British armed forces and all QFIs are trained centrally at CFS to ensure
commonality of training and the maintenance of extremely high
standards. The course is of three months duration and covers all
aspects of aeronautical air and ground instruction. No. 202 Flying
Instructors Course consisted of thirty pilots from every flying
discipline, including two army officers, an army sergeant and two
naval officers. In the rooms flanking me in the Mess were two young
pilot officers called Mike Graydon and Andy Jones, so called 'creamed
off' graduates from the RAF College at Cranwell, who were to be
trained as flying instructors instead of going onto operational flying.
They were both assessed as having special skills and qualities which
proved highly accurate because not only did they become lifelong
friends but Mike eventually became the Chief of the Air Staff and Andy
became the Chief Test Pilot of British Aerospace at Dunsfold
Aerodrome.

The course was split into two groups of two flights each and my
instructor on A Flight of Group II was a really friendly individual
called 'Timber' Woods who would handle me on the basic stage
conducted on Piston Provosts. The pattern of the course was simple in
that one group spent the morning flying and the afternoon on ground
instruction whilst the other group reversed the process. The work on
the course was comprehensive and designed to make you apply

yourself hard, with study in the evening being essential, as all aspects of aviation-related subjects were covered and I flew twenty-six times during the month of March. In the air you were taught by your instructor how to fly really accurately, whilst at the same time learning how to teach someone with no previous experience how to fly. Every other trip you would fly with another student and practise your new-found techniques on him as well as acting as a 'student' for him. It was a remarkably effective process as it encouraged criticism from people you trusted and you could feel your confidence and skill improving with every trip.

Standards required on the course were high and by the end of the first week of April, four students had been suspended, all of them for lack of flying ability. I celebrated my twenty-third birthday by passing my Intermediate Handling Test given by Flight Lieutenant Chris Horn and obtaining above average marks in a similar ground-school exam. Life was looking up and particularly so because I was selected to become an Advanced Flying Instructor and moved on to the Vampire for the final stage of the course. I clearly enjoyed being back on jets from the enthusiastic way in which I described my feelings and my assessments all reflected this with High or Above the Average ratings and a final overall ground-school mark of 78.5 per cent, which placed me fifth on the course out of the twenty-four students who graduated. There is a certain knack in being able to maintain one's own flying standards whilst allowing the student to do the vast majority of the flying by limiting your own handling involvement to that required for demonstration: the demonstration does, of course, have to be as near perfect as possible and you also have to be talking the whole time. I found the whole process fascinating and derived enormous satisfaction from getting it right, which does perhaps explain why I was to find the job of being a Qualified Flying Instructor so enjoyable.

The course finished on 1 July in a flurry of activity and on a high note with the Officers' Mess Annual Summer Ball at which we really let our hair down. Amongst the highlights of my time at CFS was a feature on the course where we were allowed to fly frontline aircraft so that we could go to our Flying Training Schools with at least a recent touch of operational flying in our minds. I did three flights in Hunter F4 (XF973) from RAF Kemble and can remember trying to push the aircraft and myself to the absolute limits but more prophetically had a hugely enjoyable flight in a Canberra T4 (WJ991) and enthused about its responsive handling: little did I know that three years of operating this 'Queen of the Skies' lay in wait for me in the not-too-distant future.

There was, however, a sting in the tail with the news of the postings, which caused huge amusement to all my friends. I had deliberately cultivated a scruffy dress code with a devil-may-care attitude, a reputation for all night partying and a disregard for normal conventions which I believed epitomized a 'fighter pilot' approach to life. I believe, therefore, that there was an element of mischief and tongue-in-cheek in my posting to the RAF College at Cranwell, a place which was known for the orthodox, rules before common sense, and strict adherence to dress codes and conventions. Mike Graydon and Andy Jones could hardly contain themselves and there was a book opened on how long I would last there – as it turned out, a fair question with an answer of: less than a full tour!

Never having been to the RAF College I started on the wrong foot when, arriving in the early evening I mistook the college itself for the Officers' Mess (on a normal station the Mess is the grandest looking building and this is what misled me). Driving through the gates at speed I tried four-wheel-drifting my sports car round what I later found to be called 'The Orange' and skidded to a halt in front of the entrance, jumped out and was accosted by someone who asked me who on earth I was. I explained that I was 'Flying Officer Evans and most probably the greatest fighter pilot in the world.' This apparently clarified matters for he looked at me with distaste and, pointing vaguely to the south east, said: 'Ah, well this is the Royal Air Force College and if you are an officer, I believe the Officers' Mess is over there!' Thus put firmly in my place by a College retainer, I started my uneasy relationship with Cranwell.

The first and most important thing was that there were no problems about keeping Hassan in my room in the Mess (which is now called York Mess because a second large and modern monstrosity of a Mess has been built). The Mess was a delightful building from the 1920s and its present name derives from the fact that the Duke of York (later to be King George VI) lived there during part of his service in the Royal Navy. I was posted to A Flight, commanded by Flight Lieutenant Vic Radice, of No. 3 Squadron commanded by Squadron Leader Peter Terry (later Air Chief Marshal Sir Peter Terry). However, it was to be two months before I started instructing because of the peculiarities of Cranwell, abetted by the fact that HM The Queen was to make a formal visit to the college on 25 July with everything subordinated to practising for this. I managed to become involved in the Royal Fly Past by volunteering to ride in the back seat of a Meteor Mk7 (WH169) flown by Flight Lieutenant Peter Harding (later Air Chief Marshal Sir Peter Harding).

The peculiarities of the college came into play because it was run on a three term basis like a school/university and it broke up immediately the royal visit concluded and did not reassemble until 2 September. During the five week stand-down I flew ATC cadets in Piston Provosts and rode horses from the College stables to keep them exercised. As a bachelor living in the Mess I was also an easy target for all the odd jobs that needed doing so I did get to know the station and its personnel well. I also found that there was a very active social whirl and I made friends with two couples who were to become very close: Jake and Audrey Barclay, and Dennis and Eileen Southern. They took me into their homes and invariably included me in their social events, which made a great impression on me. Lincoln was our local entertainment centre and a pub called the Green Dragon was the focus of our activity. I also kept in contact with Andy Jones who was instructing on Vampires at the nearby airfield of RAF Swinderby, and Mike Graydon who was in Yorkshire at RAF Linton-on-Ouse and whose girlfriend Elizabeth I occasionally gave a lift to when I went to a thrash up there. The best one that August was a 'Roaring 20s' barbecue and dance with a jazz band playing Charleston type music and everyone in flannels, blazers and boaters and Liz looking beautiful in a flapper outfit.

Flying started in earnest for me at the beginning of September when the cadets returned from leave and after a five-day familiarization period on 'Standards' Flight I flew my acceptance check with Peter Terry and was allocated my first student, Flight Cadet Gerald (Gerry) Crumbie. Little did I realize that the student/instructor relationship would develop into friendship and then become such a close one that it has lasted to this day, and that I would eventually become godfather to his daughter and end up living four miles from his home in Croydon. I was impressed immediately by the standard of his flying, as you only had to show him something once and you could sense that he understood what was involved in the manoeuvre or exercise and had the innate skills to perform it to a high level. Unfortunately, flying took a pretty low priority at the college (drill and ceremonial rated a much higher position) and we only flew with our own student about ten times per month with a very short period prior to and after the flight to brief/debrief him and get to know him, and we were never allowed to fraternize socially with cadets. This was a matter that I took into my own hands later with disastrous results.

As it was I settled into the instructional world easily and really enjoyed the challenge of bringing along a student who knew the basics but was uncertain how to extract the maximum performance from a fighter-type jet aircraft and be prepared to take it to the edge and, if necessary, beyond it. I was concerned with Gerry because he knew that he could finish the course as one of the very best pilots but did not seem to be prepared to make the effort to claim the Number One spot: I set out to make him work harder, to set himself more demanding goals and to achieve his potential. Part of my plan was to get under his skin and to get to know him better on a personal basis, and this is where I came unstuck as I broke the college's rules by taking him out for an evening. Against his protestations I took him into Nottingham, where we had several beers in the famous pub called The Trip to Jerusalem, which is built into a hillside, and then set off to The Silver Slipper, where there was an excellent traditional jazz band playing with Humphrey Lyttelton fronting. We not only had a good time but I got to know him as an individual and managed to get my feelings about his potential across to him. Flushed with success I was quickly brought up short when Peter Terry told me the next morning that I had been reported for going out socializing with a flight cadet and was to report to the Commandant's office at once in my No. 1 uniform. I was subjected to yet another one-sided interview in which Air Vice-Marshal Denis Spotswood (later Marshal of the Royal Air Force Sir Denis Spotswood: Chief of the Air Staff) informed me that I had broken the code of the college, clearly had little idea of the protocols involved, and was setting a very bad example. He became coldly angry when I attempted to explain why I had taken Gerry out, cut me off short and told me that he would look at the wisdom of retaining me at Cranwell. As it turned out the opportunity to move me came about eight months later because there was a need to reduce the number of Vampire QFIs when they started to phase out the aircraft and I was posted to RAF Leeming in Yorkshire to help open up that base as a Jet Provost flying training station. This move, however, was to be the best thing that ever happened to me because without it I would never have met my future wife.

The evening out with Gerry did, however, despite the Commandant's 'misgivings', bear fruit because Gerry and I began to work wonderfully well together and I was proud as punch on his Passing Out parade in December when the Reviewing Officer, the 1st Sea Lord, Sir Casper John, presented him with the Flying Trophy: I felt vindicated.

The course ended with a 'jolly' on 6 December for the cadets when we flew them to RAF Valley in close formation, had lunch there and came back in the afternoon. And this trip vindicated even more the trouble that I had taken with Gerry because on that day I was flying as Red 6 on the port of the leader but unfortunately had a monumental hangover and when we took off in close formation I was looking across the two-seat cockpit of the Vampire T11, and had considerable difficulty focusing on the leader. We became airborne in very tight 'Vic' and as I retracted the undercarriage we lurched dangerously at the leader; Gerry quickly grabbed the stick and with an: 'I have control Sir' stabilized us at a correct and respectable distance from my unintentional victim. The rest of the flight was unexceptional, mainly because I let him do the flying!

Christmas passed in a blur of parties with, as usual, three days spent at Dad's in Chestfield and three days from Boxing Day with Mum and Carole. Back at the college we had one week of getting ourselves back into shape in the air whilst getting to know our new students and giving them all the ground briefing on the aircraft before their first flights. During this period I notched up my 1000 hours of total flying and celebrated in the Mess with a drinks party. My new students, John Swaine and Phil Burton, made a very good impression on me and both did indeed turn out to be diligent and steady and no trouble at all. I did not, however, discover in them the spark that I had with Gerry Crumbie. What was pleasant, however, was taking someone who had never flown a jet aircraft before (Gerry had already done some flying with another instructor) and see the student copying and learning from you; even replicating some bad habits. I also like to think that I was able to implant some of my enthusiasm and love of flying and open up to them the sheer delight of flying an aircraft with reasonable performance which handled so responsively. And also, when we reached the formation stage, the thrill of tucking an aircraft in tight against another and holding it there no matter what the leader did. Phil turned out to be a steady if not inspired pilot but John Swaine emulated Gerry by winning the flying trophy and then surprised me by opting to go onto transport aircraft when, with his flying skills, he was eminently suited for fighters.

I now began to have some problems as, although I loved the social life at the college and made some wonderfully close friends, I felt out of kilter with the rigid formalities and was left in no doubt how badly I had blotted my copybook over the evening out with Gerry. I was also disciplined over the behaviour of Hassan, who had chased sheep in the local area and killed a large number of hares on and around the airfield, which brought me into conflict with the College Shoot. This all affected my flying and my re-categorization went poorly, leading to a retest. Whilst re-sitting this I was told that as I had clearly not settled into the ethos of the college I would be posted off the unit at the end of August to RAF Leeming in Yorkshire; unsurprisingly I began suffering a crisis of confidence and my ACR by Peter Terry accurately reflected this:

'Flight Lieutenant Evans is chronically under confident. He has an inferiority complex, with the Service being particularly unkind to him because he never stays long enough in one place to become good at a job and build up his ego. Just when he was set to take his A2 (the advanced QFI exam) he was posted to Leeming and I feel he is giving up on the Service.'This report was endorsed by the Chief Flying Instructor and the Station Commander, but the latter's comments are worth recording: 'I agree entirely with the assessments and remarks.

Evans is a very pleasant young man and very good company socially. It is difficult to understand why he should be so under confident (perhaps his chronically under confident Saluki has something to do with it and maybe he should get a placid sheep dog instead!). If he could only develop more assurance he would be a much more effective officer.'

The long breaks between terms enabled me to spread my wings and I spent a great deal of time with Uncle Bill marshalling at various aviation meetings for the Royal Aero Club. We spent three hilarious nights at the Chase Hotel in Coventry for the King's Cup Air Race and helped supervise the Shoreham Air Meeting. I also started playing tennis seriously and went out to Malta in June with the Station team on a Varsity aircraft via Orange in France to play a series of matches with the RAF units on Malta. Best by far, however, was a holiday spent with Andy Jones in August in the South of France. We drove down there in his VW Beetle and camped near Nice. His prospective father-in-law (Air Marshal Beckwith) owned a cottage called La Bergerie at Sclos de Contes near L'Escarene in the Alpes Maritimes just north of Nice. We slept in camp beds on the terraces under the stars, spent all day in bathing trunks and water ski'd every day using the Air Marshal's boat and skis at Antibes. In the evenings we ate like kings (I was introduced to escargots), and drank red wine under the stars until it was time to get our heads down prior to another exhausting day on the skis. All too soon it was back to reality and the formality of Cranwell, but with the prospect of a fresh life at Leeming.

Group Captain Lynch-Blosse had been a wonderfully humane Station Commander, had invited me into his home on many occasions and never failed to encourage me. His example remained with me and in my later career I know that I drew on my experience with him in my relationships with others. Be that as it may, although I was very upset at being posted away in the manner that I was, I have no doubt that the college was not the place for me to develop and allow my natural strengths to come into play. There is no doubt that I was immature but the rigidity of the regime, requirement for absolute conformity and denial of any attempt to use initiative were all totally alien to my natural instincts. RAF Leeming was in contrast a unit at which I would be encouraged to do everything that the RAF College had denied.

Chapter 6

Love in the Dales

In love, as in war, we must come into contact before we can triumph
Napoleon Bonoparte quoted 1842, after his death

On 18 September I packed Hassan and all my kit into the Ford Consul that I had bought after selling my mechanically troubled Triumph Roadster, and drove up the A1 to RAF Leeming. I was with friends because there were five of us from Cranwell amongst the dozen or so who were detailed to initiate flying training at the newly formed No. 3 Flying Training School. Leeming had been a Javelin Operational Conversion Unit but the only evidence of their presence was a very bent Javelin in one of the hangars, caused by it flying into the arrester barrier on landing!

The Officers' Mess was a classic 1930s style and the PMC encouraged dog ownership. I was lucky to get a ground floor corner room which meant that Hassan could jump in and out of the window whenever he needed to relieve himself. Dennis Southern, Jake Barclay and I were on 'A' Flight of No. 1 Squadron under the command of Squadron Leader Paddy Glover and after two familiarization trips on Jet Provost T3 (XN598) I went solo. I started instructing after a further twenty-five trips which we used to practise the patter and techniques required for students who had never flown before. Unlike Cranwell, where I had been an advanced instructor, at Leeming we were tasked with taking our students right the way through from scratch until they reached 'Wings' standard on the same type of aircraft; the Jet Provost. The JP was remarkably easy to fly; too easy in some ways as it did not build up the stress loading in the way that occurred when going from the basic Piston Provosts to the relatively slippery Vampire. It had, however, a very comfortable cockpit and whilst much less powerful than the Vampire it was more comprehensively equipped and a pleasure to instruct in.

I was not too impressed with my two students, Moore and Nelson, and they were understandably of very different quality from the cadets at Cranwell. Nelson I found to be very shy and under-confident, whilst Moore was just the opposite, so I was faced with developing two diametrically opposed instructional techniques to impart the same information. I found it fascinating to see them develop and gain confidence as their skill levels improved and to coach and coax them into achieving higher standards. Not only were we allowed to try our own ideas but I was given a free hand to run the Station squash and basketball teams and also (as the senior living-in Mess member) to organize most of the social events in the Mess. My previously commented upon under-confidence disappeared and I began to realize that I could motivate other people and gain a tremendous amount of pleasure in the process.

The social life was terrific and A Flight was pre-eminent in partying as well as flying, with our Flight Commander, Flight Lieutenant Ian Chalmers, setting the standard and myself, Dennis Southern, Jake Barclay, Lofty Lance, Thorney Thorneycroft, Wally Norton, and Bill Bailey, ably supporting him and spurred on by our Boss, Paddy Glover. The Fancy Dress New Year party to welcome in 1962 was a real highlight as the quality of costume was extraordinary: I had been to Chestfield (where Dad and Auntie Norah now had their homes) and Normandy for my usual Christmas break but could not get back by car because of blizzards, so travelled by train. Having left King's Cross at 1455 hours we ground our way slowly north and I decided to warm things up in our compartment by opening a bottle of Scotch, which was gratefully received and led to others unearthing their bottles and starting an impromptu party. I was persuaded to don my fancy dress Charlie's Aunt costume that Mum had made for me and by the time I got off at Northallerton in a blinding snowstorm I was also pickled, much to the amusement of the taxi driver who delivered me to the Mess. I was greeted rapturously by my friends on the Flight and we all reckoned that 1962 was the best New Year of all.

Flying took several different turns as, despite all my efforts on his behalf, Nelson was suspended for lack of general ability. It was the first time a student of mine had failed and I felt very bad about it, because it made me feel that I had failed him. Fortunately, Moore was making steady progress which was reassuring and I also upgraded to A2 standard of QFI after two very full days of examination by Flight Lieutenant Brimson at the Central Flying School. This was a significant step forward and enabled me to accept more responsibility and have much more authority: I did wonder if I would have achieved it had I stayed at Cranwell. Exuberance overtook me on the flight back and I performed more than twenty minutes of continuous aerobatics including three consecutive slow rolls through the smoke from the brickworks near Peterborough: with little visible horizon it was not the most sensible thing to do. The wonderful end to the flight was when I landed and taxied in; Ian Chalmers had arranged for the whole Flight to clap me into the crew room from the aircraft and then what a party we had!

The pace of life quickened in every respect as the number of students increased with the arrival of a course consisting of ex-members of University Air Squadrons and, with my new 'A' category, I became involved in check flights and dealing with students who were having difficulties. I relished the opportunity and in March I flew forty-two trips and broke the forty hours of flying in a month barrier. At the same time I was captaining our Station squash and basketball teams and having reunions with old friends and ex-students. I journeyed down to RAF Swinderby for a weekend with Andy Jones and then up to RAF Acklington, north of Newcastle, for a weekend with Gerry Crumbie who had started instructing there on Jet Provosts, whilst Phil Burton came and spent the weekend at Leeming, prior to going out to Singapore to fly Shackletons. Whatever may have been said about my relationship with students at Cranwell, I did feel vindicated that they all seemed to want to keep contact with me and clearly enjoyed my company.

The new course of students started in June following the graduation of the first course to have started at Leeming and it contained a large number of NCOs. This was a trial that the RAF was carrying out because of the difficulty they were having in recruiting enough potential pilots who possessed acceptable 'Officer' qualities. I was responsible for three of the sergeants on the course and the difference in quality from our officer students was as marked as they had been from the RAF College students. The three young men were all charming and keen but lacked drive and initiative and became steady but uninspired performers. Several found the demands of the course beyond them and one of my students (an ex-airman) even found the demands of living in the Sergeants' Mess too much for him and resigned from the course to continue service in the ranks. All in all the entire scheme was not a success and the RAF very quickly reverted to all officer training.

My return from my summer holiday coincided with the arrival of a new Officer Commanding Engineering Wing and this event was to change my life permanently as he brought with him his lovely 18-year-old daughter Therese; hereafter for ever to be called Terry. I was alerted to her presence on the station on 10 August when Jake Barclay burst into the Squadron Crew Room and told me that: 'There is a terrific looking girl just installed as one of the Station Commander's secretaries and you'd better get down there quickly or she'll be snapped up by one of the students.'

I grabbed his bike and hurtled down to the Station Headquarters to be confronted by the Adjutant 'Black' Paddy English who told me to push off. I eventually persuaded him to let me see the new girl and was immediately bowled over by her good looks. I refused to take her 'no' for an answer when inviting her out and guaranteed that we would make up a foursome to go to the pictures that night so that we would be chaperoned. It was only after I had left that I realized the address that she had given me was one of the senior officers' married quarters and I began to question the wisdom of what I had done. I then had to persuade Jake to accompany us with Audrey his wife and this he did after blackmailing me into paying for their cinema tickets and a meal! It did work out extremely well, however, as we got on wonderfully well and I was smitten enough to announce publicly in the crew room the next day that I had found the girl that I was going to marry.

The RAF attempted to put a spoke in my wheel by detaching me on 17 August to London to run the RAF stand on the Radio Show at Earls Court for two weeks. But before departing I persuaded Terry to come down to London for the weekend of the Farnborough Air Show and, even more importantly, persuaded her parents, Wing Commander Douglas Goodrich and his wife Joan that my intentions were honourable and that she would be meeting my family and would be extremely well chaperoned. I then set off for London and stayed with friends at 357A Finchley Road in the company of eight other residents; my bedroom being the kitchen in which I slept on a camp bed in company with an Italian and Hassan, who did not think much of the set-up at all. I could not wait to get back to Leeming to see Terry and saw her every evening of the week of my return until it was time to set off to drive her down to London on the Friday to stay in the Strand Palace hotel and take in the show *A Funny Thing Happened on the Way to the Forum* with Frankie Howerd. On the Saturday we went to the air show, where my Uncle Bill made the biggest fuss of Terry imaginable, and then went to Normandy to show her off to Mum and Carole. On the Sunday we sunbathed in Green Park listening to the band which was playing in the forecourt of Buckingham Palace, had lunch at a restaurant in Leicester Square and then went to the National Gallery to see the Leonardo da Vinci cartoon that had just been purchased by the nation for £800,000. It was a weekend to remember and by the time it had ended I was in no doubt whatsoever that I had met my future wife.

Back at work our flying was interrupted when the aviation doctors became concerned that the amount of flying that we were doing at high level in the unpressurized Jet Provost could lead to medical problems.

It was decided that all QFIs should undergo testing in the pressurization chamber at the Royal Naval Station at Lee-on-Solent and on 23 October we spent all day being tested after a very thorough medical examination. We underwent the normal anoxia testing whilst being kept at a simulated altitude of 35,000ft for three hours. Luckily no one showed any signs of ill-effects apart from the hangovers resulting from a night out in Southsea where I paid a memory-triggering visit to the Pomme d'Or.

My romance with Terry progressed very smoothly as her parents encouraged us and all my friends on the squadron, who couldn't wait to see me married (I was the only bachelor), engineered events such as babysitting requirements which brought us together. Visits to York, Harrogate and Darlington for shopping and the cinema; Ripon for Chinese meals, a terrific social programme in the Mess, and many an evening spent at the Goodrich's playing Mah Jong, meant that we saw each other nearly every day and I found that I just could not get enough of Terry's company. Not only was she gorgeous but was tremendous fun and seemed to really enjoy what we did together. At long last I found that I was enjoying my life because I was thinking of someone other than myself and getting fun from seeing the enjoyment that I could bring to another person. I missed her so much when I went south for the 1962 Christmas with my parents that I felt that it would be silly to wait any longer and proposed to her on 15 January 1963.

I took the precaution of obtaining her parents' permission first and then reserved a table at The Leeming Garth Motel, which was reckoned to be the best local restaurant, before spending a wonderfully romantic evening with her, at the end of which I dropped to one knee and proposed. Her acceptance was greeted with universal delight by all our families and friends and we made arrangements immediately for our marriage on 15 June. We went into Leeds and bought a three-stone diamond engagement ring, reserved the Mess for the reception and obtained agreement from my cousin the Reverend Hubert Butcher, for him to marry us in the local church, St Gregory's of Bedale. The most important thing in some ways was that both Dad and Mum agreed to come as a couple to the wedding, which, with my sister Carole acting as bridesmaid, meant that I would have my whole family around me for the day.

It was at this time that Douglas Goodrich played a very important part in my life by having a chat with me about my future career intentions. I trotted out some half-formed ideas about leaving the RAF at the end of my 12-year engagement and joining civilian airlines: the truth was that I was having so much fun that to think of anything more than six months into the future did not even feature. This was not good enough for Dougie and he let me know so in no uncertain terms. He did, however, go further and tell me that, after discussing me with my superiors he was convinced that I could have a very productive career in the RAF if I could obtain a Permanent Commission (PC).

In general terms the only 'career' officers in the RAF were those that had been through the RAF College at Cranwell, but a limited number of PCs were on offer each year to enable the RAF to take advantage of officers on short service commissions who nevertheless had the potential for higher rank. I gave in to the pressure exerted by my future father-in-law and entered the competition to the amusement of most of my peers. To my surprise I found the interviews and tests both interesting and enjoyable and none more so than the one with our AOC, Air Marshal Cole, who encouraged me to give my views on the future shape of the RAF and the equipment required to support it. To my delight I was one of only two officers in our Group to be offered PCs and accepted with alacrity: I really did not give much thought to what effect it would have on me but it did get Dougie Goodrich off my back and enabled me to get on with things that mattered like flying and Terry!

The months did seem to pass slowly, but I did an incredible amount of flying and in May completed fifty-six sorties for a fifty-three hour total. The highlight of the month, however, was a trip to Middleton St George on 2 May where my friend Andy Jones gave me a flight in a Lightning T4 (XM997) in which we did a speed run of Mach 1.6 to qualify for the 'ten ton' club for people who have travelled at more than 1,000mph (M1.6 equated to 1,075mph). The flight was a revelation as I had clearly 'down-tuned' to Jet Provost speeds but the whole impression was startling, beginning with the sheer size of the aircraft and the height of the ladder that you had to climb to get into it. The acceleration on take-off using afterburners was extraordinary and the 3½G rotation after take-off (done to slow the acceleration in order to allow the undercarriage time to retract before exceeding its limiting speed) completely disorientated me. My next surprise was the extraordinary steep angle of climb as Andy rotated the aircraft and the horizon disappeared from view and, with the extreme sweep of the wings, I found that I had no way of assessing my climb and had to convert immediately to the roller blind artificial horizon. Just as I was becoming accustomed to this Andy levelled off, punched the stopwatch and said: 'One minute fifty-six seconds from take-off, not bad for 36,000ft, eh! Well let's go for the fast run.'

The mach meter moved steadily up to Mach 1 with the only indication that we had gone through the Sound Barrier being an apparent loss of 300ft on the altimeter at the moment of transition to supersonic speed in level flight. Andy throttled back and there we were at the magic 1,000mph with M1.62 on the dial; at which point he handed over to me and let me do the rest of the trip under his tutelage except for the final circuit and landing. As the brake chute popped out and we were thrown forward into our harnesses I truly believed that it had been the most exciting ride of my life and, after an emotional farewell with Andy, I flew back to Leeming inverted in my JP for most of the time and interspersed this with as gut-wrenching a series of aerobatics as I could manage. I was exultant. What a day, and one that I rammed down my friends' throats at every available opportunity! Little did I know that three years later I would be going solo on a Lightning at RAF Coltishall whilst Terry would be giving birth to our first child. In June I did 14 trips up to the day before our marriage and then did not fly again until 1 July.

Terry and I were up to our ears organizing our wedding and although her parents agreed to pay for the reception they left all the payment for the wedding gown, bridesmaids' dresses and incidentals to me, which practically exhausted my reserves of cash. I had booked our honeymoon in Majorca at Cala San Vicente, flying out of Gatwick, and reckoned that we might just have enough spending money, if we were careful. The Goodrichs agreed to look after Hassan and my cousin Hubert invited us both to his home in his parish of Bradford so that he could go through the marriage preparation with us. He was superb except for causing Terry to get uncontrollable giggles every time we practised the actual ceremony.

All the family arrived on 14 June and although I flew during the morning, Paddy Glover gave me the afternoon off to go and collect them. At the same time all my mates started to arrive and the visiting aircraft park was soon full of Lightnings, Canberras and Jet Provosts, and the noise level in the Mess started to rise as the party got underway. Terry had her hen night at her parents' whilst my stag night in the Mess really took off with games breaking up the drinking. I was eventually recovered from the bottom of a Mess rugby scrum unconscious and carried to bed on a door that had been ripped off its hinges with lit candles all around the edge in the style of a Viking funeral. I was later charged for this door, a settee damaged beyond repair and two bicycles that had disintegrated during 'corridor jousting'! Far too soon the dawn broke and Paul Houselander dragged me unwillingly from my sleep and helped me dress in my No. 1 uniform before escorting me to Bedale for the wedding.

Terry took my breath away when she appeared in the church as she looked quite the most beautiful girl imaginable. Her dress was modelled on that worn by Princess Alexandra whilst she was carrying a beautiful bouquet in which freesias were dominant and gave off the most wonderful smell. The wedding passed in a blur whilst clear blue skies and sunshine enhanced the ceremony and my friend Win Harris flew a Jet Provost overhead at the moment we came out of the church under the crossed swords of our guard of honour: my own sword became a very necessary prop as I struggled to keep a smile on my face whilst coping with a throbbing hangover. The photoshoot went well and provided some lovely pictures of my mum and dad together as a permanent reminder of my real family, but the star of the show was Terry who was absolutely radiant and the object of a vast amount of male adoration; grudgingly permitted by the accompanying wives and girlfriends. It was followed by the reception in the Officers' Mess (slightly marred by the fact that Jack Pollard had sprayed most of the floral decorations with lighter fluid the previous night before setting fire to them).

Our honeymoon was perfection with a lovely hotel overlooking the bay and a huge macaw called Jacko on a perch just below our window who chatted to us constantly and became our real favourite. We hired a motor scooter, which Terry persuaded me to let her drive and which she immediately crashed, but used all her feminine skills to avoid paying for the damage. It was a heavenly break in which we got to know each other properly, made plans for the future (most of them wrong), decided on two children (correct) and wondered where my next posting would be?

The answer to that last question was quickly resolved on our return as my Wing Commander Flying, Basil Lock, worked wonders to overturn a posting to Vulcans on the V-Force and had me re-assigned to Canberras in Germany. I was not ecstatic about bombers, even if they did have an interdiction role, but Germany sounded good and so we looked for a short term lodging until my move in September. We were really lucky in finding a two-bedroom flat 'Stabann' in the market place at Bedale, overlooking the church in which we were married, at £5.5s per week.

My flight commander, Ian Chalmers, decided to squeeze every last bit from me during my final two months at Leeming and I did 48 flights in July despite being away for one week at Plymouth doing the Sea Survival Course. Fifty hours of flying in three weeks was hardly the start to married life that Terry and I had anticipated, and neither was she happy being left alone for a week. I then did thirty-three flights in August before we left for RAF Bassingbourn after an immense party in the Mess.

And so came to an end a most eventful tour in which I re-established myself on the flying side, regained my confidence, had more fun than it was decent to experience, and met and married a most beautiful and wonderful person who would give me more love and support than anyone ever should expect to receive.

Canberras and Germany beckoned.

Chapter 7

Operational at Last

Make no mistake. There is no such thing as a conventional nuclear weapon
Lyndon B Johnson in Detroit, August 1964

With Hassan on the back seat and most of our worldly goods piled around him as well as in the boot we drove south on 25 August to the village of Barrington near Cambridge, where we were going to stay with Paul and Di Houselander at The Boot, Boot Lane, during my time on the Canberra Conversion Course at RAF Bassingbourn (No. 231 Operational Conversion Unit). They lived in a thatched cottage with timbered ceilings, sloping floors and a central staircase. We had our own little lounge where we could cut ourselves off and this became very necessary as Di's new baby Peter (born on the 20 August) developed colic and screamed every evening from 1800 hours onwards which made my study and homework rather difficult.

Having been trained initially as a fighter pilot I was now about to move from the defence of our country to being part of the force that would engage in attacking the enemy. In the event of an attack on the UK the heavy strategic punch would come from our V-Force but the first to be thrown into the attack in a quick response would be our Canberra force stationed in Germany. Situated close to the Warsaw Pact borders they could be airborne within minutes and would attack vital enemy positions with nuclear weapons. If, however, the war did not develop into a nuclear exchange the Canberras could also deliver conventional bombs or fire guns or rockets: this was termed its 'interdiction or (I)' role.

The course started on 28 August with four pilots and four navigators and we all had to do four weeks of ground school before starting the flying phase. The ground school was quite tough but as nearly all of it was new to me I found it very interesting, particularly on the weapon side. As the Canberra could carry nuclear weapons we undertook a short course at RAF Wittering where there was a nuclear facility so that we could actually see, touch and smell them, as well as learn about the style of delivery, which in our case would be Low Altitude Bombing System (LABS). With the ground exams behind us we were left to crew up and I paired with the only NCO among the navigators because the others were all straight from training whereas Jack Stewart had had two tours as a signaller on Neptunes and Shackletons before converting to navigator and I reckoned that this would give him an edge in airmanship. He and I became very good friends and combined to make an extremely efficient team: the only downside, which I had not taken into account, was that we had rather different social lives because officers and NCOs used different Messes and married quarters. We did, however, take every opportunity to go out together with Terry and Esme, his wife.

The Canberra was very different from any aircraft that I had flown before, although it was a classic design enabling it to fulfil the many roles to which it was assigned. The T4 dual-controlled trainer was powered by two Avon Mk I engines, each of 6,500lbs static thrust, and the performance was surprisingly lively with a take-off speed of 100 knots and a climb of 330 knots until .72 Mach was reached: the top speed was 450 knots or .84 Mach. The aircraft was also fully aerobatic and with well harmonized controls and light aileron forces I looked forward to performing the loop from low level, from which the weapon was released in the LABS delivery: the loop was converted into a diving roll from the top so that the aircraft could achieve maximum distance from the nuclear weapon at its point of detonation.

The strangest and hardest part for me, however, was learning to rely on someone else to do the navigation. I also found the two-hour flight durations quite tiring but after five flights in the two-pilot T4 Trainer I went solo and then started flying on operational conversion using the B2 bomber with Jack acting as navigator. Asymmetric flying was interesting and demanding but I loved the low-level aspects and the bombing brought out a very competitive edge in me. We bombed from 10,000ft at a ship target in the Wash but practised our LABS deliveries from 250ft but without releasing weapons. Night flying was a delight but I did manage to have one incident that caused me to have a rap over the knuckles and derision from my peers. The B2 Canberras were all parked on the far side of the airfield on 'D' shaped dispersal pans outlined with blue lights at ground level. After starting the aircraft in the pitch dark I taxied out and followed a line of blue lights which I mistook to be the inside of the taxi-way but which turned out to be an optical illusion caused by a number of pans lining up to form an apparent straight line edge to my imagined taxi-way. This caused me to taxi onto the grass where I got stuck up to my axles in mud and had to shut down with the aircraft having to be de-fuelled to lighten it, so that it could be pulled out: not an impressive end to my Conversion Course! The good news was that our posting was to No. 3 Squadron at RAF Geilenkirchen in Germany flying the B(I)8 Canberras which had the dual role of low level nuclear strike/interdiction: the interdiction role used cannons mounted in a pack in the bomb bay and conventional (iron) bombs which were dropped from wing pylons.

Complications preceded my move to Germany as the squadron contacted me to say that there was no married quarter available and I would have to find my own accommodation in the local area. Until I did that I was not allowed to bring Terry out with me and I was to live in the Officers' Mess at RAF Geilenkirchen. Feeling very upset about this I was relieved when Mum said that Terry could stay with them until her move to Germany. In the meantime we spent my last three days at Chestfield and it was from there that I set off on 20 January in my Ford Consul with Hassan on the back seat and waving goodbye to Terry, Dad, Auntie Nor and Nana Evans with unashamed tears rolling down my cheeks. How little did I realize how many times this event would take place over the next twenty-five years with the sight of 131 Chestfield Road receding in the rear-view mirror as we embarked on yet another adventure. I drove to Dover, used the cross Channel ferry to Calais and then drove through Brussels, Liege, Louvain, and Aachen to Geilenkirchen where I found a room reserved for myself in hutted accommodation.

The chaps on the squadron were very welcoming and it was good to be reunited with Jack Stewart, but morale was not high because of the demands of maintaining aircraft on permanent nuclear alert, the difficulty of finding accommodation off base, and the prickly nature of the Squadron Commander. The primary role of the squadron was to respond with great speed to any aggression by the Warsaw Pact (WP) and mount nuclear strikes into WP territory if nuclear weapons were used against us. This meant that all squadron members had to be on constant call (at various readiness times) and live within ten miles of the base: unfortunately as the base was right on the Dutch border and the border closed at midnight we were limited to finding somewhere to live within a ten-mile semicircle.

The Canberra B(I)8 was powered by two Avon Mk 109 engines of 7,400lbs static thrust and although the airframe limitations were similar to other models, these more powerful engines gave it a much more lively performance. As it was also heavier, however, it proved to be a very stable aircraft and well suited to the long low-level sorties that we were required to undertake in order to practise for our war role.

I got quickly into my stride with the flying as I fell in love with the B(I)8 Canberra because it handled so well and was so versatile. With its offset bubble pilot's canopy the view was superb and a comprehensive suite of navigation aids meant that Jack could settle quickly into achieving a good navigation standard. After two trips in a dual T4 (WJ846) with, first, the squadron QFI (Flight Lieutenant Greg Marsh) and then my Deputy 'A' Flight Commander (Flight Lieutenant Eric Denson), I went solo in B(I)8 (XH208) and then concentrated on doing nothing but low-level flying all over northern Germany. We were part of RAF Germany which at that time consisted of the RAF bases at Geilenkirchen, Bruggen, Laarbruch, Wildenrath, and Gutersloh. We always flew north across the Rhine at 3,000ft and then let down to 250ft above the ground which we maintained for two-and-a-half to three hours of the flight. It was exciting and demanding and usually took in four runs down the range at Nordhorn, where we released practice bombs using the LABS delivery of pulling back at 3½g with micro-switches triggering off the release at 45° or 60° so that the bomb was tossed down the range whilst the aircraft rolled off the top of the loop (usually in cloud) and then dived at full throttle in order to escape the effects of the blast, heat, and light that would occur if it had been an actual nuclear release. The low-level flying was exhilarating and we used the 250ft rule merely as a guide and quite arrogantly and illegally spent long periods at treetop height, with adrenalin really pumping through the body: there are few thrills greater than rolling into a turn and seeing people gaping up at you as you flash just over their heads.

Our big drawback was the winter weather, which, over the North German plain, could be dreadful with low cloud, freezing rain and fog, and snow. The former could cause appalling problems with visual navigation and the latter obliterated many of the landmarks we needed for that navigation. It was for this reason that, after about sixty hours of B(I)8 flying, on 22 March Jack and I took XH228 down to Idris Airfield on the outskirts of Tripoli, Libya. King Idris was Libya's monarch at that time and had very friendly relations with the West, unlike his successor. With absolutely perfect weather it meant that we could concentrate on practising our LABS weapon deliveries and were able to deliver forty practice bombs on the Tarhuna range just south of the airfield before returning to Geilenkirchen on 26 March. Idris had been an old Italian Air Force base prior to the Second World War and was built in a delightful colonial style: the hangars even had patterned tile floors. With palm trees and exotic flowers everywhere it really was a different world but the heat and resulting turbulence meant that we flew very early in the day with our first take-off at 0700 hours so that we could finish by midday. Afternoons were spent exploring Tripoli, and buying strange Arab items in the souk before bathing in the pool at Idris and getting a winter tan. All too soon the desert dunes, orange groves, and sparkling blue sea were receding in our rear-view mirror as we settled down for the three-hour flight home.

The big news in February, however, was that Paddy Malooly, who was the navigator of my friend John Ambler, had vacated his flat in the village of Geilenkirchen and I was able to negotiate the let with the landlady Frau Franken (John and another pilot, Tony Oldfield, had both been students of mine at RAF Leeming). The flat consisted of a large kitchen with an electric cooker, a large lounge separated from the main bedroom by a sliding glass door, and a second bedroom upstairs where there was also the bathroom, which we shared with Frau Franken and Berndt (her son). They were so welcoming and friendly that it turned out to be one of the happiest periods of our lives, particularly as Hassan was adored by them both.

Terry arrived on 1 March at the RAF terminal at RAF Wildenrath and received a rapturous welcome from me and a less enthusiastic one from Hassan who turned his back on her and wet on a tree! After punishing her for two days by ignoring her, he then forgave her and from then on for the rest of his life became devoted to her. I had decorated the flat with potted plants and bunches of flowers and our friends the Amblers gave her some beautiful tulips. The weekend was a constant round of introducing her to all my squadron friends and their wives as well as going across the Dutch border into Heerlen where we tended to eat out and buy most of our goods that the NAAFI could not supply.

John and Annie Ambler did, however, treat us to a welcome meal at a restaurant near RAF Wildenrath called the Molzmulle where we started with snails, followed by roast chicken and asparagus washed down with some excellent Rhine wine, and then coffee and cigars with dancing on a highly polished dance floor to a superb small jazz style group. All in all we were settling down to life on an operational squadron, with its tight-knit friendships and sense of common purpose, and starting to enjoy being in a foreign country. Not least this involved Terry starting to accompany Frau Franken to her Geilenkirchen Women's Club at the local Gasthof where they played nine-pin bowls in the cellar. The twist to this was that anyone who rolled a bowl into the gutter had to drink schnapps and as Terry was inexpert there were several occasions when she and Frau Franken rolled home, pickled and singing merrily together. Frau Franken also invited us to the dinner party that she gave for her son's twenty-first and made us feel a real part of her family. They came down to join us for drinks after my twenty-seventh birthday dinner at which Terry excelled by serving me a lemon chicken main course washed down by a very fine Moselle wine and all under candlelight, aided by the soft illumination of a beautiful bedside lamp as my present. She had also baked me a wonderful birthday cake which even Hassan deigned to sample: it was a memorable first birthday for me as a married man. The boys, however, got to hear about it and descended on the flat the next night so that at one time we had more than twenty of them drinking our liquors and serving impromptu food from the kitchen: I noted that they disposed of ten cans of soup, twenty-four eggs and all our cheese, bread and spaghetti! They were clearly in a mellow mood as they allowed me to play my Modern Jazz Quartet and Dave Brubeck records as party music.

I took a major step forward on 27 April when my Flight Commander, Squadron Leader Hirst, flew with us and declared us operational. This meant that I was included in the Squadron War complement, given a target in one of the Warsaw Pact countries for the delivery of a nuclear weapon in case of war, and required to take my turn on the Quick Reaction Alert (QRA) roster. This was a 24-hour tour of duty inside a compound near the eastern end of the runway in which there were two shelters each housing a Canberra B(I)8 loaded with a live nuclear weapon. Two crews were required to be on alert at all times and capable of getting airborne inside four minutes from the time of the alert hooter sounding. As well as the two crews inside the alert building we had eight ground crew, an American Release Officer (because the weapons were American) and a US and British guard on each aircraft. If you decided to sleep the only concession made was that you could take your flying boots off and I can recall several occasions in the middle of the night flying headlong after tripping on my laces when racing for the aircraft during a practice alert, having pulled my boots on after being dramatically woken by the hooter from a deep sleep. The QRA targets were always pre-planned and we were tested regularly on our knowledge of the route to them which I had to be able to carry out, even if Jack was incapacitated. It was all very professional in some ways, but had elements of the ludicrous as we were required to carry eye patches to be put on after take-off so that if we were blinded by the flash from a nuclear explosion (there would be quite a lot going off if we were ever called upon to do the mission) then we would be able to take it off and carry on with the good eye: no-one ever explained what we were meant to do after the next flash!

We shared the base with two Javelin squadrons, Nos. 5 and 11, and began to make friends with some of them and join in their parties. A particular success was a No. 5 Squadron 'pirate' party at which they served a suckling pig on a spit, supplemented with roast chickens and corn on the cob. Equipped with masks, swords and headscarves we looked a villainous crew and had sufficient to drink that we slept it off in a spare room in the Mess – much to Hassan's disgust when we returned home next morning. With the approach of our Summer Ball I 'misused' a Canberra by taking it on a training navigation exercise to RAF Leuchars in Scotland where, mysteriously, 80lbs of salmon was loaded into a pallet in my bomb bay for the return flight. It did enable me to spend a couple of hours during the turnaround with Gerry Crumbie, who was on No. 43 Squadron, Lightnings. Being in the RAF was living up to my expectations of the Service existing as a special extended family with friends everywhere you went. The sting in the tail for me, however, was that the Squadron Commander put me on QRA for the night of the ball, as I was the most recently qualified operational crew, and so I missed out on the salmon. Terry was distraught and I insisted that she went with our friends the Muloolys so that she at least could enjoy what she had been looking forward to for so long and for which she had made a new ball gown and Mum had bought her some new long gloves. At midnight the phone in the QRA compound went, and it was a very tiddly wife calling from the Officers' Mess to say how well she was being looked after. When I arrived home at 0900 hours I found her in the kitchen in her ball gown having coffee after having breakfasted in the Mess and just being driven home by the Muloolys.

Our big excitement, however, was in collecting our new Ford Zephyr 6 from the garage in Heerlen: white with red trim, it was the first new car that I had owned and it really was very smart. It was to give us tremendous service in the two years that we owned it as it was big, fast, and wonderfully comfortable, with a huge boot; all these features were to be much appreciated during the time that we owned it.

The workload on the squadron was stepping up and I detailed in a letter to Mum on 9 August that during the previous week I had spent a total of 125 hours 45 minutes on duty. I spent all Saturday on QRA, had Sunday off before going back on QRA on the Monday, from which I spent all Tuesday as Orderly Officer on base. I did two flights on Wednesday but did manage to sleep at home before going back on QRA on the Thursday. One hour before being relieved on the Friday (0715) the Station Alert hooter sounded which meant that we had to remain on QRA and go through full testing, readiness, and examination. Quite what a union representative would have made of that I do not know, but Terry's language was florid. I was also on QRA for the August grant but was given the next Friday off so Terry, Hassan and I got in the car and drove away for the three days down the Rhine. We visited the US Forces BX in Wiesbaden where we stocked up with all the canned food and gramophone records that we could afford as they were only a third of British prices. We then drove to Rudesheim where we used the cable cars looping over the vineyards to reach the monument on top of the hill and basked in sunshine whilst taking in the wonderful views of the Rhine valley. After a meal in Rudesheim we then started a wine cellar crawl that got out of hand, as we went from one to the next being seduced by the easy way that the wine slipped down and the intoxicating 'oom pa' music that filled each tavern. We suddenly realized that it was late, we were drunk, we had not fed Hassan, and we had nowhere to stay. I can remember cutting up lumps of meat for Hassan, on a wall overlooking the Rhine and then driving erratically up the road along the river for about five miles until we found a side road with a lay-by, in which we parked and went to sleep. Waking up shivering with the cold in the grey light of dawn and with the car stinking from Hassan's breath was not the perfect start to the day. But then there was the visual delight of seeing the superstructure of the barges showing above a solid white cotton wool of fog covering the Rhine under cloudless skies as they moved slowly up and downstream. After two magnificent cups of coffee at a riverside restaurant life returned and we motored slowly home.

Back at work I was detailed to take two aircraft down to Gibraltar via Malta which meant two legs of three and two-and-a-half hours on the Friday with Saturday off to enjoy the delights of the Rock and a three-hour direct flight home on the Sunday. My landing at Gib frightened Jack as he elected to remain in the nose and I failed to realize just how short the runway was and came to rest after a maximum braking effort with Jack's nose almost over the end of the rocks looking onto the sea: he was not amused. John Ambler, Paddy, Jack and I went on a pub crawl in Gib on the Friday night but on the Saturday we concentrated on shopping and sunbathing before crossing the border for a night of sherry drinking in La Linea and the acquisition of large amounts of melons and peaches. Breakfast in the Mess was enhanced by the sight of a school of dolphins playing in the bay right outside the windows and gave us something to talk about on the flight home.

In November I had to take three aircraft down to Malta for a week where we based ourselves at RAF Luqa and made daily excursions to Idris and Tarhuna for LABS training. It was very pleasant to leave the rains of Germany for the hot sun of the Mediterranean and cold beers drunk under starlit skies on the patio of the Mess. Back at Geilenkirchen I was tasked to pick up our Station Commander, Group Captain Rixon from RAF Thorney Island, and had a splendid flight home coaching him on flying the Canberra and talking him through the let down, circuit, and landing. We got on well and this was to play an important part in correcting what could have been a damaging moment in my career.

For reasons that I have never understood the Squadron Commander disliked me and made this clear in the way that he spoke to me and handled me. He chose to write my Annual Confidential Report (ACR) in October as First Reporting Officer instead of leaving this to my flight commander, and gave me a very poor assessment and write up. This report landed on the Station Commander's desk just after my trip with him and he savaged the Squadron Commander, amended upwards no fewer than twelve of the numerics, and wrote 'This is not a fair report and I have not seen this side of his character suggested by his Squadron Commander – if it is indeed there – but have found him to be outgoing, sensible and with an above average potential.' Who knows what my future would have been if I had not flown with Group Captain Rixon and he had not corrected my ACR?

My fighter background now came into play because the squadron's conventional weapons instructor was due for a posting and I was selected to fill his position. To qualify for this I had to complete the Day Fighter Combat School Course at the Central Fighter Establishment at RAF Binbrook near Grimsby. Once again leaving Hassan with Frau Franken, Terry and I went by train and ferry to Chestfield where I left Terry on 7 November, whilst I reported for the course. She spent time with Dad before going to Mum and Carole's and then up to RAF Leeming for a spell with her parents. The course was fantastic as it consisted of twenty-five sorties in the two-seat Hawker Hunter T7 (XL573,593,595) (which I had never flown before) doing nothing but air to ground deliveries with guns, rockets, dive bombing and skip (napalm) bombing. How I loved the feeling of being back on fighters and reefing the aircraft around in high 'g' turns with the pressure suit inflating hard across the stomach and down the legs. I received well above average assessments for my ground work and flying results and it was exciting and fulfilling to see the explosions of your rockets, bullets and bombs as they plastered the target and then experience the hard 'g' as you pulled violently away from the ground. All too soon it was over, but there had been one twist, because right in the middle of the one-month course I had to sit the 'C' Promotion Exam for promotion from Flight Lieutenant to Squadron Leader. It was rather a distraction but I gritted my teeth, stuck my head in a few books and relied on luck: it worked and I just scraped a pass, which at least got the hierarchy off my back. Terry celebrated her twenty-first birthday at her parents and we had a huge party in the Mess with all our old chums enhanced by the news that Terry's father was being promoted and going to HQ No. 1 Group at RAF Bawtry. Back to Chestfield to spend a day with Dad and then back to Geilenkirchen and a rapturous reception from Hassan.

We now had two new Flight Commanders, with Squadron Leader Dave Collins as my 'A' Flight Commander and Squadron Leader Pete Little with 'B'. Both were splendid characters, full of drive, humanity and charisma with Peter being an old friend of mine from QFI days at

Cranwell and also a double Olympic participant at the pentathlon. Both were to make a huge difference to the squadron's morale and efficiency and it was a tragedy that Dave killed himself when he moved on to Buccaneers and Pete did not make the career progress he merited because of a disagreement with the upper echelon about representing the country for a third time at the Olympics. The best news for me, however, was that we were to have a new squadron commander in the Spring and that heralded a wonderful last year for me on the squadron.

My new found skills were soon put to good use because I left for RAF Akrotiri in Cyprus on 5 January 1965 in my role as the squadron's Conventional Weapons Instructor in order to qualify six new crews in the Interdiction Role. I flew T4 (WT846) down the old familiar three-hour route to Malta, refuelled and then due east along a route that was new to me for one-and-a quarter hours to RAF Akrotiri. I set up the weapons camp, made sure that we had all the equipment, hangarage, operations facilities, air and ground crew accommodation, and range slots, and then had a whole day to explore the island of Cyprus with Jack before a Britannia brought in our ground crew and the B(I)8s arrived. What a change the weather was from Germany and we basked in the sunshine whilst embarking on an intensive qualification programme using targets at RAF Larnaca range for gunnery, and the bay at Episkopi for dive bombing using 25lb practice bombs. We also took aircraft across the Mediterranean to RAF El Adam, just south of Tobruk, for the dropping of 100- and 1,000lb bombs on a big range in the desert. We also used this range for dive-bombing at night, illuminating the ground targets by dropping 16x5in flares from our own bomb bays at 5,000ft which then drifted down to earth under parachutes but gave us enough time to dive down under them to drop our bombs. This was actually one of the most dangerous routine training missions that we performed because, if a flare hung up in the bomb bay, then the Canberra, with its fuel tanks surrounding the bomb bay, would undoubtedly explode. There was considerable relief every time we counted the same number of flares burning as those we had released.

Strangely enough it was not this manoeuvre that caught me out but straightforward ground strafing at Larnaca. I took the very early morning slot on 18 January which was the best time for gunnery because the temperature was too low to cause much turbulence and there was little wind. I rolled into my third pass and because I could see that I was scoring very heavily was reluctant to stop even though my navigator called that I was through the 'foul line'. With my finger firmly on the firing trigger I suddenly saw what I thought was a bird in front of me which, as I disengaged and pulled hard upwards, flashed past me accompanied by a large bang. I immediately returned to Akrotiri and upon shutting down was faced by a grinning flight sergeant who couldn't wait to show me a huge hole in the side of my fin. Delicate negotiations and two crates of beer ensured that the aircraft appeared on the next day's flying programme in pristine condition but every time I passed any of the ground crew I was greeted with a muttered 'bang' and a huge grin. I was, however, better placed than the Squadron Commander who came down on a visit, took off, had an engine failure and crashed in the overshoot area at the end of the runway, demolishing the aircraft but, luckily, not injuring himself or his navigator.

With all my crews qualified satisfactorily in the conventional role I despatched them back to Germany, wound up all the administration and returned with the ground crew on board a Britannia on the last day of January. I had an ecstatic welcome from my wife and my dog who had stayed with our friends the Tompkins during my absence. Wendy and Neil (who was the navigator crewed with Tony Oldfield) lived in a house in a remote location about six miles from the base, but had provided a wonderful home for Terry whilst I had been away.

It came as a particularly nasty shock, therefore, when I was contacted the very next day as duty operations officer by HQ RAF Germany to say that one of our aircraft had crashed and that both crew members were dead and I had to confirm that it was the one with Neil in it. Tony had a cold and his place had been taken by the most experienced pilot on the squadron, Sid Townsend. I contacted the Station Commander, Squadron Commander and both Flight Commanders and set the accident procedures in motion. When they had all gathered it came to light that none of them knew where Neil's house was, so I accompanied the Station Commander after picking up Terry so that we could look after Wendy once the Station Commander had broken the appalling news to her. She broke down in my arms and Terry and I almost carried her and their small son James to our car before driving her home with us. She stayed with us until the funeral as did her mother and father and I took it upon myself to sort out Neil's personal effects, whilst Terry did a fantastic job of looking after her and James and giving her the support and strength she needed. Neil and Sid were buried with full military honours at the RAF cemetery at Rheindahlen under leaden skies with snow settling across the graves. It would appear that they crashed into high ground on the Osnabruck Ridge whilst attempting to continue with a low level exercise when the weather had gone well below limits: a tragic and senseless loss of life.

Our domestic situation suddenly changed as we were offered a beautiful bungalow, ten miles from the airfield in the village of Dremmen, near Heinsberg at No. 7 Wolkaulstrasse, which was one of the Station's hirings. Frau Franken broke down and wept when we told her we were leaving because she had become so fond of Terry and did, I believe, look on her almost as a daughter. We drowned our collective sorrows by demolishing a bottle of brandy with her and Berndt, made our move on 1 March, and then had them round for a meal so that they could see why we had felt the need to move.

With the departure of the Squadron Training Officer I was appointed in his place and became responsible for the checking and training of all crews on the squadron. As this also included LABS training I was effectively responsible for the flying standards of the squadron and its capability for nuclear and conventional weapons deliveries. I also had to return to RAF Bassingbourn for a week to be certified as the squadron's QFI with Jack Stewart as my navigator, despite having achieved the squadron's only 'Above the Average' rating from the Central Flying School 'trappers' when they made their annual assessment of the squadron.

Keith and Judy Webster arrived for a week's holiday with us and helped to celebrate my twenty-eighth birthday, which had to be held on 20 April because at 0600 hours the following day I was airborne in (XH204) on a trip to the Mediterranean but had to divert to Luqa in Malta for a quick repair before continuing home. I did get home in time to do a string of checks on the crews and take part in rehearsals for the grand fly-past for Her Majesty who was visiting Germany at the end of May. The fly-past took place on 26 May at RAF Gutersloh with eighty-seven aircraft taking part and each RAF Germany station represented. It was quite impressive to be part of such a large formation of aircraft and involved some very accurate timing to bring us all together at the right moment because the aircraft speeds varied so much from the Javelins right down to the Chipmunk that momentarily led the whole lot as the formation passed the dais on which the Queen stood.

Jake and Audy Barclay stayed with us for ten days in June and we had a hilarious time, particularly as they were able to attend the Summer Ball. There was also extra cause for celebration because we said goodbye to Wing Commander Field and welcomed in our new squadron commander, Wing Commander Hugh Scotchmer. He turned out to be just what we needed and a superb leader who managed to raise the morale of the Squadron within weeks of taking up his command.

With the departure of Flight Lieutenant Eric Denson I was appointed the Deputy 'A' Flight Commander to Squadron Leader David Collins and as he went on leave I had to pick up the traces at once. We also lost a navigator on medical grounds which left the Flight with only four QRA qualified crews and this meant that we had to do the 24-hour duty every fourth day on top of all of our other duties: three nights at home per week with only one day off now became the norm.

Life suddenly became more complicated and exciting in early October when the Families Officer told us that as the Javelin squadrons were disbanding there would be no need to have hirings and we would have to move into a married quarter. We were so disappointed as we had come to love our bungalow but suddenly the move became a godsend because on 1 October Terry discovered that she was pregnant with the baby expected in April 1966. We were so excited and Terry immediately wrote to Mum asking her for all her tips on carrying a baby. She looked absolutely radiant and her only immediate symptom was that she became very tired and started having to have a sleep during the daytime. She was reassured by Mum telling her that she slept every afternoon whilst carrying me and was overjoyed when Mum sent her a girdle and a 'first gift' of a nappy pin; as well as a promise of a Karricot as a baby present.

We had to move into the married quarter on 2 November which was the very day I had to take six aircraft down to Akrotori for another weapon's camp. I took Terry on to base with me and John Ambler acted as my proxy by 'marching in' to the married quarter for me whilst I flew down to the Mediterranean.

I was away for the whole of November and the added bonus of getting away from the poor weather of Germany was that I was reunited with my old friends John and Edwina Downs as he was a Fighter Controller at Cape Gata Radar but lived at Berengaria, which was where Terry went to school when she was out there with her parents in the 1950s. I spent the weekends with them and we toured the island visiting Nicosia, Limassol, Paphos and Keyrenia; the latter I liked best of all, with its picturesque harbour, the beautiful castle on the hillside and Bellapaise Abbey which was built in 1150 AD and was in a very good state of repair. All the crew conversions went well and there were no dramas or accidents which meant that I could fly home in a B(I)8 (XH204) on the 27 November and be met by a radiant wife on the tarmac, as she had been able to walk down from the married quarters at the Squadron Commander's say so: rather a change from the previous regime.

In January No. 92 Squadron Lightnings arrived to take over the Air Defence role from the Javelins. It seemed very exotic to have these huge sleek machines sharing our base and we integrated with them well although we were made very aware of just how perilous their fuel state would be and that we must never interfere with their landing patterns. It was with relief that I took a detachment down to Luqa at the beginning of February because the weather at Geilenkirchen was unbelievably poor and the flying, when we could get airborne, quite hazardous. After four days I received a mysterious signal summoning me home to be interviewed by the Station Commander. Fearing the worst I flew back on 15 February and was sent directly to Group Captain Headley's office where I was welcomed like a long-lost friend – even more mysterious.

After being served coffee, he beamed at me and told me that I had been selected as the RAF pilot to go to the USA for two years and fly the brand new F-111 fighter bomber, fifty of which our Government had contracted to buy, and then bring the first one home to start the F-111 OCU. He explained that my unique above-the-average qualifications on both fighters and bombers, linked with my General List PC, QFI rating and weapons' instruction background had filtered me out from my competitors and that after a refresher course on Lightnings at RAF Coltishall starting on 15 April we would be off to the States. It was, however, all classified Secret at that moment and the only person that I could tell was Terry: she was bewildered and quite overcome by the news as she tried to temper her excitement with concern about how she was going to have a baby in the middle of all the turmoil. In the meantime I took another bombing detachment to Luqa and Idris where we dropped a total of ninety-six bombs and qualified four more crews before returning and being told that my move had been confirmed and everything was now out in the open following the publication of the Defence White Paper confirming that the UK would be purchasing fifty of the F-111 swing-wing fighter bombers, instead of the now cancelled TSR2.

The role of the F-111 would be the same as that of the TSR2 which itself was essentially an updated version of the Canberra's role. It would provide a long-range, low-level, very high speed strike aircraft to intrude under the enemy's radar and destroy vital targets with nuclear or conventional weapons. I would, therefore, be the single RAF pilot at the very forefront of aviation technology and performance. I could not have been more excited.

Suddenly it was all hands to the pump in starting to pack up our possessions, make medical arrangements for Terry to have our baby in the UK and also to have Hassan placed in quarantine kennels near Oxted at a cost of £2.12s.6d per week.

I did my last QRA on 22 March and supposedly flew my last flight on 23 March in T4 (WJ868) carrying out an interdictor check on Flight Lieutenants Fradley and Gardmen, when the Squadron Commander asked me if I would do one last flight for the squadron on the RAF Germany bombing competition the very next day. It is the sort of thing that you should never give in to, but I agreed and Jack and I did a superb timed exercise with excellent photographs of the turning points. Climbing up from the Rhine, however, for the ten minute flight at 5,000ft in cloud back to the airfield, disaster struck. Without warning a lightning bolt hit the aircraft, entering via the pilot's canopy and my helmet and exiting through my heels and the floor, where it punched two small holes. There was an enormous bang, my head was driven down on to the control column, half the circuit breakers popped and I lost all my electrically-driven instruments. Jack yelled that he had lost his equipment and came back along the tunnel trying to reset the circuit breakers, but nothing worked. I then made the mistake of calling Geilenkirchen to let them know that I had been struck by lightning, which they misinterpreted as my saying I had 'struck a Lightning'. At this point they lost all interest in me and started emergency procedures for the loss of one of their shiny fighters. Using my air-driven instruments I let gently down and, after breaking cloud at 1,000ft, did an emergency landing. The aircraft had turned itself into a bar magnet and when I left the base on 1 April the engineers were still trying to degauss it, with no success. It was a salutary reminder not to reschedule your flying life or be talked into doing something outside your proper plan.

Terry and I had the most emotional farewell from the squadron, as during our last year we had developed into a true family in the very best traditions of the RAF. For the last time we drove through the guarded entrance to the base, along the straight tree-lined roads to Geilenkirchen, Aachen, Louvain, Liege, and Brussels. We crossed from Ostend to Dover, bade Hassan a tearful farewell as he was crated en route to quarantine kennels and drove slowly to Chestfield where we had a rapturous reception from Dad and Auntie Nor. After a week we drove to Mum's for five days before going up to RAF Bawtry where I left Terry in the care of her parents who would supervise her attendance at the RAF hospital at Nocton Hall near Lincoln, in which she would have our baby. I then drove to RAF North Luffenham in Rutland, which was the School of Aviation Medicine, and went through a gruelling week of High Altitude training as a pre-requisite for flying Lightnings, culminating in a special birthday present for me on 21 April when I was subjected to a High Altitude Decompression to a simulated 56,000ft in their chamber.

With all the ticks in place, I drove to Norwich, turned north and on 25 April reported for duty at RAF Coltishall, the home of No. 226 Lightning OCU. The aircraft's performance and my career stakes were moving inexorably upwards.

Chapter 8

Lightning Interlude

'Better to live like a lion for a day, than live like a sheep for a hundred days'
Italian Maxim

A delightful and compact airbase, RAF Coltishall was one of those 1930s airfields that represented all that was aesthetically best in military airfield design. A classic small airfield with a three-wing design layout, traditional Officers' Mess and three substantial hangars, the beautifully landscaped grounds instilled a feeling that all was well. This was enhanced by the snarl of Merlin aero-engines overhead because the station was host to the RAF's historic flight of Spitfires and Hurricanes and these could be seen and heard on most days of the week as they practised or performed for the public.

What a contrast these old aircraft made to the large gleaming Lightnings adorned with No. 145 Squadron insignia with their thunderous engines and ear-splitting afterburners. We collected as a course on 25 April and, before we had chance to draw breath, were squeezed into immersion suits, marched out to the two-seat Lightning T4s (XM988 in my case) and treated to a 40-minute high-speed introduction flight. It was almost a repeat performance of my flight with Andy Jones three years before, featuring a reheat take-off, rapid climb to height and a 1,000 mile (Mach 1.6) run before a TACAN descent and a couple of circuits. With our appetites thoroughly whetted we were then subjected to an intensive ground school and simulator phase before starting our flying conversion on 9 May.

Before this, however, I was more than preoccupied waiting for the birth of our first child, which agonizingly ran later and later; albeit Terry had several false alarms which kept her parents on the hop. It started happening for real on Monday, 2 May when Terry was taken by her father into the RAF hospital at Nocton Hall where they assessed her as being nine days overdue. On 7 May after a very tough labour

Guy Scott was delivered by Caesarean section, weighing 7lbs 4ozs and looking absolutely beautiful. We were now parents and the wonder of it never ceased to amaze us.

I returned to RAF Coltishall desperate to celebrate my fatherhood with someone but the Mess was empty on the Sunday at 2300 hours. I was too excited to go straight to bed so decided to wind down by watching the television and, as a result, I started a lifelong love affair with the music and artistry of the pianist Jacques Loussier, when the room filled with the wonderful sound of his jazz interpretation of J.S. Bach.

I started my flying conversion onto the Lightning the very next day, but with two or three flights every day during the week and learning and revision in the evening I was unable to get to see Terry; in my place good old Mum and Carole made the journey up to Lincoln and stayed at the Eastgate so that she would have company. I drove to her on the Friday and bought twelve huge bundles of tulips from a roadside stall so that she was inundated with flowers when I arrived at the ward. I also took a day off so that I could march into a married quarter at the satellite housing located at the ex-RAF airfield of Horsham St Faith. Number 3, Douglas Close, Fifers Lane, was going to prove to be ideal short-term accommodation as all the other residents on the 'patch' were Lightning pilots, including my close friend Mike Graydon, who had acquired me as his student – 'Just to get my own back and cut you down to size,' he grinned as we started a really happy two months on the conversion stage.

Powered by two Avon 210 engines developing 23,000lbs of static thrust, which increased to 29,000lbs with reheat, the Lightning represented a spectacular advance in performance to all previous British fighters. Capable of over Mach 2 at 35,000ft it had a ceiling of 60,000ft and was equipped with two Firestreak infra-red missiles instead of guns.

After five dual flights on XMs 974, 968 and 971 I solo'd in a F1A, (XM 173) on 10 May and then alternated between dual and solo trips, gradually coming to terms with the aircraft and its quite extraordinary performance. I fell in love with it at once and found the whole process of kitting up and bringing the big beast to life a spine-tingling process leading up to the surge down the runway and the exhilarating performance which just begged you to tame the aircraft and make it work for you. You also became acutely aware of fuel because you could actually see the fuel gauges moving and with only one landing circuit left to you after you dropped to 800lb of fuel you found that your mind was wonderfully focused. After a successful standardization check with my flight commander, Squadron Leader Peter Vangucci, I moved onto No. 2 Flight on 7 June as the student of

Flight Lieutenant Don Oakden, another old friend who had trained with me at RAF Oakington.

Whilst all this was going on I was trying to cope with being a new father and getting to see my wife and baby, who had returned to Terry's parents. The 150-mile journey each way was a pain but luckily Guy was turning out to be a good baby and feeding very well so that Terry was not too stressed. We moved into our married quarter on 30 May and found that Guy loved being outside in his pram. With the doors open the garage provided a marvellous suntrap and he insists that it was this that started his love affair with cars! Terry started driving lessons with the British School of Motoring in Norwich, spurred on by the news that Carole had just passed her test and that Mum was also driving: little did I realize just how valuable and important it was going to be for Terry to have her licence. With Terry feeling better we started taking advantage of the excellent social life at RAF Coltishall and, apart from formal events such as the magnificent Summer Ball, we went with the squadron on an evening local boat trip on the Broads with a jazz band in the bows and dancing on the saloon roof; frequent stops were made at waterside pubs for pasties and pies whilst drinks were supplied from our own sources, and the atmosphere was terrific. The USAF officers on the base threw a Mexican night where we all ate Mexican food and drank Tequila in the proper native fashion – becoming highly pickled in the process. How prophetic this evening was to be for our time in the States.

The flying continued to go well and I finished the course in the middle of July feeling confident in my ability to use the Lightning as a weapon system. The radar and fire control system was crude and made you work extremely hard to achieve good results because the heat-seeking Firestreak missile demanded that you get in close within a narrow cone at the rear of your target, but once you had the hang of it you could do the job and really enjoy the tremendous performance of the aircraft. My posting to the States had been delayed because the F-111 was not progressing as expected in its development phase and the RAF did not want to send me until the first squadron started to form. As a result I was seconded to the Lightning weapons flight and asked to fly about twenty flights per month for them acting as a target for practice interceptions. I leapt at the chance and continued doing this until the end of the year whilst bringing my total of Lightning hours up to about 100.

Guy was christened at the Bawtry Church with Carole, Tony Oldfield and Paul Houselander becoming his godparents. By an immense piece of mistiming the Christening took place on the day that England beat Germany at soccer in the final of the World Cup and all the way through the service I could see the men sneaking glances at their watches and willing the priest to hurry things up. The moment the service finished there was a Le Mans start to get back to the house and get the TV switched on, with Guy being ignored and all the men in the lounge watching the TV whilst the women were shunted off to the kitchen. Once the match was over, normal service was resumed, drinks and eats were served and everyone suddenly remembered we were there to take notice of Guy who, one has to say, had behaved beautifully and undemandingly throughout.

My idyllic flying life was suddenly interrupted by my having to attend the Officers' Command Course at RAF Tern Hill for eight weeks. This was a precursor for Staff College and was designed to reintroduce aircrew officers to staff work. A neighbour, David Jones, and I shared a car for the weekly journeys and by working in the evenings ensured that we had all the weekends free to be with our families. It was great fun re-visiting RAF Tern Hill with all its memories of my flying training and I was even accommodated in the same hut that I had used in 1955 and with the same batman – it made me feel very nostalgic. The 200-mile journey took us nearly six hours as it was all across country so our weekends didn't start until nearly midnight on the Fridays, but I found the work easy, if a bit tedious, and the spoken exercises very good value. It was pleasant, however, to get it all behind me and return to flying as well as a settled home life with our rapidly growing son.

Our posting to the States was confirmed for January and so we started our round of farewells to family and friends. What was nice, was that I was able to get permission for one last flight in a Lightning on Terry's birthday and, as John and Annie Ambler had come up to help her celebrate, I was given permission to take him up for a ride. I gave him the full works in XM 974 and qualified him nicely for the Ten Ton Club by doing Mach 1.6 at 36,000ft and then with great regret taxied in and, after a final long look round from the elevated cockpit position, climbed slowly down the ladder, gave my faithful steed a final pat and said a sad farewell to a wonderful aircraft.

As usual we spent Christmas with Dad and then moved on to Mum's for Boxing Day. The only blot on the happy time was a sudden newsflash, backed up by TV coverage, of the death of Donald Campbell whilst on his attempt in the jet-powered Bluebird to break the world water speed record: the sight of the boat flipping through the air was appalling and put a bit of a damper on things.

All too soon the holiday was over and our farewells to the family were sadder than normal because we had decided that it would be unfair to Hassan to have him crated up and sent to the States. Mum had very kindly agreed to look after him for us, but we gave him extra hugs and pats as we said our goodbyes. What we did not know was that we would never see our wonderful pet and companion again as he was not to live to see our return. How fortunate it is that we cannot see into the future.

We were driven down to Southampton on a typical British winter's day with snow drifting in the air and fog shrouding the hills and then with the whole family walked up the gangway onto the SS France for the start of our United States adventure. Life would never be the same again.

Chapter 9

The American Dream

'The most vital quality you can possess is self confidence'
George S Patton – Letter to his son 6 June 1944

How many young couples get the opportunity to spend three years in the United States at government expense, with a transatlantic liner cruise thrown in for a bonus? Not too many, that's for sure but that is what faced us as we gathered at Southampton on a snowy day in January 1967 waiting to board the longest liner on the Atlantic crossing: the SS *France*. How lucky we were to travel out prior to the advent of RAF air trooping.

We drove down on 6 January with Mum, Carole and Uncle Bill. Knowing that we were going to a desert area of the USA we revelled in the atmospheric journey through heavy driving snow with ghostly white trees climbing the hills on either side of the road. Arriving early we all went for tea at the Dolphin which Mum insisted on paying for because 'You never know when you are going to get the next decent cup, because I know they use tea-bags over there!'

At 1800 hours we drove down to the imposing building of the Ocean terminal, which catered for all the big Atlantic liners, collected our embarkation cards and moved on board where a crowd of red-coated bell boys swooped on our baggage and whisked it away to our cabin. There to our surprise and pleasure we were presented with a vast bouquet of flowers which had been sent by our friends and neighbours at Douglas Close, Mike and Liz Graydon; a small spray of flowers with a beautiful card had been sent by Paul and Di Houselander and our cabin suddenly assumed a festive atmosphere. After a quick drink we roamed like a group of excited children all over the ship, including the luxurious first class area before the call came for visitors to disembark. We said our farewells with many hugs and kisses, opened a porthole, and were thus able to shout down to them as they emerged onto the balcony of the terminal: they were all so close but seemed so far away that the great adventure suddenly seemed not to be such a good affair. At 2130 hours we cast off and with streamers fluttering down from the upper decks the tugs moved us gently away. Mum and Uncle Bill walked a long way along the quay waving until they had to sit down but Carole ran along to the very end waving her handkerchief and calling out to us until the ship turned and hid her from view: my last memory was of a little white handkerchief slowly disappearing into the darkness behind the bulk of the SS *France*. We turned to each other with tears streaming down our faces, hugged each other and agreed we needed a drink. Our adventure had really started.

The four-and-a-half days of the crossing were a revelation because neither of us had ever been so cosseted before and on an Atlantic crossing there is nothing to do but eat, sleep and enjoy yourself, which the crew ensured that you did. The standard of cuisine on the SS *France* was exceptional and they provided free red and white wine from the company's own vineyards at every meal, including breakfast! Terry breakfasted in the cabin, whilst I used the dining room and we then whiled away the days waiting for the excellent social programme of dances, fancy dress parties and 'casino' nights that were arranged for every evening. Terry managed to become involved with the ship's officers (I'm not surprised because she looked stunning) and as a result we were invited to cocktails in the officers' quarters and also given a private tour of the bridge where to my delight I was able to talk knowledgeably with the navigator about the ship's Decca navigation systems, as they were almost identical to those on the Canberra B(1)8. I was very impressed with the speed of the SS *France* at 30 knots, which the navigator said could be increased to 32 knots, but they rarely pushed it higher because they would use too much fuel. What I could never really get over, however, was the sheer size of the ship (316m long), with vast promenade decks, malls of shops, an enormous two-storey dining room and a theatre which, at 800 seats, seemed bigger than most that I had used ashore. We went through boat drills with little Guy encased in a mini lifejacket, hoping that we were not going to end up like the *Titanic*. On a daily basis Guy would spend his mornings in the beautifully equipped nursery, where he was fed, played with, and changed: which all meant that Terry and I had the freedom to really indulge ourselves and enjoy every aspect of the crossing.

We docked at 0500 hours on 11 January and were thus denied the opportunity to see the famous New York skyline come into view or to see the Statue of Liberty slide past, but we were suitably impressed when we woke up and found skyscrapers towering over us in our berth. Customs and immigration went smoothly except for one amusing incident when the immigration officer refused to process

My Uncle Bill who became a pilot in 1938 and inspired me to follow in his footsteps.

My uncle (front row, centre) in Stalag Luft 1 in 1945 after 5 years as a POW.

The day after my first flight in 1952, at HMS *Daedalus*, RNAS Lee-on-Solent whilst in the Army Cadets. I am fourth from the left in the front row.

In the cockpit of a Piston Provost T1 prior to going solo at RAF Tern Hill, May 1955.

Sitting proudly in my first car, an MG PB, at RAF Oakington in August 1956. A Vampire T11 is in the background.

Graduation day for No.117 Flying Course on 24 September 1956. I am second from the left, middle row.

About to fly the Hawker Hunter Mk 1 for the first time, at RAF Pembrey on 20 February 1957.

Care-free days at Exeter Airport with No. 4 AEF in April 1959.

A Balliol T2 at RAF White Waltham on 21 April 1958.

Flying in a Chipmunk T10 with No. 4 AEF on 26 April 1959.

Leading a formation of Jet Provosts for a 'photo shoot' at RAF Leeming on 18 May 1962.

Our wedding day at St Gregory in Bedale, Yorkshire on 15 June 1963.

Overflying the Tarhuna range near Tripoli, Libya in a Canberra B(I)8 of No. 3 Squadron on 29 April 1965.

Looking rather chuffed after a good weapons sortie in my Canberra B(I)8 at RAF Akrotiri, Cyprus in January 1965.

A wonderful welcome from Terry upon my return to RAF Geilenkirchen on 27 November 1965 following a month's weapon detachment at RAF Akrotiri, Cyprus.

A truly supersonic steed – Lightning F1 at RAF Coltishall in May 1966.

A happy family arrive at Cannon AFB at the start of my exchange tour with the USAF in February 1967.

I have just linked up with a KC135 tanker ...

... and am now taking on fuel from it.

Starting my flying with the F-111A at Nellis AFB in December 1967.

The Cessna 172 that refused to get airborne because of water in the floats, at Lake Mead, Nevada.

Congratulating a USAF pilot after qualifying him on the F-111A in October 1968.

"SHAVING IS NO PROBLEM," says Squadron Leader Clive Evans as he explains to his friend Arvin Lankenau, principal, 6th Avenue School, that he just hasn't cut his beard since being confined to Fitzsimons General Hospital with a broken neck. The Royal Air Force F-111 pilot was just finishing a two-year tour at Nellis Air Force Base, Las Vegas, when he and his family were involved in an auto accident outside the Nevada military base on January 16. He was flown to the Aurora hospital two weeks after the accident and put in the head traction shown here.

Squadron Leader Evans (same rank as a U. S. major), will be put in a body cast tomorrow (Thursday) for an estimated eight weeks. It is anticipated that the congenial faster-than-speed of sound pilot will be assigned to a post with the Ministry of Defense, London, after he is fully healed.

During the recuperation period, his wife Terry and their 3-year-old son, Guy, will be staying with Squadron Leader Derek Crompton, and his family, 901 Hanover St. Crompton is a liaison officer with the Air Force Finance Center, 3800 York, Denver.

Arvin Lankenau became a welcome and regular visitor during my recovery time spent in Fitzsimons Hospital in Denver, Colorado. (*Aurora Sentinel, Denver, Colorado*)

With Captain John Phillips in the right-hand seat, I am about to say my farewell to the F-111A in January 1969.

Fronting my entire Hercules Squadron on the occasion of its sixtieth Anniversary on 1 September 1975.

Approaching a link-up with a Victor tanker in my Hercules C1 on 21 June 1982 …

Link-up complete and fuel flowing ...

Job well done and time to relax after the refuelling.

With the family at Buckingham Palace after receiving the CBE from the Queen on 8 February 1983.

Receiving Princess Anne in her role as Honorary Air Commodore of RAF Lyneham: Air Vice-Marshal Don Hall, as AOC 38 Group, stands beside me.

After Sir Rex Hunt and General Sir Peter de la Billière lay their wreaths at the war memorial in Port Stanley, Falkland Islands I lay mine, on 14 June 1985, the anniversary of Liberation Day.

As Chief of Staff British Forces Falkland Islands, I visit the battalion stationed at Goose Green, West Falklands in May 1985.

Full circle. Reunited with the Hawker Hunter after 43 years, at the Brooklands Museum, August 2010.

As Representative Deputy Lieutenant for the Borough of Sutton I escorted the Duke and Duchess of Cambridge when they opened the children's wing of the Royal Marsden Hospital on 29 September 2011. (*The Royal Marsden NHS Foundation Trust*)

Terry because she had no middle initial and we had to agree to her being given one ('A' for anon) so that he could complete his paperwork. We were met by an RAF flight lieutenant who guided all nineteen members of the RAF group through everything and then saw us safely ensconced on a 45-seater luxury coach. After an extended tour of New York, which took in Broadway, the Empire State Building, the UN Building and Central Park, we departed the city through the Lincoln Tunnel under the Hudson River. The coach party was rather quiet because, I believe, we were all quite overwhelmed by the sheer size and quantity of the buildings and the huge number of cars that were all bigger and flashier then anything we had ever seen.

The weather was perfect at 65°F with a cloudless sky and we just sat back and enjoyed the views from the New Jersey turnpike which changed from flat and industrial, to residential with many broken-down clapboard buildings, to rural with rolling countryside with ranch style houses and paddocks full of horses. After crossing the Delaware we stopped at a Hot Shoppes restaurant where we had a marvellous chilli con carne with little salty biscuits and, to our amazement, as many cups of coffee as we could drink as well as a huge jug of iced water; it suddenly seemed like a land of milk and honey to we impecunious Brits!

We covered the 236 miles from New York to Washington in five-and-a-half hours, which included the lunch break; a dramatic difference from travel in the UK. The Embassy had booked us into the Windsor Park hotel at $20 per night and whilst I received my briefings at the Embassy, Terry and Guy spent the time with an RAF family who were living in the suburbs. I was given a $450 loan to enable me to buy a car and then, with travel orders issued by the USAF, we were taken to Dulles Airport and flown on a Braniff International Boeing 727 to Dallas in Texas where we changed to a little Convair 240 piston aeroplane and set off for Clovis airport, New Mexico, which was the civilian airfield close to Cannon AFB (Air Force Base) where I would join my squadron in the USAF.

We were met at Clovis by two young lieutenants in a huge staff car who whisked us straight to our married quarter on the base at 1714A Juggler Loop. It was a sparsely furnished three-bedroom bungalow, but equipped with a huge fridge freezer, automatic washing machine, tumble drier, large cooker and a double sink with garbage disposal unit: Terry could not believe her luck. The squadron had completely stocked the fridge for us and we were then handed the keys to the Volkswagen that was standing in the car port, for us to use until we bought our own car. They could not have been more hospitable and made us feel so very welcome; as did our next-door neighbours who were round to us the next morning to insist that we eat with them and let them do everything until we found our feet. High on their agenda was to have us with them the next day to see the very first ever American Football Super Bowl in which the champions of the American Football Conference (the Kansas City Chiefs) were playing the champions of the National Football League (the Green Bay Packers). It was rather like the British FA Cup Final except that it pitted the champions of the two different leagues against each other, with the received wisdom that a Conference team would never beat a League team.

Work started at 0730 hours and I checked into my unit, the 474th Tactical Fighter Wing, for a very warm welcome by the Commander, Colonel Ivan Dethman, who looked most imposing behind a large desk in a movie-style wood-panelled office with large UK and USAF flags in holders flanking him and many photographs of him with various aeroplanes covering the walls. He explained to me that the F-111s were not coming into service as quickly as had been planned so that I would have to fly T-33 jet trainers and F-100 Super Sabres to keep my hand in, whilst helping him plan and bring the first unit of F-111 designated personnel up to strength and speed. The next weekend he threw a party at his quarters to welcome us to the unit and into the USAF and to introduce other officers on the unit that I had not had a chance to meet because of the lengthy booking-in and induction process that I was subjected to. We were the only Brits on the base, a fact that intrigued everyone, but this seemed no bar to our incorporation into their affairs and I was made to wonder if we went to as much trouble with foreign aircrew on exchange to the RAF: I hoped so! From our first foray into town we quickly realized that Clovis was a real cowboy town situated on Route 66 with the biggest stockyards outside Dallas/Fort Worth. We were given our civilian driving licences by the Sheriff, who we found in his office with his cowboy boots propped up on his desk and a shotgun resting across his thighs. With his large Stetson tilted down on his forehead, he could have come from casting at MGM, but he was friendly and helpful and, armed with our new licences, we went to a car lot and bought a dark blue Chevrolet Impala Super Sport. It was the biggest car I'd ever seen but its power steering and automatic gearbox made it so easy to drive that Terry had no difficulty in driving it back to the base.

I spent the first month of my time on the base going through the F-111 ground school which was a more sophisticated set up than anything that I had ever seen before, with every system on the aircraft having a complete instructional room to itself. With its swing wings, terrain following radar (TFR), bypass engines, pilots' escape capsule, and enhanced avionic/weapons suite, it was the most complex aircraft imaginable and I really had to get my head down and study very hard.

The effort was worthwhile because I came top of my course with a mark of 81 per cent and was able to join my unit, the 474th Tactical Fighter Wing, with head held high.

The whole F-111 programme continued to suffer delays and I was told that I would be unlikely to check out before the autumn. It was at this time that the first fatality occurred in the programme (19 January 1967) when F-111A No. 9 crashed on landing approach at Edwards AFB because the pilot pushed the wing sweep lever the wrong way and swept the wings instead of moving them forward. The aircraft stalled and crashed with the co-pilot being uninjured but the pilot was trapped in his ejection seat (the early aircraft had seats and not an escape capsule) and was burned to death when escaping fuel caught fire. Aircraft were immediately modified to make wing sweep accord with movement of the lever: until the accident, moving the sweep handle forward actually swept the wings rearward.

I started my conversion onto the T-33A (529145) on 17 February with Colonel Hoy and suffered several shocks. The first of these was the number of aircraft on the base, which was a main F-100 conversion base preparing pilots for their tour of duty in Vietnam or South East Asia (SEA) as they preferred it. My eyes nearly popped when I started to count the tail fins on the ground because there were more than 100 of them with at least a dozen more in the air over the base; and there were also the odds and sods like the T-33s and C-47s. It seemed to me as if someone had gathered all the aircraft of RAF Fighter Command together and crammed them onto one base. My second shock was the terrain: Cannon AFB was on the so called 'cap rock' of New Mexico and, no matter what height we climbed to, the land was absolutely flat to the horizon and, apart from Clovis, without another town in sight: it was an instant lesson in just how big the USA is. With no clouds and an azure sky it was a perfect day and I explored the full range of the little trainer's capabilities. It was easy to fly and very responsive (a little too much at altitude where it was twitchy) but very antiquated in its equipment. It was, however, to be my sturdy little playmate until I checked out in the F-111 and I came to love her for what she was.

On 1 March I began a lasting association with a newcomer to the unit, for whom I was to work, Lieutenant Colonel Dean Salmeier. He finished my conversion on to the T-33 and started taking me all over the USA with him in the aircraft. We started with a trip to Davis-Monthan AFB near Tucson in Arizona, which just happens to be the storage area for every USAF aircraft that becomes obsolete and is retired. There were literally thousands of aircraft on the ground including B-52s, F100s, F105s and so on, models of which were still on frontline service. It was the most amazing sight of my life. We then went on a jaunt to Nellis AFB which is on the outskirts of Las Vegas,

Nevada and spent two nights there so that he could show me the town and introduce me to the US style of gambling. It was an amazing trip and a friend of his loaned him his car which was waiting for us by the operations room, right by a big arch on which was a huge legend reading 'Through these portals pass the finest fighter pilots in the world'. Wow! The first night we spent going from one end of the 'Strip' to the other, visiting all the famous night clubs such as the Tropicana (which at that time was the very last building on The Strip), Sands, Dunes, Golden Nugget, Sahara, Aladdin, Thunderbird and Caesars Palace. Every casino had shows that were taking place on stages located by the bars so that you could drink and see them for nothing with artists of the calibre of Fats Domino, Debbie Reynolds, the Ink Spots and Eartha Kitt. He taught me how to play craps (shooting dice) and refused to go back to base until we emerged from the Caesars Palace at 0630 hours in blinding sunlight. I could hardly believe it when I was dragged from a deep sleep in my room in the Visiting Officers Quarters (VOQ) by the Colonel telling me to get up as we had to fly down to Luke AFB near Phoenix in Arizona for my day/navigation check and on my return for my night check! Somehow I managed to do this and imagined that we might have a few beers and go to bed on return – not a bit of it as he barely gave me time for a shower before we were off back to Las Vegas for a steak meal in 'The Flame' restaurant and another night on The Strip – starting at the Silver Slipper for a fantastic burlesque show, then on to the Stardust for a three-hour big show featuring the Blue Bell Girls from the Lido in Paris, magicians, trampoliners, jugglers, comedians, singers, a skating rink that appeared out of the floor, and an aquarium with semi-naked girls swimming about in it. After all this we started our gambling and although I ended up with $10 profit, Dean was at one stage more than $15,000 up and ended by losing it all by the time he consented to go back to base at 0700 hours. At midday I was once again dragged from my bed as Dean said he needed to get back for a party in the Club that night, so I left him to it and gently dozed in the rear seat for the two hour flight back to Cannon AFB. Apparently he had a whale of a time at the party whilst I went straight to bed.

We took advantage of our widening group of friends to leave Guy with Lieutenant Colonel Cliff Carter and his wife Jane (who were to do more for us in the future then we could ever have imagined) and spent a long weekend on a visit to Mexico. We drove down to El Paso via Roswell, Artesia, and Carlsbad. It was a distance of 375 miles, with no motorways to help, and we stayed at a Ramada Inn with an open air, heated swimming pool and a bizarre belly dancer show in the evening conducted by a girl who had to change her own gramophone records to which she was dancing. We spent the next day touring across the border in Juarez listening to mariachi bands and bargaining for typical Mexican goods in the colourful market. The contrast with the clean US side of the border was a shock as Juarez was dirty with dust blowing everywhere, a general air of decay, beggars trying to get money from you and every shopkeeper imploring you to buy their goods. In the evening we went to one of their up-market clubs and saw the singer Jack Jones and Nancy Ames and had an excellent Mexican meal with very cheap tequila drinks. We returned to Cannon Air Force Base the next day, visiting the Carlsbad Caverns (one of the seven natural wonders of the world) on the way. We started the tour in the great Bat Cave where millions of bats roost and then descended along narrow paths for over an hour until we were 800ft below ground level. A further forty-five minutes of walking through caverns enabled us to see thousands of stalactites and stalagmites, many illuminated to reveal their beauty, before visiting the Big Room which is 1,250ft long with 250ft-high ceilings and the Bottomless Pit which is actually 138ft deep. It also contains the Totem Pole stalagmite at 37ft tall, which is growing at one inch every 5,000 years. All too soon we were climbing rapidly to the surface in an elevator but with tales to tell and marvellous memories.

I took every opportunity to stretch my wings and get around the States and flew up to Griffis AFB in New York State via Richards Gebaur AFB in Missouri and Wright Patterson AFB near Dayton, Ohio with a friend on the squadron called Bob Waldbillig (later killed in a helicopter crash in Europe in 1974) as he was speaking at his old university (Syracuse) and we were hosted by the Officer Training Corps on the campus. Then off to Barksdale AFB in Texas, and Birmingham AFB in Alabama for discussion on the introduction of the F-111 as well as to Holloman AFB, Arizona with Dean Salmeier to discuss missile tests before going on to spend the weekend at Boise AFB in Idaho where we stayed with Dean's parents who owned a farm and let me ride their very frisky horses. Then on to Hill AFB in Utah to evaluate the supersonic low-level flying facilities at the Bonneville Salt Flats.

Our plans took on a suddenly different shape when we were told that the whole squadron would be relocated to Nellis AFB in Nevada in August and that if we wanted to get any leave, then we should take it now. By a strange coincidence we had been contacted by a lady called Tomye Clausen who was a cousin on my father's side of the family, who lived near Los Angeles. As a result we planned a tour to the West Coast which would enable us to stay with her.

We set off for the Grand Canyon on 11 May on Route 66 via Albuquerque (the capital of New Mexico) and had a very good run through desert country all the way to Flagstaff, Arizona. A feature that intrigued us was that every petrol station that we used had a snake pit shielded by a little 'wishing well' roof, full of rattlesnakes which writhed, hissed and rattled at you when you looked over the edge of the pit. The next day we arrived at the Grand Canyon village where we spent two nights in a plush little log cabin. We were overwhelmed by the size, beauty and panorama of the Canyon with all the varied differently coloured strata of rocks, whose colours changed as the sun changed position. We took full advantage of the lectures and guided tours but had one heart-stopping moment when Guy managed to disengage the brakes on his buggy as a result of his violent rocking, and we saw him suddenly start to roll towards the edge of the Canyon. No parents ever reacted as quickly as we did to arrest his movement. The next day we drove to Las Vegas via the Hoover/Boulder Dam which is a structure that defies belief because of its colossal size as it climbs up the sides of the valley that it spans. Arriving at Las Vegas we went into the Caesars Palace with Guy to stake his claim for being in a casino at one year of age, before checking into the VOQ at Nellis AFB and spending the evening at the Club with our RAF friends Don and Majorie Oakden, who showed us their married quarter so that we would have an idea of what ours would be like when we moved to the base. They baby-sat Guy for us the next night so that I could show Terry the town, starting with a full show at the Dunes, followed by exotic Aku Aku drinks in the Polynesian Room at the Stardust and then a spot of gambling before a final bar show.

The next morning we drove north west to Beatty before crossing Death Valley. It was 103 miles to cross the valley and I was so thankful to put it behind me as it was absolutely desolate with no one else about and broadcast temperatures of 115°F and the knowledge that if the air conditioning or the car broke down then your small child was extremely vulnerable. We really did question our wisdom in deciding to undergo the experience and we were very thankful to leave the Mojave Desert and go through Bakersfield to Fresno, California. Then on to San Francisco and the start of our love affair with that wonderful city. After sightseeing and spending time in China Town we made arrangements for babysitting with the hotel and caught one of the famous trams to Fisherman's Wharf where we had a truly memorable meal in a restaurant which overlooked the marinas. Crab starters followed by oysters and whole lobster washed down with an excellent Californian wine and view of the illuminated Golden Gate Bridge as a perfect visual backdrop. With great reluctance we said goodbye to the city but were immediately entranced by the stunningly beautiful coastal road south of Santa Barbara via Monterey and Carmel: it is cut into the hillside with sheer drops of hundreds of feet into the sea on the

Pacific side and with no protective barriers to give you a sense of security. Terry was not impressed!

Guy started having trouble with his teeth and developed very nasty bronchitis so I drove into Vandenberg AFB, on the Californian coast, checked into the VOQ and had him examined at the medical centre where he was given antibiotics. Once he had recovered we set off down to Los Angeles and after confirming that there was no 77 Sunset Strip we looked round the Hollywood Studios and visited the zoo. We captured on film the moment when, in the children's area, an acquisitive sheep stole Guy's milk bottle from his pram and ran off guzzling from it, with Terry trying to pull it from its mouth. After a night at Redondo Beach we spent four magical hours at Marine Land watching whales and dolphins leaping huge heights from the surface of their pools and Guy having differences of opinion with the penguins. Then it was off to Tomye's where we received the most wonderful welcome from the whole family: a bundle of energy, she worked full time at Collins Radio and was raising three children as a single mother. After a night of nonstop chatter we realized a personal dream by spending the whole of the next day at Disneyland which was within fifteen minutes drive of her home in Costa Mesa. We were all entranced but Guy was transported by the magic of the colours, the experiences and the personal contact of all the Walt Disney characters. He was less impressed by our next day's 130-mile drive to Palm Springs but enjoyed the cable car lift to the top of the 8,500ft Mount San Jacinto and the chipmunks and squirrels which came up to him to be fed by hand. The views from the top were spectacular and the combination of pure clean air and lush green forest and vegetation was a wonderful contrast to the desert environment to which we had become accustomed. All too soon we were revisiting the desert, as we said our goodbyes and left for an overnight stop at Phoenix, before a final one-day run from there of 650 miles to Cannon. It had turned out to be quite a holiday and we had recorded 3,850 miles of travel, using 240gall of fuel in the process.

Hardly had we settled back in than I was sent for by Colonel Ivan Dethman and reported to him in his office in my flying suit. He looked up slowly and gave me a roasting for looking so scruffy and not having the manners to change before presenting myself to my Commanding Officer. I was taken aback but before I could say anything he said: 'That's why it surprises me that the Queen should promote such a slovenly officer.'

As he burst out laughing the doors opened and all the squadron officers came in shaking my hand and clapping me on the shoulder and pinning on two huge cardboard squadron leader shoulder boards. We then all went to the Officers' Club where we drank ourselves to a standstill with Terry being collected so that she could join in the surprise celebrations. With no advance warning about promotion being given in those days it was a terrific but exhilarating shock and we really let our hair down with about twenty of my friends coming back to our house to continue the party. We were in no condition to drive and so a friend offered to do the honours but Terry and I decided to sit on the bonnet and serenade our friends during the drive, much to the amazement of two USAF Air Police who flagged us down and tried to arrest us for dangerous driving. They were summarily dismissed by Dean Salmeier who told them in choice language that they had no jurisdiction over Brits, and anyway we weren't driving!

Almost before I had become used to being a squadron leader it was time to start preparing for our move to Nellis AFB. The whole move was generated by the sort of internal fighting within an Air Command in the USAF that could not take place in the RAF. Nellis AFB is the Tactical Fighter Weapons Centre of the USAF and was commanded by a general who was a friend of the General Commanding Tactical Air Command and had lobbied for the F-111s to enter service on his base. I had become intimately involved in the in-fighting by preparing the papers to support its introduction at Cannon AFB and even though we lost the battle, the general had been impressed enough to demand my move onto his staff at Nellis AFB. It was, therefore, with some regrets but a sense of excitement that we prepared for our move to Nevada.

Ironically I started my F-100 conversion with the certain knowledge that I would be leaving the unit in the near future. My first flight was in F-100F (63865) with an old friend, Major Glen Cheney, as my instructor. Although it was good to get another type in the logbook I was not all that impressed with the Super Sabre, which had none of the performance of the Lightning and flew like a lead sledge. The most extraordinary feature was in doing aerobatics at high level when the application of aileron induced a large amount of drag which yawed, rather then rolled, the aircraft. This trait was also evident at low speed on the landing approach making you use rudder to counteract it which I found uncomfortable. The aircraft was, however, a very solid platform for the delivery of air to ground ordnance.

My farewell to Cannon AFB was marked with a monstrous party in our neighbours' house which saw me pass out in the lounge, because they spiked my drinks with tequila, and with the house opposite being set on fire because my chums set off a salvo of aircraft distress flares which toppled over and went horizontally across the road. I was eventually carried to my car which Terry drove back to the VOQ and she then goaded me on all fours down the corridor to my room where I slept the rest of the night on the floor. In the morning I had an appalling hangover and when I went to the car I found a litre bottle of tequila on the driver's seat with a farewell card from the boys on it: I nearly threw up at the sight. I was in no condition to drive so Terry had to take control, which was no easy matter as we had hired a U-Haul trailer to carry all our large items, and she had never driven the car with a trailer attached. After about fifteen minutes of abortive reversing manoeuvres which caused the trailer to go in the wrong direction we eventually got out of the car park and I slipped gently into oblivion. Somehow or other she drove us to the Flagstaff motel where we night-stopped and I then took over for the drive on 21 August which ended with us installed in the VOQ at Nellis. Another chapter of our lives completed and the real adventure was about to start.

I reported for duty to Colonel Gabriel P. Bartholomew (Bart) commanding the 4481st Tactical Fighter Squadron which would become responsible for converting all new crews onto the F-111. He was a huge larger-than-life character and he and his wife Jeannie were to become dear and close friends of ours. He had been shot down in both the Second World War and in Korea and was immensely experienced as well as being one of the most understanding and humane men that I have ever met. He explained that the aircraft was still experiencing delays and although I would not convert until late in the year I would be his deputy (he and I were the only members of the unit at that time) and responsible for defining the whole conversion programme. As others were posted in, according to their seniority they would assume positions of authority on the squadron and I would gradually slip down the authority ladder but would assume the mantle of 'guru without portfolio' answerable to no one but him. I could hardly take all this in as but a month before I had been a flight lieutenant who had never even been a flight commander on a RAF squadron. I did not demur, however, and never once did any USAF officer question my position or treat me with anything other than respect and friendship. My golden operational period was about to start.

I also took advantage of the relaxed US approach to flying to qualify myself for a light aircraft licence and with a friend we took to hiring a Cessna 172 with floats and retractable wheels from the local Thunderbird airfield, so that we could pop up the thirty-five miles to Lake Mead for days out with our wives. The first of these ended in a farce when, after a wonderful day out we found that we could not get airborne because the floats had leaked and were full of water. No matter how much we pumped them out the water was forced back into the floats on the take-off run and the aircraft became too heavy to become airborne. We decided on a drastic solution and hailed down a passing cabin cruiser, and the three of us swam across to it leaving Jim to try to get airborne: in its lightened condition he just managed it and, as he zoomed overhead waggling his wings en route for Las Vegas, his wife cried out: 'Oh look, I've got both sets of car keys in my purse!'

We were landed at the marina and sat shivering there until after midnight when Jim returned in a foul mood driving a hire car. What he said to his wife does not bear repeating. We used Lake Mead as our recreation centre and went there repeatedly with friends to make use of its facilities to hone our water skiing skills and gorge ourselves on barbecue food. Guy would come out with us in the boat in his lifejacket and spend endless hours building sandcastles on the beach. Our evenings were spent mainly in Las Vegas going to the big shows, seeing stars such as Ella Fitzgerald, Sammy Davis Junior, Frank Sinatra, Dean Martin, Schnozzle Durante and Harry Belafonte. The evenings were all very cheap because the casinos tried to entice you in with low cost tickets and then make their money from your gambling.

At work I was becoming more and more involved with the planning into entry of the F-111 and spending a great deal of time in the air acting as airborne range scorer for the unmanned ranges on which the Nellis aircraft dropped their bombs, using my time airborne to work out the navigation routes for the F-111s which were starting to appear at Nellis in their pre-production form. All my old friends from Cannon had been formed into a separate Harvest Reaper squadron under Colonel Dethman and were tasked by Secretary of Defence McNamara to deploy six aircraft to Thailand in March 1968, under the code name of Combat Lancer, to start operations against North Vietnam. To this end all the early flying was earmarked for these crews, from which I, as a Brit, was excluded. Truth to tell I could not have been busier with preparation for the normal training programme and the T-33 flying did keep my hand in.

An interesting diversion occurred in October 1967 when Mr John Stonehouse, the UK Minister for Aviation, visited Nellis AFB after having a flight in an F-111 at the General Dynamics plant at Fort Worth. I spoke to him about the aircraft and the way I was preparing the conversion, which I would then adapt for the RAF, and then took him to lunch at the Dunes casino. He was interviewed by CBS, NBC and ABC with me beside him and gave an irrevocable commitment to the RAF's purchase of the aircraft which cheered me up no end: the sad commentary on this commitment was, however, that the Labour Government cancelled the order on 16 January 1968 without warning and it was only because I was so embedded in the programme that the USAF would not let me be returned to the UK and I did, therefore, remain in the States. As Stonehouse had affirmed to me personally that the aircraft order would not be cancelled you can imagine how I felt and his actions confirmed my already low opinion of politicians!

At long last I started my conversion on 19 December 1967 when I took to the air in a pre-production model F-111A (655708), with Captain John Phillips as my instructor. As one of the cadre of instructors who would have to convert both left and right seat crew members our training consisted of twenty-five hours in the left seat and then twenty-five hours in the right so that we could practise exactly what we were going to preach: this occurred by the end of February.

Finally getting to grips with the F-111 fulfilled all my wildest imaginings as it was so far in advance of anything that I had ever flown. The first impression you always had of the aircraft as you approached it was its sheer size as a fighter. The aircraft is a mammoth, at 80,000lbs it is heavier than a Lancaster and its 73ft length equals that of a B-17 bomber. The cockpit was wonderfully comfortable as it was so roomy and well planned. With no ejection seats, because in an emergency the crew would eject in a capsule, one sat on a red-cushion seat that adjusted up, down, fore and aft, and even reclined.

John required me to do all the handling on my first flight and merely talked me through my actions which was a terrific confidence booster. Once on the runway I moved the throttles past the function detent signalling the start of after burning and felt the gentle nudge from the rear as each of the five separate stages of the after burner lit. With none of the violence of the Lightning we accelerated down the runway and at 140 knots I eased the aircraft into the air and felt the feather-light but steady pressure of the controls. At 180 knots I raised the flaps, at 250 knots swept the wings to 26°, at 400 knots pulled the throttles out of after burner and then swept the wings further back using the 'trombone' slide lever under the left lip of the canopy. The one thing that did catch me out was the auto-trim which was required to cope with the change of gravity when sweeping the wings but which operated the whole time so that, for example, you ended up with zero stick load in turns without doing any trimming (I kept on tightening my turns by trying instinctively to keep a constant stick pressure – but I learnt quickly!).

Once I was happy with my handling John asked me to descend to 500ft, re-engage the after burners and continue sweeping the wings to their fully swept position as speed moved above 500 knots. Suddenly, and with no real sensation in the cockpit, we were supersonic. The sensation of speed was fantastic and I found the aircraft to be quite responsive in pitch but at supersonic speed very reluctant to turn: it seemed to be on rails. We then did a power climb to 30,000ft and accelerated smoothly to Mach 2.2, at which point we had to slow down because the aircraft skin temperature had risen to its limit. Then it was a roller coaster descent for thirty minutes of exhilarating automatic terrain following radar (TFR) controlled low-level flight at 200ft above the ground. We climbed hills hugging the ground and barrelled along valleys and all the time with our hands and feet off the controls. I was in seventh heaven and it was with enormous reluctance that I agreed to return to base and land. John demonstrated a landing using nothing more than the angle of attack indicators in the cockpit to guide us down to a feather-cushioned landing. I must have had a grin like a Cheshire cat when I climbed from the cockpit for the routine PR photographs and presentation of an F-111 model which all pilots received after their first flight. Then it was off to the bar and much later a very disgruntled wife's arrival to join in the celebration and eventually drive her paralytic husband home; luckily, a mere five minutes to our new married quarter at 27A Riggs Parkway on the base which we had moved into in early December.

We finished 1967 and started 1968 in Los Angeles with my cousin Tomye and family as they were insistent that we should celebrate Christmas in a family environment. We flew down and had a moment of magic coming in to land at Los Angeles when we descended over the rooftops and were amazed to see them all covered with Santa Clauses, sleighs, reindeer, Christmas Greetings and coloured lights. We had never seen anything like it before as every house seemed to be decorated and provided a fairy-tale vista. We quickly transferred to a cross-city helicopter and flew at low level across the city to Orange County airport where Tomye collected us and then had a wonderful, relaxed and very happy Christmas holiday. It was unlike any that we had had in the past because the weather was so beautiful and we woke on Christmas Day to the sight of butterflies in the garden as we sipped our freshly pressed orange juice. We became very close to Tomye and it has been no surprise that forty years later we are still in regular correspondence and have constant visits from her daughter Marie.

Once back from our Christmas break I cracked on with my conversion programme and really fell in love with the F-111. It was a complex aircraft but the systems were so well integrated that, providing everything was working, it was an easy aircraft to fly. The problems started if a major system started to go down because of its effect on so many other systems, and that was what sorted out the pilots who really understood the whole aircraft and those that did not. I did all my initial conversion in pre-production aircraft (block numbers 655701 to 655710) but on 15 February flew to the General Dynamics plant at Fort Worth/Dallas in Texas to collect our first block 2 production aircraft 66025. We received a tremendous welcome at the plant and after a magnificent piece of ceremonial Colonel Bartholomew and I signed the acceptance forms and started the engines on the aircraft which had just thirty-five minutes total flying time. I set up the inertial navigation system with great care and after a completely uneventful flight of two-and-a-half hours to Nellis AFB, after shutting down the engines on the pan, recorded an error of about 85ft in the navigation system: and this without updating it during the flight.

By the end of February I had completed my conversion and became the fourteenth qualified instructor pilot on the aircraft. I immediately started my instructional career by converting two pilots into the delights of ground attack and rocket firing. The extent of the activities undertaken by this multi-purpose aircraft was extraordinary as it ranged all the way from air combat and air-to-air refuelling, to nuclear and conventional bombing, and the full suite of ground attack manoeuvres. At the same time the inertial navigation and fantastic ground mapping radar enabled pinpoint attacks to be made after spending two to nine hours at very low level using the TFR. I loved the low flying and the adrenalin rush of doing this at night in pitch darkness, knowing that there were obstacles and valley sides within a few feet of the aircraft and, the knowledge that a single mistake by you or the equipment would be fatal, gave an edge to the flying that I had never before experienced. I also relished the fact that I became expert in all aspects of the aircraft, its systems, and its weapons and that hugely experienced USAF pilots respected me and turned to me for advice. To my last days on the tour I got a thrill out of the flying and on looking out of the cockpit at the USAF insignia on the wing, I always found it hard to believe that the President of the USA was actually allowing me to fly one of his country's most precious aircraft.

On 15 March I waved 'goodbye' to all my friends from Cannon AFB as Colonel Ike Dethman led them in a ceremonial fly-past on their departure to Thailand, as the six aircraft Harvest Reaper detachment, to take part in the war against North Vietnam. With no external assistance they flew to Hawaii, then to Guam, and then on to Takhili AFB in Thailand. All the crews were friends of mine and I was devastated to get the news that three of the six aircraft had been lost by 27 April. The wrecks of the first two were never found but the third crew used their capsule to escape when the aircraft went out of control because of a technical fault, with the main control-valve rod snapping at a welded joint. Just before this was established we lost one of our aircraft when Major Chuck van Driel had to eject because of a similar fault, and the whole fleet was grounded whilst the faulty components were replaced by units made from a single piece of metal.

Whilst all this was going on, Mum came across to stay with us and made her first ever flight in the process, bravely changing planes at Chicago O'Hare Airport before arriving at McCarran, Las Vegas. She was amazed at Las Vegas and we took her to shows, gave her gambling money for the one-armed bandits and let her visit as many casinos as she could manage. The squadron wives really looked after her and she was treated to an extra delight when she attended the monthly Officers' Wives' Lunch at the Club. Our squadron wives were providing the main entertainment and when one of the stars withdrew at the last moment I was prevailed upon by Milly Bartholomew to help out. The girls dressed me up in female clothing with heavy face make-up, wig, gloves and dark tights and introduced me as Anna Romane, a Hungarian Show Girl from the Lido in the Stardust. I used a breathy husky voice and, despite one or two suspicious looks, got through the complete reception and lunch without being unmasked. The compere then introduced me and after a few questions said: 'I'm sorry but I have to say that you remind me of one of the fighter pilots on the F-111s,' to which I responded by dragging off my wig and saying: 'I've never been so insulted in all my life!'

There was a deafening silence for about three to four seconds followed by thunderous applause and Mum being ushered forward and with a bemused look on her face, being introduced as my mother. Perhaps all those POW stories about people getting through the lines in disguise are true after all? By far Mum's most exciting experience, however, was going with Terry to the Tropicana and taking part with Terry in their Annual Exotic Hats contest: both wearing hats that we designed and 'built'. She ended up on the famous stage having reached the final wearing a 'Fire' motif with burning buildings and fire engines and came home clutching her prize. After visiting Warm Springs, fifty miles north east of Las Vegas, where there is an oasis in the desert with wonderful tepid water in natural basins, we departed for Tomye and Los Angeles. Here we not only visited Disneyland but also went to Knotts Berry Farm which is a fair and zoo, but more celebrated for its Ghost Cowboy Town which is recreated from actual cowboy buildings and structures. It also features a real Wild West railway system and stage coaches on which you can ride. There is a training barn used by James Jeffries when he was the heavyweight champion of the world which is packed with boxing memorabilia, and a real Red Indian village with scores of redskins in costume who perform tribal dances. All too soon, however, we were waving 'goodbye' at McCarran Airport and watching until her United 727 vanished from sight in the direction of the Grand Canyon.

The week after Mum departed we had Dad out for two weeks and more or less repeated the package that we had created for Mum, except that I did not have to appear in drag. But much more to his taste I took him on a boy's night out in Las Vegas starting off with the burlesque show at the Silver Slipper where he got to see real girls take all their clothes off! Additionally I took him on an air flight up the Grand

Canyon, landing at Grand Canyon airfield and spending the whole day on The Rim. He was bowled over by the whole experience and reckoned it to be amongst the great experiences of his life.

Our fifth wedding anniversary occurred whilst the F-111 was still grounded and so we had a babysitter so that we could really let our hair down. We started with a terrific meal at the Alpine Village Inn where all the bowls and plates are made from pewter and a potato soup trolley circled the tables serving as many helpings as you wished. Then off to the Flamingo to have a stage-side table for the Ella Fitzgerald Show (fantastic) after which we gambled for nearly two hours, with Terry hitting a $20 winning streak on the slot machines and putting my $5 win into the shade. Bar shows then claimed us until 0200 hours but left us with an unforgettable memory of our 'fifth'.

But now back to flying and I volunteered to air test the first F-111 (66033) to be fitted with the re-machined rod and did this on 20 June with Major Fitzgerald. We put the aircraft through its paces but were forbidden to use the TFR below 1,000 feet AGL just in case a problem occurred: they didn't say anything about 'g' loading or speed so we went supersonic at 1,000 feet AGL and pulled the aircraft to blackout point. I did the same to F-111 (66025) and as the authorities were convinced that all was well we were released back to unrestricted flight operations. I collected two more new aircraft from Fort Worth (66036 and 66052) and we started accelerating the conversion programme which now included Australians from their first squadron scheduled to receive their F-111s. The accuracy of the weapon delivery was amazing and it was very disappointing to see a bomb fall more than 100ft from the target, no matter what type of delivery was used. The temperature on the airfield was higher than anything I had known at about 126°F on the pan and, as one had to gyro compass the INS for about ten minutes before starting the engines, you, literally, had to sit in this temperature and sweat it out; it was no surprise that I quickly lost all surplus fat and, with a regular exercise programme, reached peak physical condition. This was to play a significant part in my ability to cope with the shock and injuries that I sustained in our forthcoming car crash.

Flying continued to be demanding and interesting because the aircraft developed some problems that involved me. On 12 July after a two-hour low-level flight as I switched on the Armament Master Switch, prior to carrying out bombing runs at a range north of Nellis AFB, there was a jolt and the complete container with its four practice bombs was jettisoned from the aircraft. Very fortunately it fell in open countryside and no one was injured but it was a dangerous incident and I had to undergo an enquiry. The engineers quickly established that with certain switch selections on the weapons panel stray electrical currents could be induced; a fleet-wide inspection and modification resulted.

I then had a very dramatic flight during which I suffered major systems failures whilst about forty minutes flying time from base, when the electrical system started to go off-line followed by major elements of the hydraulic system. More and more warning lights illuminated and my student began to press me to initiate an ejection because he feared we might lose control. I began off-loading and bypassing systems and eased the aircraft back to Nellis AFB for an emergency landing because I was convinced we had enough reserves and was determined to save the aircraft and let the engineers have all the evidence in one piece. I was proved to be very lucky because as we slowed to a stop on the runway with ambulances and fire tenders flanking us, the aircraft gave a final convulsion and dumped all the remaining hydraulic fluid on the runway. It was as close as one could get and my student would not talk to me in the crew room and demanded a change of instructor – which he was given. Bart interviewed me and praised me for my handling of the situation but then chastised me for hazarding our lives and stressed that in the USAF they would always discard the aircraft in a similar situation to ensure the safety of the aircrew. One lived and learned.

On 30 August we had the most wonderful news that Terry was pregnant, little realizing the heartache that would follow in five months time. The whole family was ecstatic and as the due date was in early May there was intense speculation as to whether she would give birth on Guy's birthday!

On 23 September there was a spectacular crash of one of our F-111s (the 10th) involving a close friend of mine, an Australian navigator, Flight Lieutenant Neil Pollock. The cause was, incredibly, a faulty fuel gauge. Unfortunately, the pilot did not appear to have understood that the actual needle positions controlled the tanks from which fuel was removed when he selected 'fuel dump'. As a result, when he dumped fuel because of another malfunction, the aircraft became unbalanced and rotated uncontrollably nose-up when on the final stages of landing. He froze on the controls and it was Neil who pulled the ejection handle at 300ft AGL with the capsule having time to swing just once under its canopy before hitting the ground just as the aircraft crashed in a huge fireball alongside them. Neither of the crew was hurt and, although we were grounded until the cause was determined, we were back in the air in the middle of October. Interestingly, I noted that the unit cost of the aircraft at the time was $7,300,000.

Once we started flying there was an attempt to recover lost ground and I did forty-six hours flying in November with the knowledge that I was into my last three months on the aircraft before returning to the

UK. Not only did I try to get as much flying as possible but pushed the aircraft to see just what it could do and had a memorable read out of 972 knots TAS (True Air Speed) at 200ft AGL flying up a valley towards the Great Salt Lake. The aircraft felt as though it was on rails and very difficult to manoeuvre but the sense of speed was breathtaking and it was hard to assimilate details of the approaching terrain. At altitude I managed to get up to Mach 2.25 before the temperature limitations brought my high speed jaunt to an end and I decided to go on a TFR extravaganza down the Grand Canyon, much to the concern of my right-seater. I have to admit that I did have some nervous spasms myself as we streaked down parts of the Canyon with the rim above us on both sides but the excitement it generated was well worth it. And I had the childish feeling that there was nothing anyone could do to discipline me as I was returning to the UK in a month's time at any rate.

Our imminent departure was being marked by the squadron as the wives gave Terry a wonderful going away party combined with a baby shower at the top of The Dunes and presented her with a silver dish, a Snoopy scrapbook of her time in the USA with a squadron crest on it and a mass of baby items. Milly Bartholomew made a tear-jerking speech about Terry and the fantastic person she was; to which Terry responded. She then had her twenty-fifth birthday, which started well because I had a late take-off and was able to take her tea in bed. Guy joined us and we piled all her presents on the bed so that he could help his Mum open them. We had bought her a fur hat and luxurious negligee; Mum had sent her earrings; Dad material for maternity clothes; Carole a brooch; and Jan and Bob Saffel some battery-operated scissors. I bought a surprise birthday cake with roses all over it and Guy made such a fuss that he was entrusted with the knife to cut the slices: his, surprisingly, was by far the biggest. Leaving Guy with friends we then went for a meal at Paquito's Mexican Restaurant and then gambled and danced the night away at The Mint.

I did sixteen hours of flying during the first part of January but our focus was on selling our car ($600) and cleaning and moving out of our married quarter. Our crates were collected on 15 January and we moved into the base Guest House with our remaining belongings in suitcases. I did my last flight on 13 January in 66052 and was greeted at the ramp when I shut down with a guard of honour of all my friends and colleagues that stretched to the crew room. Every single member of the squadron shook me by the hand and it was a very emotional moment when I looked over my shoulder for one last time at the F-111 before getting into my car and driving through the main gates to be with my family.

With our flight back to the UK starting with our departure from Las Vegas on 16 January we borrowed Bob and Jan Saffell's VW Beetle car to go round to Colonel Bartholomew's home to spend the evening and say our final farewells to a select group of twenty close friends. A wonderful meal complemented the nonstop reminiscence of friends, who were relaxed, happy and confident in each other's company. They were undoubtedly the most talented group of pilots with whom I had ever flown and everyone, except myself, had a distinguished and glittering war record with most of them having completed at least 100 missions over North Vietnam in the F-105 Thunderchief. That they accepted me and made it clear that they respected and liked me made me feel very special, and nothing that would happen would ever tarnish that memory.

At midnight we called a halt and, with a final hand-clasp and hug, we squeezed into the car, covered Guy with a rug on the back seat and set off for the Base. The time was fifteen minutes past midnight on 16 January when I turned on to the Salt Lake Highway from Nellis Boulevard.

Our lives were about to be changed forever and I was to find that the challenges in surmounting the pain barrier that were awaiting me were to be every bit as great as those of going through the Sound Barrier.

Part III

Chapter 10

Munich or Bust

January 1969

> '*It is war that shapes peace, and armament that shapes war*'
> John F. C. Fuller, 1945

My actions since the accident had been passive, dictated by circumstance and the decisions of others. Now, however, with the arrival of Bill Fisher, my life began a new chapter in which I would make decisions, start to take active measures to assist my recovery and establish an independence from the painkilling drugs that had dulled my intellect.

Bill Fisher was a captain in the US Army who, having completed his year in Vietnam, was completing his two-year draft by working in the neurosurgical team at Fitzsimons hospital. A skilled neurosurgeon he seemed to have modelled himself on the anarchic doctors in the M*A*S*H television series and, whilst excelling in his professional performance, did everything in his power to distance himself from career officer behaviour. With a large pipe clamped in his mouth, wearing outlandish clothes, and spending as much time on the golf course as he could, he was the despair of the regular staff but got away with it because of his ability. This became immediately apparent when he sat by my bed and started discussing my treatment, because he began involving me in the decision making and showed clearly that he had a real appreciation of my particular needs.

He explained that, although I was very seriously injured, the immediate post accident care had saved my life and stabilized me. The tongs in my head were, however, incorrectly located and would have to be moved and then there was a need to consider the type of treatment to which I would be subjected. The standard procedure would be for bone to be taken from my hip and plated to the three broken vertebrae which would stabilize the spine, prevent the spinal cord from being cut and should ensure a safe path to recovery. The drawback, however, was that this would lead to a rigidity in the spine which would severely restrict neck movement and, in his opinion, would prevent me resuming flying duties. Having engaged in flying sorties in Vietnam he realized how important it was to have this rotational mobility for lookout and general flight safety and in his estimation this 'safe' surgical procedure would jeopardize this. There was, however, a riskier alternative which he wanted me to consider which should result in enough movement returning to enable me to fly again; this would entail a lengthy period of complete immobilization without surgery but he believed from the nature of the breakages, and his past experience, bony spurs could form which would provide sufficient stability. The risk element was that they would never be as strong as the artificial bridgework and if they failed, the cord could be cut and paralysis would occur; the risk would be assessed at 25 per cent. How I wished that Terry was with me but she was not and a decision had to be made, so I crossed my fingers and said: 'Let's go with the flying option.'

He roared with laughter and said: 'You've just made my day as I reckoned no Limey would go the safe route and I've set up surgery already to go the flying route. I hope you don't mind drills!'

He had me wheeled down to a theatre where a team was waiting and set to work. I immediately understood his reference to drills because they gave me a local anaesthetic into the scalp, cut away circles in this area and then hand-drilled through the outer layer of cranium so that an umbrella device could be inserted in the gap between the inner and outer skull bones to which were attached the rods supporting the 10lbs weight bag. Bill worked fast and with enormous certainty and although I was in a certain amount of pain I managed to keep up a running dialogue with him as we swapped stories. The grinding and reverberation of the drill as it cut through the bone was extremely unpleasant but I was determined not to let anyone see my apprehension and discomfort. Suddenly it was over, the old tongs were then removed and I was positioned in a vertically rotational Striker frame. This was to be my home for the next eight weeks with two positions only: flat on my back looking at the ceiling, or flat on my face looking at the floor. I was then moved to a two-person room and started to acquaint myself with the cracks in the lino and the holes in the peg-board style ceiling: visually these were to be my sole companions on a regular basis for two months and I got to know them very well.

Now, however, I began to think about things other than myself and to worry about Terry, Guy and the baby. I began to fret and make a real nuisance of myself but no one seemed to be in a position to tell me what was happening to them and then, wonderfully, a telephone link was established with Nellis and I was able to speak to Terry. Just to hear her voice was the closest thing to heaven for me and to learn that she and Guy were out of hospital and doing well without major injury was the best tonic I could have had: she then very gently told me that she had lost the baby and part of me collapsed. I know that I cried but she kept on reassuring me and stressing that she could still have children and that we must keep looking forward. How she did it I just do not know, particularly, as I found out later, she had had to name the little boy who she had delivered in a natural manner and then go through a formal funeral service for his interment. Her strength was amazing and to this day I just do not know how she found the fortitude to cope with everything that was happening, and look after Guy and sort out all our affairs with absolutely no assistance from me. She became the rock to which I clung and all I could think of was for her to be with me in Denver.

Very fortunately things began coming together because the British Embassy contacted an RAF exchange officer stationed in Denver and Squadron Leader Derek Crompton came straight round to the hospital and started looking after my affairs at that end. At the same time our very dear friends the Carters sprang into action and, whilst getting Bob and Jan Saffell to look after Terry (insult to injury as it was their car that had been wrecked in the accident), their daughter Candice accompanied Terry and Guy to Denver on 29 January where they stayed with Colonel and Mrs Locke, who were close friends of the Carters.

Candice came in with Terry and Guy (who was allowed in on just this one occasion as there were concerns for him about infection and the visually appalling casualties he might see) and Terry's presence made anything seem possible and made me even more determined to live up to the standard she had set. Guy, of course, was hugging his teddy bear and Terry told me that he was lucky to still have it because after the accident it was lost and he became almost hysterical because no other toy would do. Eventually Cliff Carter drove down to the wrecking yard where the Beetle had been taken for disposal and found Teddy lying under the pedals of the car: what a reunion it was when he was returned to Guy and it is rather wonderful that Teddy still lives with us to this day and has been on so many adventures with Guy since the accident.

It was fantastic to see them both again and I felt my spirits rise immediately and I no longer had any doubts about making a recovery and resuming our life as a family. I felt devastated for Terry about the loss of the baby and on subsequent visits we spoke at length about this, but for that first reunion it was a time for rejoicing, touching each other, reassuring ourselves and talking about the future. Guy was fascinated with the rotating Striker frame and made me go from face down to face up again and again but much preferred me in the vertical position! All too soon the visit was over and, although I was not to see Guy for the next two months, Terry came in to see me every afternoon and evening.

My principal problems whilst waiting for the neck to heal were boredom and trying to get my limbs to move properly. Bill Fisher solved the first of these by ensuring that I always had a companion in my two-person room, and I had to work hard at exercising to improve the second. My first roommate was a 24-year-old helicopter pilot called Mike Steer who had been shot down in Vietnam and suffered spinal damage during the crash. Cheerful and, following his operation, quite active, he fascinated me with his combat tales which were so very different from those of my companions at Nellis who had conducted all their operations from bases outside Vietnam. Just having someone to talk to was a therapy in itself and helped keep my spirits up in between the visits by Terry. At the beginning of February she moved to stay with Derek and Eunice Crompton and this meant that Guy had two small boys as playmates whilst she was out of the house. It also gave her the close contact with Derek that was useful in his running of our affairs: the British Embassy proved to be singularly unhelpful as they appeared to take very little interest in my affairs apart from the Defence Attaché, who intervened personally to prevent Terry being made to return to the UK. Apparently an archetypal civil servant from MOD London instructed the Embassy to initiate her return because my tour was officially finished and, because I was in hospital accommodation, there was no official requirement for me to be accompanied and this was, therefore, an unnecessary financial drain on Treasury resources. Air Vice-Marshal Crowley-Milling told them that under no circumstances would he allow Terry to be sent home as my recovery was dependent on her presence and, if they cut off funding, he would make good from Embassy funds. He then travelled to Denver (officially he told me, to visit the USAF Academy at Colorado Springs) and spent more than three hours with me, reassuring me about his support.

All was proceeding as planned until 10 February when a rather dramatic event occurred during Terry's evening visit. I was face down with Terry sitting in a chair by my head when the right side of my skull cracked, the tong jumped out and I was wrenched round by the weight of the bag. Thinking incredibly quickly Terry grabbed the bag, took the load off the weight, and, because my body's nervous system was convulsing so strongly as to jerk me all over the place, Terry then had to lay on top of me to dampen the movement whilst screaming for help. Nurses and a medical team arrived but the situation was too delicate for me to be moved to theatre, so they settled Terry in the corridor and set up an emergency theatre in my room. Bill Fisher was not available so another surgeon operated and subjected me to three hours of the worst pain that I have ever known: he was not experienced and seemed unable to make progress with the two new holes that had to be drilled. The local anaesthetic did not seem to be effective and the pain of the drilling was so intense that I began to believe that I could not take it any more. Blood seemed to spurt everywhere and covered me and the bed and I ended up by having to be physically restrained by the medics. To get through it I began focusing on one thing alone and that was, seeing Terry. Eventually it was over and after the tongs were inserted into two new holes Terry was allowed in to see me but before they had cleaned up the room: she held my hand for a moment but was so unnerved by the sight of all the blood everywhere she had to go out until they had cleaned me up. The remarkable thing was that by her prompt action and their emergency surgery the whole episode did not affect my recovery in any way.

On 10 March, following a series of x-rays that showed that the spine was perfectly in line and that bone growth was occurring as planned, I was encased in a body cast called a Minerva jacket. They covered my body in soft cloth and then applied layer upon layer of plaster until I was encased from my hips to the top of my head with portholes for my face and ears and a vent on the top of my head and at my throat. As it left my arms free but extended to my shoulder ends, I was completely immobilized when I lay down on my back as I could not exert any pressure or purchase to roll myself up or over. Initially I could not believe how uncomfortable the Minerva jacket was because it was heavy (26lbs), so tight that normal breathing was impossible and I had to learn to shallow breathe, and eating was a slow and laborious process because I could only just open my mouth in the very restrictive headpiece: all necessary because my spine and neck had to be prevented from moving at any cost. I was determined to fly the British flag, however, and when they produced a wheelchair to take me from the plaster room, I pushed it away, stood up and walked in a very wobbly way back to my room.

I worked assiduously at my muscle-strengthening exercises and after a week I was given permission to move to a local motel with Terry and Guy and report back to the hospital as an outpatient for physiotherapy. My joy was unconfined and we established a proper little home at £60 per week in which we could restart our family life. Snow kept falling heavily, as it had done every day since my arrival in Denver, but as I was still very limited in my mobility we stayed indoors, watched television and played games with Guy. My legs strengthened rapidly as did my arms except for my triceps: the doctors reckoned that the weakness would be permanent because of the massive shock to the nervous system that I had received and in this they were proved correct. The progress that I made and good results from x-rays satisfied them that I would benefit from a break and on 1 April we all flew by commercial airline down to Las Vegas where the Carters and Saffells were waiting for us. The first person I went to see was Gerry Garrison and presented him with a bottle of malt whisky as a small measure of my thanks for saving my life in the crash. Wearing loose clothes that masked the cast I was able to get out and about and we even spent several evenings out in Las Vegas seeing shows and gambling. The highlight, however, for me was a formal squadron dinner given for me in the Officers' Club where I was treated like the prodigal son and made to feel like a returning hero. I made several nostalgic trips to the flight line and the squadron and paid my respects to the F-111 in a very tearful ceremony, following which I was presented with a wall plaque and a commemorative album and Terry was given a 'Bat-Girl' certificate (the squadron emblem was a bat!). Quite suddenly our break was over and we were once more in our motel back at Denver with the exciting news that they would be taking the cast off in two weeks providing the x-rays were satisfactory.

On 8 May my cast was cut off and my pallid, puffy body exposed to view, accompanied by the most appalling smell. Terry washed and washed me and the smell disappeared but the body would take months before the muscle tone improved and I dared take off my shirt in public. My neck ached beyond belief and although I wore a neck brace for a while I found that I could turn the neck and also flex it backwards and forwards. Greatly heartened I started to work at neck-strengthening exercises and muscle tone activities and we celebrated by being taken out by Bill Fisher for an Italian meal followed by an evening at the Denver Dog Racing track: notable for one of Terry's selections stopping to have a fight with another dog on the far side of the track. Things went so well that I received my hospital discharge on 17 May and we left Denver on 21 May for Washington DC and New York. The RAF VC-10 flight to RAF Brize Norton was due to depart New York on 31 May and we planned to do some serious sightseeing before departure. I was also having fun shaving because when I emerged from the cast I had grown a full dark beard and had been trimming it back in stages to give different styles from full to Van Dyke, Goatee, Mafia and lastly just a moustache: I liked the full set best but to my chagrin it made me look far too naval.

We spent five days in Washington in a hotel and took in every tourist stop on the map, being very affected by the newly-turned soil on the grave of Bobby Kennedy in Arlington Cemetery alongside his brother's with its eternal flame reminding one of the unfulfilled promise of the brothers. In New York we stayed with an RAF exchange officer and his wife on Staten Island and travelled every day by the famous ferry to New York City where once again we acted the tourist role to perfection with a trip up the Empire State Building, dining in O'Henry's in Greenwich Village, and taking in shows on Broadway. All in all the final fortnight helped to expunge much of the pain and agony which stemmed from the January crash and enabled us to leave the United States with positive thoughts for the future and memories of good people and exciting times.

Only Guy really slept on the flight home and I can recall the excitement and wonder with which we saw the chequerboard of green and yellow fields slide into view as we broke through the overcast sky near Oxford. After two years of flying over the desert regions of the south-west USA it was a revelation to see such a verdant countryside and the feeling of being home was palpable. As we made our way slowly down the steps from the VC-10 we scanned the crowd waiting behind the barriers and our hearts leaped as we saw Mum, Carole and Ralph. Laughing, embracing, crying and just holding each other – we were home and it meant everything to us.

We were driven down to Cocking, south of Midhurst, where Mum now owned and ran the village shop, and settled down to a real homecoming rest where we re-acclimatized to the UK and I made my number with the RAF, MOD, and the RAF's medical authorities in the shape of the Head of Orthopaedics, Air Vice-Marshal Mckenzie Crooks.

The Air Vice-Marshal proved to be likeable and thorough, but sceptical about the prognostication of my American neurosurgeon because he felt that I should have received neck fusion to ensure stability. After x-rays and further examinations he stated that he was concerned that he could not see the bone growth predicted by Bill Fisher and that he needed to take me into the RAF hospital at Halton and perform a fusion because he was fearful that a sudden sideways blow could cause dislocation and paralysis: arrangements were set in train.

Meanwhile we returned to Cocking to enjoy the pleasures of family reunion which were enhanced by the delivery of the new car that we had ordered whilst in the USA. It was a top-of-the-range Triumph 2000 Estate in British Racing Green with red leather upholstery and all the available safety devices. Little did we know that this faithful piece of machinery was going to remain as our principal car for the next sixteen years but we certainly enjoyed the luxury of it at the time and it seemed to swallow all our luggage as we packed it for our journey to

Chestfield, where a similar joyful and tearful reunion with Dad and Auntie Nor awaited us.

We really did relax whilst at Chestfield, but all too soon the MOD called and I reported for duty whilst being given a married quarter at RAF Northwood in Middlesex from which I could commute into London and the Main Building of the MOD. I was debriefed thoroughly on my F-111 experience and told that, directly I was fit to travel, I would be posted out to Munich, Bavaria to use my experience as the project pilot on the new Multi Role Combat Aircraft (MRCA) that the UK were going to build with Germany and Italy, following our cancellation of the F-111 purchase. This aircraft would have most of the features of the F-111 with Terrain Following Radar (TFR) and variable geometry (swing wings) and it was essential to bring my knowledge into play when defining the new systems.

Before this exciting tour could commence, however, I had to get my operation out of the way and on 3 August I went into Halton, after a 'farewell' day in London with Terry, during which I bought her some expensive pearls from Ciro's in Regent Street to remember me by in case something went wrong! Having settled into my ward I was prepared for the spinal operation, had some x-rays taken, and was wheeled down to the operating theatre where I waited with some trepidation. A sudden commotion resulted in my trolley being turned round and a doctor informed me that Mckenzie Crooks would not now be operating but that I should dress and report to his office; which I did. Much to my surprise he said that he had spoken to Bill Fisher on the telephone and that, following this discussion and reviewing the latest set of x-rays, he could now see sufficient evidence of bone growth to enable him to take the considered judgement to grant a reprieve from surgery. He would x-ray and review me every two months and if all progressed satisfactorily he would take no further action. Terry's surprise was total when I called her with the news and returned home by tea time: she refused to hand back the pearls!

From then on it was a mad rush to get all the arrangements made for my departure on 25 August, ferry tickets bought, and accommodation booked in Munich. We then went through the by now familiar routine of family farewells, staying overnight at Chestfield and then driving down to the docks at Dover in the pouring rain. Guy was in seventh heaven on the ferry as it was not crowded and we were all able to run about the decks and climb the ladders pretending to be sailors. The drive to HQ RAF Germany in Rheindahlen took five hours and it was a real relief to be welcomed in by Terry's parents, given a good meal and then, surprise, surprise, be whipped off to the Mess for a party. I stayed there just long enough to take and pass my German driving licence and then, leaving Terry and Guy with her parents, set off on the

420-mile journey to Munich: nine hours later I pulled up at the Hotel Lettl, Amalienstrasse 53, unloaded my bags and locked the car. Our Bavarian adventure was about to start.

Munich
I was on the fourth floor in a medium size room costing 23DMs per night B&B and next door to Squadron Leader Ken Hancock, who was the project navigator and who became a close friend of mine. With an evening meal costing 10-15DMs I wrote with some alarm that my very basic living, without going out or doing anything else, would be costing me £110 per month which would exhaust all my money! Work was from 0800 to 1630 hours in the Interim Management Organisation – MRCA HQ at Arabellastrasse 16 – and I would be answering directly to Luftwaffe Lieutenant Colonel Kahtz with an upward chain of Group Captain Roger Topp (No 111 Squadron and RAF Coltishall), Air Commodore Ray Watts, and Luftwaffe General Kroger. Squadron Leader Don Oakden, who had trained with me and been at Coltishall and Nellis with me, had been holding the fort in my absence and I eventually took over the job fully from him on 5 September. Terry had returned to the UK and spent her time between RAF Northwood, Dad and Mum, with trips to the beach at West Wittering.

I rapidly became used to doing the first true desk job that I had had in the RAF since joining fourteen-and-a-half years before and I could not have had one that was more interesting. I had to co-ordinate the Air Staff Requirements from the three participating nations and hold such meetings as were necessary to resolve the differences before arriving at a common requirement which could then be passed on to the manufacturers. This involved a lot of horse trading because one eventual design would have to cater to separate demands of the three nations and, whereas the Germans and Italians wanted a fighter replacement for their ageing F-104s, the RAF wanted a fighter/fighter bomber. I found myself in a very powerful central position, particularly as all three air staffs knew that I was talking with three years' F-111 experience and was the only European to have flown TFR and used VG. I was given full responsibility for all the aircraft systems, with Ken looking after the avionics. In particular I ran the cockpit design committee which meant going to the British Aerospace (BAe) factory at Warton, Lancashire, every six weeks to chair the meeting there with all the contractors and surrounded by the developing hardware. I also visited the German Messerschmitt, Bulkow, Blohm (MBB) works at Manching and the Italian FIAT works in Turino where the swing-wing and the TFR were being developed.

In some ways it was all for the best that Terry was not there initially as I could work all hours of the day to get everything sorted out and a really good system established without feeling guilty. Ken and I enjoyed each other's company and as he was not yet accompanied we not only worked well together but explored Munich and ate and drank together. The late summer in Munich was perfect with wonderful weather and we lunched in the gardens of the Hofgarten, sunbathed on the banks of the River Isar as well as taking raft trips on the river and went to a large number of concerts in the evening; both classical and jazz (Dave Brubeck was one such memorable event). And then on 21 September we went to the Oktoberfest, which is a two-week mad period in Munich when the seven major breweries of the City dispense their double strength brews at a huge fair held on the Theresienwiesse. Interestingly, however, during the preceding week we were invited to the German premiere of the famous *Battle of Britain* film and mixed with the stars, actresses and scores of real Luftwaffe pilots, most of whom were wearing Iron Crosses and rows of medal ribbons and all clearly having a marvellous reunion. Outside the cinema there was a real Messerschmitt on a stand with large models of Spitfires and Hurricanes, but the thing that amused us was the high good humour and laughter during the early part of the film which gradually died away and was replaced by a subdued almost sullen atmosphere – just as though they did not realize how it all ended!

The biggest news, however, was that on 15 September Terry was confirmed as being pregnant with an expected delivery date of mid-March 1970. We were ecstatic because, despite the reassurances, we had never been truly convinced that the after-effects of the crash might not prevent pregnancy. Although nothing could ever replace our lost son or eradicate the terrible memories, we now had something wonderful to look forward to. As I had been given the medical clearance to continue with my tour, I immediately started house hunting so that I would have a home suitable for a pregnant mother. The latest x-rays showed bony growth occurring between the vertebrae and as my range of head movement was gradually increasing Mckenzie Crooks said that he could foresee me getting my flying category back in two to three years' time. Our joy was unconfined.

On 7 November, laden with carnations and irises I arrived early at Munich airport and saw Guy and Terry in the line at the customs desk. I called out and Guy looked up and before anyone could do anything, dashed past the customs and threw himself at me, with everyone clapping. What a reunion we had and how Terry loved our house and the location: Guy started playing with Christina Harsch from next door and, as she spoke no English he started picking up German immediately. We also visited the other UK members of the IMO team who also lived in Neubiberg and were both engineers: Dusty and Margaret Saunders and Dave and Bess Sledge. The RAF wives then got together and gave Terry a welcoming coffee party so that she was made to feel one of the team and able to get to know them all.

Terry's twenty-sixth birthday came with snow blizzarding down as though to give her her own gift of the most beautiful scenery that one could imagine. A perfect white blanket with all the pine trees which surrounded our house holding out their snow-dusted boughs in welcome. The Bavarian houses with their steeply-pitched roofs and shuttered windows looked like something from Hansel and Gretel with yellow bars of light stretching out and illuminating the snow fields. And then the most perfect sight and sound of Saint Nicholas in full ceremonial dress followed by a long snake of children all singing carols, crunching their way through the snow. It was a magical experience and we all thought how blessed we were to have come through the accident and be able to be together to witness such scenes.

We were becoming seduced by the beauty of Bavaria and the winter season became a delight rather than the doldrums that it was in England. The snow remained deep and pure with cloudless blue sky giving the countryside a storybook effect and causing the snow to glisten brilliant white on the fir trees. We explored the local area and found a fairy tale area near Tegernsee with classic Bavarian lodges, unmarked snow fields and, high above, skiers snaking down towards us. The memories were indelible and our time in Bavaria became a treasured passage in our lives. We had also joined the local Anglican Church which was an American Episcopalian, just like the ones we attended whilst in the United States. I quickly became involved in the church affairs and was talked into becoming the Church Treasurer. The church was originally located in Blumenstrasse in Munich but moved out to the suburbs, where the friendly family-orientated atmosphere became an important element of our life in Munich.

A very dramatic event occurred on 10 February when I had to fly from Munich Airport with Lieutenant Colonel Kahtz to chair a meeting of the cockpit committee at Warton. As we were in the taxi on the way to the airport Palestinian terrorists infiltrated the passengers and mounted an attack with machine guns, pistols and hand grenades in an attempt to kill Israeli passengers, amongst whom was Moyshe Dyane's son. As we arrived the German police were going berserk following a huge gun battle resulting in many dead and wounded: we innocently got out of the taxi and were grabbed and slammed up against a wall with guns in our backs. Luckily for us the German trait of response to higher authority came into play as Kahtz started to shout at them with much mention of his rank and we were suddenly released and ushered into the building. It was chaos with wrecked furniture and glass and pools of blood all over the floor, although all the dead and wounded had been removed. The sight was terrible but little did I realize that this was the precursor to the sustained and continuing conflict between Israelis and Arabs that would still be claiming so many lives forty years further on.

Our lives were about to be enriched, however, by the arrival of our second child. With none of today's technology we did, of course, have no idea about its sex and waited with growing excitement for its arrival. Terry had been told categorically by Doctor Bobbitt that she would have to have a Caesarean as there would be too great a risk to try for a natural birth, and was provisionally planned for admission on 2 March with an anticipated date of 7 March for the delivery. Mum had agreed to come to us to help and arrived by BEA on 27 February.

The arrival of the baby became a very protracted affair as it seemed extremely reluctant to brave the snowy Bavarian weather. However, at 1929 hours on 13 March Madeleine Patricia was delivered and I could have cried when Terry squeezed my hand, looked at me and said: 'We did it – didn't we?'

The MRCA project was beset with technical and financial problems and, with the Canadians and Dutch having already withdrawn, it was vital for the Germans and Italians to remain in the programme and agree to cost-cutting measures. This was achieved by reducing the number of prototypes and all three nations agreeing to produce only two-seater aircraft: the Germans and Italians agreed to shelve their plans for a single-seater variant. This created an immediate problem because the Italians did not have a 'navigator' branch in their Air Force and, although they would need to start to train them specifically to fly in the rear cockpit of the MRCA, they insisted that the aircraft should be able to be flown by a single pilot in the front seat. I had to sit down immediately with their test pilots and make cockpit design proposals to accommodate this and then hold a series of Cockpit Committee meetings at BAe Warton to persuade the other nations that the proposals were feasible. I became very familiar with Munich, Frankfurt and Manchester airports, as I became a regular commuter on this route, and also with the B&B establishments along the front at Lytham St Anne's! The workload was extreme because Lieutenant Colonel Kahtz had moved on and his replacement, Wing Commander Des Melaniphy, did not arrive until June. I had to run the Operational Requirements section as well as doing my own job and there was no doubt that I could not have done it all without the selfless attitude, support and hard work of Ken Hancock. He was terrific.

Once Des arrived I made arrangements for Dad to holiday with us and we took the opportunity to explore the local countryside and the beautiful city of Munich. The churches, museums, and general architecture were a constant delight as were the markets, shops, restaurants and beer cellars. We took him to see Nymphenburg Palace and all King Ludwig II's palaces and castles, as well as lunching 500 feet above ground level in the revolving restaurant at the top of the newly built Olympic Tower. Dad had a wonderful time sightseeing but his real joy was in developing a relationship with his grandchildren, as he was endlessly patient in playing with Guy and so very loving in holding and crooning to Madeleine. Highlights of his visit were a trip to Tegernsee with a cable car ride up to the top of the mountain, a lovely drive to Linderhof castle and thence to Mittenwald via Garmisch, but best of all an idyllic day visiting Ludwig's palace on the island in Lake Chiemsee. We did this on a hot day under cloudless azure skies and revelled in the boat trip across the lake surrounded by large fish that would become galvanized once you threw them bread fragments, and then relaxing in a little pony and trap to get to the palace.

Our social life was hectic as we tried to cram in as much as we could and at Oktoberfest time we were hosts first of all to Gerry Crumbie, who stayed with us for three days that incorporated two nights of revelry there with me. He did, however, treat us to a marvellous dinner at the Jagdhoff Hunting Lodge followed by dancing until midnight, much to Terry's delight. With barely a night to recover we hosted Terry's Mum and Dad who ostensibly came to see us and the grandchildren but in reality were intent on consuming vast quantities of beer at the Oktoberfest. Terry's Dad was in the process of leaving Rheindahlen on his prestigious appointment as Station Commander at RAF Aldergrove in Northern Ireland, where he would serve until his retirement and where he and Joan would buy their small farm at their retirement location.

One notable event took place prior to Christmas as the RAF element at IMO was detailed to take part in the Remembrance Day service at Durnbach Allied cemetery in the forests south of Munich. Sir Roger Jackling, the British Ambassador to Germany, attended and read the lesson on what was the first ever unified British and German act of military remembrance for the two wars. It was a service of extraordinary atmosphere in the cold, dank, misty forest with full ceremonial guards of honour from the RAF, German Air Force and Army, USAF, and Canadian Air Force. The feelings of sadness, regret, and gratitude were palpable and I suffered a sudden shock when my eyes focused on the nearest headstone, dedicated to Sergeant Leslie Evans: Air Gunner aged 20 years. To see the same name as my father's jolted me, and made me even more aware of my good fortune in that my father had come home.

The pace of the project was increasing and I not only had to make my usual trips to Warton but was given permission to spend three days in Edinburgh at Ferranti's expense to be squeezed dry of everything I knew about Terrain Following Radar because the British firm were determined to win the TFR contract for the Multi-Role Combat Aircraft. They wined and dined me without reservation but made me work very hard in return for their largesse. I was also having to go to Turin in Italy to give advice and to be squeezed by FIAT on the variable geometry aspects of the aircraft and to help them translate the operational requirements into hard design. Once again I benefited from a civilian company's expenses system, but the most enjoyable trip was to Warton, followed by another visit to Edinburgh and then a direct flight to Paris for two days to visit the Air Show. Naturally I allowed myself to go sightseeing and after the Eiffel Tower I relaxed on a bateau mouche to enjoy the full experience of a Seine river trip, before becoming involved with the aerospace contractors at the Show. Just to complicate matters I had to sit the final exam of my two-year correspondence course (the ISS) which I had started on my return from the USA. All went very well and I gained an 'A' (above the average) grade, which almost guaranteed my selection for a place on the RAF Staff Course at Bracknell. This did, in fact, occur and I was given a start date of 10 January 1972 for the course: our time in Munich was coming to an end.

Demanding though work was we had now started our long run-down to departure and as I had it in my mind that we would need to look good and entertain a lot if I was to make an impression at the Staff College, we set about equipping ourselves for the next strange (for a pilot that is) phase of college life. We used the marvellous shops of Munich to purchase a 12-place canteen of cutlery and I then used a trip to Warton to go down to London and order three pairs of handmade shoes from Maxwell of Dover Street, and three suits and a set of sports clothes from Hawkes at No. 1 Savile Row.

We then embarked on a long series of goodbyes which had a sense of real sadness about them. Colonel Bruno Von Mengden (who had taken over from Colonel Fred Obleser as Head of Military Factors) hosted a magnificent dinner at Kreitmans, which was an authentic Bavarian restaurant featuring hunting trophies on all its walls, and presented me with an ice bucket (which I use to this day) and a beautiful tankard decorated with the sights of Munich. Air Commodore Ray Watts entertained us to dinner and I began to get the feeling that I had actually made a difference to the project and by hard work, vigilance, and using my previous experience without showing bias to my own country, had moved the complex project much closer to the best design. This feeling was reinforced when at my last Cockpit

Committee Meeting at Warton I was given a surprise reception by PANAVIA and the three participating nations, where they made presentations and said some very complimentary words.

There was just time before we left to treat Terry to a really expensive night out in Munich to celebrate her birthday, starting with a marvellous meal at a Balkan restaurant called 'Opatiza' and ending with visits to a beer cellar, a wine restaurant, and a night club.

And then a final big party. Forty-eight people came to our going-away party, with Guy being allowed to show all the ladies upstairs to the powder room and the bedroom where they could leave their coats; he was so grown-up and serious about it all. At 2145 hours Terry called us to table and what a spread it was. She had cooked one 'roulade' for each person (a thin steak rolled and stuffed with spices and peppers and served with a rich sauce) complemented by chilli con carne, an unlimited supply of Uncle Ben's rice, a complete carved ham and a lavish salad. For dessert she had cooked two apple pies, two meringues, two cheesecakes, a trifle and a fruit salad. And then a cheese board and coffee. Twenty-five bottles of wine were drunk and the entertainment was dancing down in our cellar to taped music or listening to a live guitarist in the lounge. At 0400 hours the last guest left and we closed the door, looked at the address of 6 Lime Walk, RAF Bracknell, Berks painted on our crates and wondered what the future held for us.

Chapter 11

Dogsbody Days

A wise man is strong but a man of knowledge increaseth strength. For by wise counsel thou shalt make thy war

Proverbs 24, v–vi

The tension in the car was palpable as we drove along the broad dual carriageway linking Lightwater with Bracknell, where the RAF Staff College was located.

It really did seem that I had reached a pivotal moment in my career because I was now being asked to move out of my narrow pilot specialization and start to mix with and compete against officers from all branches. Not only that but I had to perform well: it was, quite rightly, said that it was better never to have attended the Staff College than have attended and performed poorly. For the first time for me in the RAF I was not going to be able to rely on my flying skills but would have to demonstrate that my all-round abilities were better than others. It was an unknown world and one that aroused considerable trepidation. The children were of course completely unaffected by all this and could not have been more excited when they spilled from the car and started to explore No. 6 Lime Walk, the semi-detached married quarter that had been allocated to us for the duration of the one-year course.

There were 120 officers on the course drawn from every branch in the RAF but also including officers from the army and navy as well as from overseas. With a rank of squadron leader, or the equivalent, the course was led by Wing Commander Ken Hayr (later Air Marshal Sir Kenneth Hayr), who had just commanded the RAF's very first Harrier squadron. We could not have had a sharper individual with more street cred than Ken and he was to remain a firm friend until his untimely death in a Vampire crash at the Biggin Hill Air Show in 2005.

The course was organized on a three-term school basis with students changing syndicates every term so that maximum exposure to other people's views and capabilities occurred. The general routine was for some coursework in the morning followed by a lecture from a prestigious speaker and then follow-up exercises conducted in a syndicate during the afternoon. The pressure was steady and there were written exercises that had to be completed out of hours, both of an individual and a group nature. Everything that one submitted was critiqued by the Directing Staff, who were all of wing commander rank, and you were kept up to date with a continuous running assessment of your performance.

It was not, however, all work in the classroom and there was a comprehensive visit programme so that we could not only see how the other Services operated but also be given an insight into how other Public Service organizations such as the police, fire, and Civil Service carried out their work. Visits to business and local authorities complemented this and we then undertook specialized visits to see every type of activity within the RAF at Station, Group, Command, and the Ministry of Defence. Commanders at every level spoke to us and politicians reinforced the fact that we were extensions of the political arm and did not exist for any reason other than that, whether it be for Home Defence or for the enforcement of overseas policy. To put this latter point in perspective we were taken on visits overseas to British and NATO organizations including the HQ of NATO in Brussels. And all the time we were being pushed hard to expand and develop our staff skills with emphasis on reasoning, logic and persuasive argument.

Halfway through the course I underwent a medical board at the Central Medical Establishment in London and was stunned when the President told me that, although my neck had healed, it would never be strong enough to survive the forces of an ejection. I was offered two options. I could either be invalided out of the RAF into civilian life or remain in the Service but be restricted to flying aircraft without ejection seats.

My reaction was immediate and predictable as I started to argue my case and insist that I could accept the risk. The President cut me off short and told me in no uncertain terms that my opinion was irrelevant and that the board's decision was final with no possibility of change: the decision as to what I wished to do in the future was mine.

My feeling of devastation was replaced by one of anger so that by the time I reached home I was almost beyond reason. In my mind I had done everything required of me and considered that I was well and fit enough to return to my chosen profession as a fast-jet pilot, with Tornadoes as my future. That a set of doctors should deny me this was beyond belief and I was having none of it! If they would not budge, then I would leave the Service.

As has happened so many times in my life, however, Terry immediately introduced a sense of perspective into my irrational world. Calming me down and making me put emotion firmly on one side, she made me consider all the pros and cons and look at all my strengths and weaknesses. After hours of discussion and several very stiff drinks we came to a conclusion very different from my original reaction.

It was clear that my career was going well and that I loved flying within the Royal Air Force. It was also clear that my low level expertise could be put to good use in the tactical/air dropping role performed by the C-130 Hercules aircraft. There could be a positive future for me there, and we agreed that I should try it. The die had been cast.

It became relatively easy to gauge from the comments and remarks of the Directing Staff as to how well one had done and yet I was still surprised when I landed one of the top jobs on offer. This was to be the Personal Staff Officer (PSO) to the Controller Aircraft of the RAF: the Air Chief Marshal who was on the Air Force Board and charged with responsibility for the procurement and development of all new systems for the RAF. It meant that I would be working in the Main Building of the Ministry of Defence (MOD) and was warned that as I would be running the outer office of the Controller (unusually for the MOD this was one of the very few outer office appointments where a Service officer took precedence over the Civil Service members), I could expect to work very long and very late hours. It came as something of a shock, therefore, when we were offered a substandard married quarter on the RAF Hendon site, which would have been completely unsuitable for Terry and the children. After a great deal of soul searching we decided that the uncompromising and unhelpful attitude of the RAF authorities towards finding us a more suitable home was perhaps the trigger we needed to move into the housing market.

Thus it was that for a cost of £18,000 we became the owners of Ringwood, Gole Road, Pirbright, a four-square Victorian detached house with two-thirds of an acre of land and in desperate need of care and attention. We completed the purchase in November 1972 and life became a blur because we had to vacate our married quarter prior to Christmas and Ringwood needed a lot of attention before we could move in. We moved into the house during the second week in December and with heroic indifference to the likely problems, Terry insisted on holding a family Christmas. And what a fantastic affair it was with Mum travelling up from Cocking and Carole and Ralph coming across from Frimley; they all brought items of furniture and furnishing because we did not even have carpets on the floor but the oven worked and with everyone pitching in it was a magical occasion.

Mum produced a large carpet for the lower room and we stained the floorboards between its borders and the walls and whitewashed the latter to complete the effect whilst our table was composed of tea chests turned upside down and covered with rugs and a cloth.

I took over the PSO job from Dickie Miller who was leaving on promotion to Wing Commander to take command of No. 36 Hercules Squadron at RAF Lyneham. My boss was Air Chief Marshal Sir Peter Fletcher and although Dickie gave me the most comprehensive handover, nothing could properly prepare you for the moment when he closed the door and you became the only link between the Air Marshal and the outside world. Learning time was nil and the learning curve vertical because there was no one to turn to and the MOD routine and demands rolled remorselessly on, whether you could cope or not. Every forty minutes a messenger deposited another load of paper in the in-tray and the PSO was the only arbiter as to what the Air Marshal should see: that which I passed to him always had to have a briefing note attached as well as a full brief on every item which would feature in the two principal weekly meetings that he attended – the Air Force Board and the Procurement Executive Management Board. As these were held on Monday morning and afternoon and the agenda was not distributed until the preceding Thursday, my activity levels on Thursday afternoon and Friday were extreme and I often did not get home until 2100 hours on the Thursday. The exciting thing, of course, was that you were privy to secrets and top policy thinking from which many air rank officers were excluded.

My home life suffered as I saw very little of the children and often had to work over weekends. My leave dates were determined by those of the Controller. There was also an added complication in that Sir Peter Fletcher retired from the RAF in June and was replaced by Air Chief Marshal Sir Neil (Nebby) Wheeler who had been the Air Member for Supply and Organisation (AMSO). In the middle of the year I had, therefore, to do my normal job but also arrange retirement courses and actual Service departure for the one Air Marshal whilst looking after the other one for four weeks once he left the AMSO job.

One amusing incident took place on the day of the handover when the Air Marshals went to the Fly Fishers Club for lunch and the driver, John, went out of his way to impress so that Sir Neil would keep him on as his driver. Seeing the Air Marshals coming down the steps of the Club he threw open his door on the sparkling, newly washed 3 litre Rover so as to be ready to usher them aboard. Unfortunately, he did not check his rear view mirror before doing so and an overtaking taxi crashed into the opening door, tore it off its hinges and deposited it 20yds down the road. They returned to MOD with a howling breeze blowing over the two Air Marshals and with the smashed door in the boot. John kept his job but remained on a yellow card for three months! The outer office hugged themselves in delight at their eminences' discomfort!

Sir Neil was a very different character from the reclusive Sir Peter, who rarely left his office, and pronounced that he could not do his job as Controller unless he had first-hand experience of the complete US aerospace industry and I was, therefore, to arrange a full tour of the top eighteen companies during the month of October, taking three weeks for the tour and using a Comet from No. 216 Squadron as personal transport. He would be accompanied by me and his senior Assistant Under Secretary, Don Harper.

Immediately prior to departure for the States disaster struck as, on 6 October, Egypt and Syria launched a surprise attack on Israel and Lord Carrington exercised his right to the use of the Comet that had been allocated to our tour. The US Embassy, however, came up trumps as their Air Attaché, Lieutenant Colonel Rich Milbourn, who had become a good friend of mine and was accompanying us on the trip, immediately organized all the internal US travel by the use of USAF aircraft. The tour itself was a blur of contact with the whole top panoply of US business chiefs as they courted Sir Neil in the knowledge that defence acquisition from the US rested in his hands. Moving in his shadow I have never experienced such continuous high level treatment and entertainment because we dined every night as the guests of a chairman or chief executive of a major aerospace company. The venues varied from the Boeing penthouse on top of their skyscraper in Seattle, to private men-only clubs where servants tended to your every need. We had two weekends of leisure, on the first of which Grumman organized a fishing trip for us in Long Island Sound where we caught blue-fish. For the second I excused myself and flew down to Baton Rouge to spend the two days with Bill Fisher, who was starting to practise neurosurgery at the Lady of the Lake Hospital. As I recall I did not get to bed and returned to Sir Neil, hungover and wearing a Stetson that had been Bill's own, much to the disgust of the Controller, who had had a rather more cultural weekend.

My one moment of glory came at General Dynamics when the President of GD (no doubt, properly briefed) clasped me warmly by the hand and informed Sir Neil that he was lucky to have one of the best F-111 pilots alive as his personal aide, and then thanked me for all my personal efforts in bringing the F-111 into service. Once again Sir Neil was not impressed. We did have a great reception at McDonnell Douglas where Don Harper was given a warm welcome and lauded as the man in our MOD who had made the US Harrier programme possible. Goodwill exuded everywhere and the trip became even better when the Comet was released for our own use and caught up with us at Fort Worth. An immense amount of work was done on the trip and many systems that we now operate can be seen to have had their genesis during those three weeks.

Back in England I was stunned to be informed that I would be leaving the MOD at the end of the year to start my multi-engine training prior to taking command of No. 24 Hercules Squadron in July: my promotion to Acting Wing Commander would take effect with my departure from MOD and would become substantive from 1 July 1974 upon taking up my new appointment.

Our world was in turmoil because despite my long working hours and absences, the family had started to enjoy some stability with Guy settling in well at the Pirbright Primary School and with all of us starting to become part of the village society and church congregation. My posting would mean a move to RAF Lyneham with two years in residence in a married quarter and another change of school for Guy; our decision to register him with Dover College as a boarder seemed even wiser. Another problem had been occurring since our return from Munich in that Terry had started to have considerable pain in her spine resulting from our car crash and had even been referred to Harley Street by the MOD doctors. Their best efforts involving corsets had not been effective and she now turned to a chiropractor in Winchester but he made matters considerably worse and thus commenced a long, continuous, and debilitating problem for her involving her spine.

In the short term we determined to have the best Christmas ever and arranged to collect Dad and Auntie Nor and then have Mum come up to us when they had returned to Chestfield. Carole and Ralph came across and we really went to town with decorations, food and drink and games. The children were completely taken in by Father Christmas and he left them the biggest stockings that they had yet seen. With the tree glowing with lights, the log fire blazing and decorations in abundance the whole house seemed to glow with warmth and happiness. The simple church service for Midnight Mass conducted by the Reverend John Cunningham seemed to underline the new start that we were also experiencing and I said some very heartfelt prayers of thanks for all that we had been given, as well as asking for God's help for my move into a totally new world in which I had no background or experience.

As we rejoiced as a family for the wonders of Christmas time, Terry and I took some very private and quiet time to reflect on our lives and the challenges that we had had to face and deal with together. There was no doubt that we generated great strength in each other and it was, therefore, with something resembling excitement rather than apprehension, that we looked to the future and said 'goodbye' to 1973–1974 would be a year of opportunity.

Chapter 12

Herculean Tasks

'Even to command a flock of sheep is pleasant; how much better a group of men'

Spanish Maxim

New Year's Day saw me packing my bags at the same time as entertaining our neighbours to New Year's drinks to welcome in 1974. My move to my old stomping ground of RAF Oakington took place the next day as I was destined to undergo my multi-engine refresher training on the Varsity aircraft based there.

My excitement at starting my new venture was affected by my regrets at saying goodbye to the family, although it would only be for periods of five days at a time with my commuting at weekends. What did happen though, which was very unsettling, was that Guy began to become more disturbed with every one of my departures and eventually took to screaming and crying at the moment I said my 'goodbyes'. No matter how Terry and I tried to comfort him and explain to him that I would be back soon, he would have none of it. There was no doubt in our minds that the car crash and all the turmoil in our lives that followed it were causing real problems. As parents we had to face this and try to cope as best we could by giving him and Madeleine even more love and as much attention as possible over the weekends. He did respond a little but we became very aware of his need for stability and the importance of our love for him.

The drive through Cambridge, along the Huntingdon straight, and the familiar turn-off to the right leading to the airfield, brought back so many memories and it hardly seemed possible that it had been eighteen years since I had last swept through the main gates to the station. This time, however, instead of a poky little room in No. 2 Mess I was installed in a suite in the Main Mess and very conscious of my new Wing Commander stripes.

I started flying on 10 January and could not believe how slow and lumbering the dear old Varsity was. Ground School seemed extremely easy and we even used the same lecture rooms that I remembered from 1956. There were memories everywhere with the ghosts of the Vampires and my old friends from No. 117 Course ever present. It was so enjoyable to view the same scenery again and although my crew would not have relished my trying an aerobatic sequence along the twin canals I did indulge in some low flying along the old remembered routes.

I completed the thirty hours and twenty-five trips by 7 February with only one disturbance. This occurred during my only overseas flight when the trip was designed to test our navigational and procedural abilities by asking us to fly from Oakington to RAF Wildenrath in Germany and after a quick turnaround to proceed along the air corridor in East Germany to RAF Gatow in Berlin. This part of the exercise went well but then thick fog developed and prohibited all flying. There I was, stuck in Berlin, but my real problem was that Terry had been admitted to Woking hospital for an operation and I was unable to play my part by visiting her and looking after the children. Eventually I overrode the Met Officer's objections and took off in conditions that one would not normally consider. I overflew Wildenrath, made Oakington in one hop, raced the car south and arrived at the hospital on the day of Terry's release. At least the other patients finally believed that she did have a husband!

With the Varsity refresher behind me I drove down to RAF Thorney Island near Chichester to start my conversion onto the Hercules at No. 242 OCU. The Hercules is the backbone of the RAF's airlift capability and was purchased from Lockheed so that the RAF could have a truly tactical transport aircraft capable of operating from short and relatively primitive airfields at reasonable speed, with a good payload, and also able to air-drop paratroopers and supplies. The aircraft is in essence a very tough airborne heavy truck and its crews rejoice in being known as 'truckies'.

We started with a solid spell of six weeks in the ground school getting to grips with the complexities of this large transport aircraft and finished with nine trips in the simulator to reinforce all the lessons that we had been taught. Working regular school hours meant that I could pop down the road to spend most evenings with Mum as it was only a twenty-minute drive. I used to get her to quiz me on some of the technical subjects even though she freely admitted that she might just as well have been speaking Chinese for all it meant to her. It was so good to have relaxed leisure time with her after such long enforced absences and made me realize once again just how lucky I was to have such loving parents and how much they meant to me. At weekends, of course, I was able to spend all my time at Ringwood but, once again, we had problems when saying 'goodbye' to Guy: because the drive was a short one, we got round this by my leaving late on the Sunday evening after Guy was sound asleep.

On 3 May came the big moment when Flight Lieutenant Burrage took me into the air in Hercules XV202 for the start of my love affair with 'Fat Albert', as the aircraft is affectionately known.

The CMk 1 Hercules could not be more different as an aircraft to the types that I had operated to date. Instead of a sleek, aerodynamic, highly powered weapons delivery platform operated by one or two aircrew, the Hercules is large, squat and purposeful and operated by at least five crew members. The aircraft is 98ft long (or 113ft in the stretched CMk 3 version) with a 133ft wing span, and is powered by four Allison T56 turbo-prop engines driving four-bladed Hamilton Standard propellers, and a tailplane that reaches up to 38ft.

I found the size of the aircraft a little disconcerting at first and the number of people on board was distracting. Having been used to doing everything myself I had difficulty in delegating responsibility for the various activities to the others, and I know that I got on the nerves of the navigator and engineer when I interfered with their functions. Although I did get better it was a trait that remained with me for some time as I felt that I should be controlling the whole lot. I found the aircraft was remarkably responsive in roll and nicely heavy in pitch so that it was easy to fly very accurately on instruments. In fact the only strange aspect was the manner in which one coped with crosswind landing by using crossed controls. The reason for this was that the Hercules's undercarriage, whilst immensely strong in the vertical sense, was not so in the transverse sense and could easily be damaged if the aircraft was drifting at the moment of touchdown. As a result in extreme crosswind conditions the aircraft could make a spectacular approach with the into-wind wing tip practically touching the ground whilst the rudder was massively in the other direction to hold the aircraft straight. I solo'd after the standard five trips and on 30 May departed for RAF Akrotiri in Cyprus for the night conversion phase and to practise route flying.

Terry came down to spend a weekend with Mum and for me to show them the station. We had a wonderful time and they were suitably impressed by the size and complexity of the aircraft. The highlight for Guy, however, was a picnic that we had on the seashore of the station when he suddenly ran up to me with a £10 note that he had found blowing across the sand: upon his return to Pirbright it was quickly converted into an Action Man! The last part of the course consisted of route flying and I was impatient for it to end as I really did feel that I could just as well be doing this on the squadron. With no real regrets, therefore, I bade my farewells to the helpful and friendly staff and the OCU and spent the last weekend of June in the bosom of my family.

As I drove along the M4 towards RAF Lyneham I must admit to having a queasy tummy at what might be waiting for me, because everything was new. I had never even been to RAF Lyneham in an operational sense, I knew no-one at all in the transport world, had only just converted onto the aircraft, and was of course without any experience of running a squadron of 120 people. When I had confided all this to Terry prior to leaving home she gave me a very old-fashioned look and a very sage piece of advice: 'Just remember Clive, that you are going to be the boss. Do things in the way you believe to be right. Don't think that you have to explain all your decisions but always be fair and let people know what the objectives are. And don't do things to be popular.'

I pondered on all this and have to say that from that time on I don't think that I have ever deviated from it. How Terry was able to synthesize all these thoughts on leadership without the benefits of all the staff training and leadership courses that I had been subjected to, I will never know! I will just add one more maxim and that is – when you have made your decision and announced it, never ever back away from it.

I turned off the M4 and, as I drove through the small town of Wootton Bassett, a Hercules came straight over the top of the car on its descent to a landing at RAF Lyneham. It seemed to be the most welcoming way of arriving and my heart lifted as I drove past the Mallard pub and the Parish Church of the village of Lyneham. Married quarters appeared on my left and then there were the station gates on the right with the guardroom and the RAF Ensign straining at its flagstaff. All of it seemed welcoming and familiar and I was impressed by the appearance and bearing of the guards and the punctilious way in which they checked my ID card. Following their directions I took the curve round to the left until the functional and unlovely Officers' Mess came into view. I had arrived.

I reported immediately to the Station Commander, Group Captain Charlie Slade, and he gave me a most courteous and warm welcome. He gave me no words of advice but made it clear that No. 24 Squadron was mine to command and he would not interfere unless in extremis. He made no comment on its current commander and gave me no clue as to the state of the squadron but suggested I get my feet under the table as quickly as possible after a two week period of acclimatization flying with the Station Standards Squadron.

I flew my Lyneham familiarization trip on 3 July and was immediately impressed with the smooth efficiency of all the aspects that were in place to handle these large aircraft and by the size and complexity of the base which housed five of the RAF's six Hercules squadrons. The station dated from 1938 when, as a grass airfield, it started life as No. 33 Maintenance Unit. The Hercules era of Lyneham started when No. 36 Squadron arrived on 1 August 1967; No. 24 Squadron arrived in February 1968, No. 30 and 47 Squadrons in February 1971, followed by No. 48 Squadron from Singapore in September of the same year. When No. 70 Squadron relocated from Cyprus, Lyneham became home to all 61 of the RAF's Hercules aircraft.

On 4 July I was handed command of No. 24 Squadron by Wing Commander Hardy in a brief ceremony and then called the whole squadron together in the crew room in order to introduce myself and set out the framework of how I intended to run the squadron, state my aims and objectives, and indicate the standards which I expected.

Although the station was organized by one administrative wing and all the aircraft were serviced centrally, the flying was undertaken by autonomous squadrons commanded by a wing commander operating from individual Squadron Headquarters' buildings. Entering the No. 24 Squadron Headquarters with its wing commander's pennant flying from the flagstaff by the doorway I admired the collection of squadron silverware in the cabinet in the hallway, the long list of past commanders scribed on a parchment honour roll, and then turned left into a corridor flanked by the adjutant's office and administrative room on one side and the busy operations room on the other before entering the Squadron Commander's office, with its walls covered by historic photographs. The largest of these behind the impressive oak desk was of Major Lanoe Hawker VC, DSO who was the squadron's first commanding officer.

No. 24 Squadron was the senior squadron at Lyneham and the sixth most senior in the RAF after being formed at Hounslow on 1 September 1915, flying DH2 single-seat fighters. Hawker was shot down and killed by Baron von Richtofen but by the end of the First World War the squadron had accounted for no less than 297 enemy aircraft. During the interwar years No. 24 was engaged in communication duties and awarded its own badge, which is of a game bird with the motto In Omnia Parati, which translates as 'in all things prepared' or as we preferred 'Ready for Anything'. Interestingly in 1947 the squadron was reorganized on a Commonwealth basis and until 1962 its commanding officers were drawn in rotation from the air forces of Canada, Australia, New Zealand, and South Africa. In 1954 the squadron received the Queen's Standard, the first transport squadron to gain such an honour and with the maximum permissible number of battle honours – Western Front 1914-1918, the Somme 1916,

Hindenburg Line and Low Countries 1939-40, Malta 1942, North Africa 1942-43, and Burma 1944-45. The squadron had assisted in famine relief in Nepal in 1973 but had had two recent accidents when it lost a Hercules in a landing mishap in snow on an iced runway in Tromso, Norway, but much more seriously when a Hercules flew into the sea at night when taking off from Pisa, Italy, with a load of Italian paratroopers: all on board were killed. The squadron had been badly shaken by these mishaps and my instruction from my group commander had been simple: restore morale on the squadron, raise standards, and prevent any further accidents.

Having delivered my homily as a precursor to addressing these issues I placed responsibility for running the squadron on the broad shoulders of Squadron Leader Keith Raynor (the senior flight commander) and set off on an eight-day trip to the Far East. I composed a crew of the senior members of each specialization on the squadron and used the trip to dig under the skin of these sections as well as getting to know them well as individuals. I also took with me Squadron Leader David Edwards from the Station Standards Squadron to act as back-up captain and informal advisor. David was a calm, knowledgeable, well-rounded individual who I got to know very well as a friend, but who tragically died in his late forties from cancer, having already had command of Lyneham and then been promoted to air commodore.

This busy trip enabled me to consolidate my handling skills and really get to grips with route planning and the operation of each of the specializations of co-pilot, navigator, engineer, and load master by understudying one of these positions on each leg of the trip.

Six hours after taking off from Lyneham on 7 July I was touching down on the familiar runway of Akrotiri in Cyprus and already anticipating the kebab and kokinelli meal at a restaurant in Limassol. On 8 July we flew to RAF Masirah, a small island airbase off the east coast of Oman, and then made the six-hour trip to RAF Gan on Addu Atoll island in the Maldives. No time on this trip to snorkel and admire the brilliantly coloured shoals of fish, because fourteen hours after touching down we were airborne for RAF Tengah on Singapore Island, where we were allowed one whole day's rest before returning to Lyneham along the same route. There was, however, a dramatic development which nobody had foreseen.

We spent the night of 14 July in a hotel in Limassol because all the accommodation at Akrotiri was full. Going out for a kebab meal that evening with the crew we thought that everywhere was very quiet but placed no significance on it: likewise in the early morning when we were driven to the airfield for the return to Lyneham. I fired up the aircraft and after take-off tried to contact Nicosia for my departure routing from the island: they refused to answer me and I could hear them telling a British Airways aircraft to land elsewhere because Nicosia airfield was closed. Suddenly my co-pilot, who was monitoring the world news on the HF frequency, broke in to say that Cyprus had been invaded by the Turks and there was fighting all over the northern part of the island following a paratroop invasion. No wonder Limassol had been quiet! Word had somehow got out that we were the first people to leave the war-torn island since the invasion and when I landed at Lyneham I felt a complete fraud when surrounded by reporters and TV crews all pestering me for news. I tried to keep a straight face when telling them that despite the dangers we flew a 'defensive' route out of the island and that British forces on the Sovereign Base Areas were adequately prepared for all eventualities. Obviously flying Hercules aircraft was much more interesting than all those silly fast jets that I'd been involved with.

What did happen immediately, however, was a sudden immersion into what Lyneham was all about in living up to its station motto of 'Support, Save, Supply'. For the next month the station went onto what was almost a war footing as we mounted a maximum effort airlift to supply our forces in the island with everything they would need if attacked, as well as bringing home all the refugees and tourists who had suddenly lost their homes or who had no other means of getting out of Cyprus. I did two trips myself on this Akrotiri airlift and took privately purchased boxes of everyday items, such as toilet rolls, washing powder and so on for the use of families in the married quarters who otherwise would have had nothing. In all, we extracted more than 5,000 people from the island before a ceasefire was declared. Terry had by now joined me with the children and found herself pressed into action helping serve meals to the refugees we unloaded at Lyneham, but who sometimes had nothing but the bathing costumes that they were wearing when they fled the fighting. She also organized the collecting of clothes so that these poor souls could be clothed prior to their departure from Lyneham. It was a true initiation into the life of a squadron commander's wife.

With the emergency over life resumed an orderly pattern so I set about developing the squadron, eradicating bad practice, building morale, and encouraging the desire to be the best squadron on the base. Much to the irritation of my fellow squadron commanders I introduced flying scarves in squadron colours and also cummerbunds for use with mess kit ('Not done in the Transport World', I was told). I also changed many of the established practices, altered the leadership of three sections and benefited from the posting in of new flight commanders who supported my efforts. Very suddenly attitudes changed and the squadron stopped feeling sorry for itself and started producing better results. I tried to fly with every member of the squadron and get to know them personally, and used a new style of social programme to bring everyone together.

Apart from the fun of running the squadron and feeling the honour and distinction of being their named representative I have to admit that I began to develop a real liking for being in charge and having the authority and responsibility that went with command. I welcomed the chance to make decisions after assembling data and analysing it, and, if necessary, defending my position by robust argument. Many of my ideas did not fit the established metier of transport squadron operation and I took a perverse pleasure in doing things that would provoke fellow squadron commanders but which I knew would result in my own squadron becoming stronger and more cohesive.

At the same time I was having enormous fun in exploring the routes and going to places that no one in the fast jet force had even thought of. The first of these trips in October was to take four aircraft to Namao Air Base, Edmonton, Alberta, to cooperate with No. 435, our sister squadron in the Canadian Air Force. It also meant a first for me in flying myself across the Atlantic to Gander in Newfoundland, where the RAF maintained a small engineering detachment for the specific purpose of handling our aircraft in transit. What I found amazing was that the journey from Gander to Namao took as long as our previous day's crossing of the Atlantic – and it was all above trees! We spent one week in Canada and had a marvellous low-level trip up to the Yukon, where we spent the night at Whitehorse (where the gold prospectors used to start their trail inland) after flying over the huge tar sands fields of Athabasca. We landed there in clear dry conditions but it started to blizzard during the night and we had an immense snowball fight of NCOs v officers, during which I was kidnapped and only returned on payment of pizzas for the NCOs.

In November, for reasons that I cannot now recall, there was a sugar shortage in the UK and it so happened that I was routing through the Indian Ocean and able to stay overnight at Mauritius, where we purchased four 1cwt sacks of sugar for distribution at Lyneham on our return. We had an emergency when climbing out of Gan when a fire warning on my No. 2 engine occurred and I had to go through the full fire drill, shut down the engine and return for an emergency three-engine landing at Gan. It proved to be a faulty warning system but the feeling on the flight deck was genuine during the emergency. Meanwhile, on my return to Lyneham the customs officers were in a quandary about all the sugar on board but took my suggestion that as they would be the recipients if it was allowed to go to the Messes, assessed it was four 'bags' of sugar with no charge made!

The New Year brought with it yet more adventures as I participated in the lift of Royal Marines and a Harrier squadron to northern Norway for the winter Arctic exercises. My first surprise was just how long the trip was, because it took us five hours from Lyneham to get to Tromso where we had a hazardous approach letting down to the airfield between mountains that were hidden in thick cloud and then landing on an icy runway in a near blizzard. My nerves were truly tested and it was a huge relief when we parked safely by the control tower. We did three more lifts using the airfield at Bardufoss as well as Tromso, where I was intrigued to see that the Norwegian fighter aircraft were all contained in hangars hewn out of the rock of the adjacent mountains. I was also fascinated to look down on the frozen fiords and see all the winter sports being played on the ice under lights, including a very adventurous form of stock car racing.

July 1975 brought a change of Station Commander from the very orthodox to the eccentric as 'Crash' Amos took over and introduced his own individual style of command. With a yacht and E Type Jaguar parked outside the Station Commander's residence he left no one in any doubt about his leisure pursuits and, when he started practising for his HGV licence using a RAF truck with his Station Commander's pennant on it, we knew we were in for an interesting ride. That said, he left us alone to run our squadrons and gave us excellent top cover from Group and their attempts to run things from afar.

Of overriding concern in August was the preparation of the squadron for the celebration of its 60th anniversary on 1 September. We had decided to invite the MP Winston Churchill as our VIP guest of honour because during the Second World War our squadron had provided 'Ascalon', the York aircraft that had been the personal transport of his grandfather Sir Winston Churchill when he was the Prime Minister. The celebrations went on for three days of flying, reunions, cocktail parties and dining-in nights and culminated in an ecumenical church service to give thanks for the squadron and in remembrance of all those who had served on and died in service on it.

Hardly had the dust settled from the celebrations than we were once more embroiled in assisting in an overseas crisis when Guatemala yet again laid claim to Belize and began positioning her troops into a possible invasion position. The irony of the timing was that the call to the station came at the precise moment when all available personnel were on parade for the disbandment ceremony of Nos. 36 and 48 Squadrons, who were being axed as a result of a cutback in the air transport fleet. With the requirement for an extensive reinforcement, aircrew were quite literally marched off the parade into the squadron HQ of the remaining squadrons and told to ready themselves for operations rather than retirement. I was tasked to establish the slip pattern and flew out to Nassau in the Bahamas via Gander on 4 November, where I established my HQ in the beautiful Nassau Beach Hotel on Cable Beach before moving to the equally good Emerald Beach Hotel on the Emerald Beach. I did the first flight into Belize on 6 November, flying around Cuba and carrying just enough fuel for the round trip to avoid using the precious fuel reserves at Belize. We were reinforcing the garrison with men, vehicles, weapons and general supplies, which were easy loads to handle with the trip taking just three hours each way. My experience of Belize was limited to the small airport building and the hutted and tented encampment of the British Forces but the heat and humidity did not make me want to linger. Once I was certain that the slip was working soundly I returned to the UK having quite an eventful trip on the way.

We were scheduled to take off at 0200 hours from Nassau but when we arrived at the airport at midnight we found that the Met Office was shut with a handwritten note on the door to us telling us that 'winds and temperatures standard for this time of year', with no details of any diversion, en route, or destination weather. We got what details we could from the aircraft's HF radio and set off, overflying Bermuda, and with what seemed like favourable fuel passed the Point of No Return (PNR). Almost immediately we started to encounter unforecast headwinds, which got worse and worse with the fuel line coming down alarmingly. In the end it was touch and go, particularly as the weather at Lyneham deteriorated and of course it became night again. I gritted my teeth as we overflew St Mawgan and decided to have a go at Lyneham despite the winds having backed and increased to such an extent that all landings had to be made on the short southerly runway. With the aircraft bucking like a wild horse in 40-knot winds and the rain lashing down from a low cloud base, my logbook shows a fourteen hours ten minutes flight from the Bahamas but does not show the fuel minimums that I had gone below or the sighs of relief from my long-suffering crew at the point of touchdown!

In the middle of all this professional activity we had gone through the personal heartache of sending Guy to boarding school. He started at Dover College Junior School, located in Folkestone, for the autumn term and looked wonderfully smart but very woeful in his new uniform. A photograph shows him trying to look very brave outside the main gates of the school but the game is given away by the white knuckles that are gripping his beloved teddy bear. Although in the end we knew we had done the right thing, we had many heart-rending months before he settled, with him writing the most tragic letters saying how lonely he was, how he hated the school and pleading with us to bring him home. After speaking with the school authorities, who gave us a slightly better picture of how he was coping, we determined to make him stay two terms and then if he was still as profoundly upset we would remove him.

That he did settle sufficiently and remained at the school as well as moving on to the main college is to his credit and eventually proved to have been of great importance to him. He absorbed enough and equipped himself with the skills that he needed to develop into a successful businessman as well as making a band of friends with whom he has remained in contact up to the present time.

In January I made my first trip to Hong Kong with a more than interesting route. On the way to Masirah from Akrotiri my co-pilot became incapacitated and had to be helped from his seat to the rest bunk. Luckily I had another captain on board and put him in the right seat for the landing and then used my authority to poach a co-pilot from a Hercules returning to Lyneham at Masirah so that I could complete my route. This was quite important because I had been asked to route prove (assess) Colombo in Sri Lanka as an alternative staging post because the RAF was in the process of giving up Gan in the Maldives and the Hercules required a stopping point between Masirah and the Far East. Colombo proved to be ideal and the local Beach Hotel was a superb watering spot but I did have one alarm during the night take-off from Colombo. The Sri Lankan Air Traffic staff quite literally went to sleep and refused to answer any of our transmissions so, having already filed my flight plan, I taxied out blind and started my take-off when, to my horror, my landing lamps illuminated a tractor towing a MIG fighter crossing the main runway. There was no possibility of stopping as I was almost up to lift-off speed so I pushed the throttles to the firewall, dumped flap, pulled back the stick and prayed. We lurched upwards and as there was no impact we knew we had made it, started easing the flap back up and reducing power to the normal climb setting – and then I believe I breathed again!

Kuala Lumpur was an exotic stop over, but Hong Kong was a revelation, as was the fascinating landing approach in which you flew your descent over the city at right angles to the southerly runway at Kai Tak until you reached the red-and-white checkerboard marked on a hillside and then rolled hard right, with hardly enough time after the 90° turn before you were crossing the airfield boundary and landing.

We had one full rest day before our return and so crammed as much into the day as we could in the way of standard sightseeing. I also took the opportunity to visit a recommended crockery shop in a back street to buy all the Chinese bowls, dishes, cups, saucers and plates that Terry had asked me to bring home. I chose one with typical dragons and it has remained in full use to this day and we always use the large bowls for our salad and the middle-size ones with the charming ceramic spoons for our soup.

On my return home I began to be aware of the very few months remaining to me in command so concentrated on making all the changes to the squadron that I envisaged would improve its performance. My efforts had already resulted in us winning both the Lord Trophy and the 47 Air Despatch Trophy, which were the two competitions for which the squadrons competed, so we did indeed sit very proudly as the top Hercules unit, but I intended that we should remain so. I did, however, want to make every effort to visit places that were unusual, so set off for Nairobi via Khartoum where we stayed in what looked like a converted lift shaft in the hotel and were repeatedly warned that the authorities would punish us if they found any alcohol on board: it was a very sober stay. Nairobi, however, was completely different and I loved the scenery, the mini-safari and the sight of the Masai tribe people: I really did somehow feel close to Dad as it was just as he had described it when he served there during the Second World War.

In April I did several fighter squadron rotations to the weapons camp airfield of Decimomannu in Sardinia and became addicted to fried squid as served with local wine in the town of Cagliari where we stayed overnight. Then off to the Azores and Lajes airfield, nostalgic returns to Luqa in Malta and Nassau in the Bahamas, before embarking on my final so called 'swan-song' when I took Hercules (XV303) on a round-the-world flight, with no spare captain so that I could do all the flying myself.

We departed Lyneham on 11 June for the standard run across the Atlantic but landed at Goose Bay on the Canadian mainland instead of at Gander. Then an overnight stay at Offutt AFB in Nebraska, which was the HQ of the USAF Strategic Air Command, before our next overnight stop at McClellan AFB at San Francisco. We had a memorable meal at Fisherman's Wharf prior to a seven-hour flight to Hickam AFB in Hawaii, where we got caught up in the celebrations marking the two-hundredth birthday of the USA (1776 to 1976) before taking advantage of the beach location of our hotel for a dip in the Pacific with Old Diamond Head as a dramatic backdrop.

We then made an unusual diversion from the normal route because we were carrying a spare engine and propeller for an RAF Hercules that had diverted to Nandi in Fiji with a major engine problem. We delivered the engine but had to stay there until the spare was fitted and test run before being allowed to proceed to Guam. This meant enduring the hardship of staying in the luxury Royal Hotel, where I occupied a full bungalow by the exquisite swimming pool and ate breakfast under a coconut tree from which one of the staff had cut my selected coconut after climbing the tree as agilely as any monkey. The scenery was glorious, the people so friendly and the surroundings so luxurious that it was a real wrench to leave the lovely island and proceed to Guam where we were greeted by the amazing sight of a USAF B-52 bomber upside down on the ground as a result of the island having been hit by a hurricane with winds of more than 120mph: the evidence was everywhere, with the golf-ball radar torn from its mountings, roofs torn off scores of buildings, and the ground littered with uprooted trees.

Hong Kong seemed very peaceful after these scenes of devastation and we made the most of our two-day break by going from Kowloon to Hong Kong Island on the Star Ferry, and then up Victoria Peak by the funicular railway. The return flight to Lyneham on 28 June was uneventful but I had a book full of memories to go with the 107 flying hours that I put in my logbook for my final month in command.

With more than 800 hours on the Hercules, a 'B' Above the Average operational category, and an assessment of Above the Average as a squadron commander, I felt very well pleased with my two years in the Air Transport Force. I was even more pleased when my AOC told me that this had qualified me for attendance at the National Defence College and I could now enjoy a most welcome 'no strings attached' break until reporting to Latimer on 6 September.

Little did I realize that it was merely 'au revoir' to Lyneham rather than the 'goodbye' that I wished all my friends on 2 July when I left the base.

Chapter 13

Tri-Service Harmony

2 September 1976 to 8 July 1977

In no other profession are the penalties for employing untrained personnel so appalling and so irrevocable as in the military

Douglas MacArthur, 1933

In 1976 the National Defence College (NDC) was located at Latimer near Chalfont St Peter, in a wonderfully picturesque part of the English countryside. The college was a strange mixture of historic and beautiful, and modern and un-beautiful structures. The Officers' Mess was the ancient manor house of Latimer with its own private chapel, whereas the tuition was carried out in wooden single-storey huts linked to a new custom-built lecture hall with all the required facilities.

The course itself (No. 6 NDC Course) was designed to build on the work of the individual Service Staff Colleges and, with the members all at the rank of wing commander or equivalent, move on from pure staff practices to developing thinking at the strategic level. It was also tri-Service with a sprinkling of police and civil servants to ensure that all views came into play and to commence the networking process which plays such an important part in decision making at the more senior levels of government.

College routine was agreeable and routine with a morning lecture by an eminent person being preceded by a syndicate exercise and followed by a discussion on the presentation. The afternoon was devoted to seminars, exercises and research, whilst Wednesday afternoons were reserved for sports. Inter-Service friendships flourished and, being maintained after the course had finished, became in the future one of the principal means of arriving at agreed tri-Service decisions: it was intriguing how many of No. 6 NDC Course came together eight years later at the Royal College of Defence Studies for the ultimate military course. We also worked individually on a thesis of about 15,000 words and I decided to use my own experiences to look into the future of the European Aviation Industry, as I had little doubt that economics and European political integration would lead to consolidation and a reduction in the number of purely national industries, with collaborative systems becoming the norm rather than the exception: I rest my case!

The course ended in July and, despite my protests, I was posted to the RAF Staff College on the Directing Staff: I had hoped for a job on the Operational Requirements branch of the MOD Air Staff or in the Procurement Executive where I could use my F-111/Tornado and international experience; but it was not to be. The advantage was, of course, very regular hours in a less stressful environment at a location which would enable us to live in our own home at Pirbright.

Our thoughts turned to moving back home and also to our holidays and, following a recommendation from one of our friends, we reserved two weeks on a houseboat at Salcombe. This turned out to be an inspired choice and provided us with a holiday that remains one of our family favourites. We took Mum with us and drove to Salcombe overnight so that we could report to the boatyard when they opened. The holiday had everything because *Gillaroo* was a fourteen berth ex-First World War hospital ship that was moored in 'The Bag' about one mile up river from Salcombe. We were provided with a motorboat and a row boat and the children were allowed to take the tiller for the fifteen-minute run to *Gillaroo*. The weather was terrific and it turned out to be a proper Swallows-and-Amazons holiday, with adventure trips up and down the river, alternating with beach and picnic sessions. Our big night out was to go to the film show held in the local hall and at which I had to sit on a radiator because there were no chairs left. The first week ended in disaster when Madeleine became overwhelmed by the tragedy of *The Towering Inferno*, burst into tears and I had to take her outside to pacify her. All too soon it was over and with the children pleading with me we made the on-the-spot decision and booked ahead for another holiday on *Gillaroo* in 1978.

Madeleine settled extremely well into the Pirbright Village Primary School, Guy was resigned (and not too unhappy) to life at boarding school, and Terry started doing part-time work at Debenhams in Guildford. With my regular hours I was often able to walk Madeleine to school through the little wood adjoining our house and this memory remains as one of Madeleine's happiest as we settled into a very stable and joyful period of our lives.

Much to my surprise I found life at the college very congenial and gained a great deal of satisfaction from assisting the students improve their staff skills. My fellow Directing Staff were drawn from all branches of the Service and were without exception pleasant, friendly and cooperative. The social life was excellent and I relished the opportunity to engage in research from the extensive library and to produce some original papers of my own. The most enjoyable aspect from a personal point of view was the chance to mix with the young and talented squadron leaders, to gain their respect, to bounce ideas off them and to engage in the cut and thrust of reasoned argument. Rather than the mundane world of repetitious teaching I found this engagement to be extremely stimulating and I formed many friendships with members on the courses that I supervised.

The glorious summer of 1978 gave us the chance to have our anticipated floating holiday on *Gillaroo* with Mum, but this time with Carole and Ralph as well. The weather was fantastic and we ventured further afield by making runs up the river to Kingsbridge where we played crazy golf and, by mistiming the tides, saw our trusty motorboat stranded on mud flats with no way of getting to it and had to wait for the next tide: lots of cakes, Cokes and cups of tea were consumed. We also had one frightening incident when the children were paddling their hired canoes near the mouth of the river and Madeleine was surprised by the outgoing tide and swept towards the sea. We were caught off guard and unable to help rapidly but Guy, with no regard to his own safety, paddled strongly towards her and managed to hold onto her until we were able to complete the rescue: he was a real hero and was given the run of the toy shops for his bravery.

In August my mother was suddenly taken ill and rushed into St Richard's Hospital in Chichester. Emergency surgery revealed that she was riddled with cancer and would be dead within weeks. She never left hospital and it was heart-rending to see her making an apparent recovery and the wound from her tummy operation healing but knowing that her body was dying. Ten days after her surgery Mum had recovered enough and looked well enough for the children to make their one and only visit to see her but she then declined rapidly and passed away on the last day of August, with me sitting quietly by her bedside and holding her hand whilst looking out of the window at a night sky filled with stars. I heard her last sighed breath and knew that she had died but her hand stayed warm in mine for so long that I did not want to believe it and kept praying for her to remain with us. At last I released her hand, kissed her gently and went to the window where I stood looking at the stars and imagining her spirit soaring and her release from all the pain and indignity of her illness. But above all I thanked God for granting me such a wonderful mother who had given me so unconditionally of her love and then chosen to do the same for Terry.

Born on 16 November 1909 and dying on 31 August 1978, Mum had tragically not reached her 70th birthday. Those six decades plus nine had enriched so many people but my greatest regret of all is that she was denied those ten vital years when she could have forged the relationship with Guy and Madeleine that she craved so much; she had adored them both.

The rest of the year passed in a blur and quite suddenly, it seemed, I was collecting Dad and Auntie Nor for the Christmas break. Rather muted because of Mum's absence the children did, however, manage to lift our spirits and the sudden and deep snow falls brought a real magic to the village. Pirbright had never looked so beautiful in a Dickensian fashion and pictures of Dad and Aunt in front of the village store could have been lifted directly from *A Christmas Carol*.

A very sad year had ended and we hoped for better things in the year to come but could never have anticipated the dramatic start when the Air Secretary rang to inform me that I was being given the acting rank of Group Captain as Head of the RAF Presentation Team.

Chapter 14

Presenting to the Nation

It is not the Army that we must train for war; it is the Nation
Woodrow Wilson, 12 May 1917

The start of 1979 was a completely blank sheet of paper for me because there was no RAF Presentation Team (RAFPT) and it was my job to design it to the requirements of the RAF Board, bring it into existence and then take it on the road.

I moved to an empty office at the RAF Staff College and started a classic piece of empire building with the acquisition of furniture, stationery, a filing cabinet and a telephone. From such humble beginnings I guessed all great things must start and armed with this elevated thought I reported to Air Marshal Sir David Craig who, as Vice Chief of the Air Staff (VCAS), was to be my boss and who spelled out what was expected of me.

The RAF was beginning to become the target of the Left and of communist-inspired organizations as a result of the intended introduction into NATO of cruise missiles and the neutron bomb (a nuclear weapon with limited radiation effects designed for specific battlefield use). The Soviet Union was determined to prevent these potentially war-winning weapons coming into service within NATO and had decided to focus their campaign in the UK on the RAF as the perceived 'owner' of the medium which would be used to deliver them. The Secretary of State had, therefore, decided that the RAF should go out to the public and make the Government's case for the need of the armed forces but in particular the RAF and these new weapons.

With VCAS as my top cover I was able to cut through a lot of red tape and my ideas as to composition and equipment were agreed without demur. I was to have a male squadron leader and female flight lieutenant as co-presenters with an airman to act as driver and equipment operator; the base team would consist of a warrant officer and a clerk typist. I interviewed for all the appointments except that of the squadron leader because the CAS had decided that I was to be given David Cyster, a Hunter pilot who was much in the news because he had just flown his own Tiger Moth from England to Australia following the route of Bert Hinkler, who was the first person to successfully make the epic journey and in a similar type of machine. I had no difficulty with this because David was one of the most likeable people I had met and had just the type of charisma needed to attract the public and help de-fuse possible confrontation. I selected Jane Dellow as my WRAF representative because she had a lot of experience of recruiting and meeting the public, and Terry Shortt because of his nous and willingness to learn how to work projection equipment. Warrant Officer Brian Yost was the model of calm experience and Corporal Bill Goss seemed dependable: all in all I had a solid team and now it was up to me.

I started writing the script and submitting my efforts for comments by the Air Staff because I was now working against very tight schedules in order to start my first tour at the beginning of September 1979. I nearly tore my hair out when I was summoned to VCAS and shown two large evenly sized piles of paper. With a smile VCAS informed me that one pile was from people who liked the content but disliked the presentation package and style, and the other pile featured those who loved the presentation but disliked ....! I eventually produced a version that satisfied most of my critics and I then proceeded to have a film made by a professional civilian outfit located in Soho and selected a superb collection of slides to back up the presentation and help with the question-and-answer sessions.

VCAS decreed that a season for the RAFPT would be similar to a school year, with presentations starting in September and breaks occurring at Christmas, Easter and the summer when the public would be less likely to wish to attend such events. He wished us to make three or four full public presentations per week to audiences of about 300 people with subsidiary presentations to influential bodies such as the unions, Rotary, councils, and large firms. Presentation to sixth forms at influential schools could be used to take up the slack in programmes and I was to get as much radio and TV coverage as possible.

On a lovely summer day in August we gave our acceptance presentation to the full Air Force Board and passed with flying colours. The road lay ahead for fame or disaster and with some trepidation I settled into the passenger seat of my staff car and, with David Cyster driving, set off for Birmingham, trailed by Terry Shortt and Jane Dellow.

The initial presentations were very successful and reasonably peaceful but as news of the RAFPT's message and success spread so did the left wing increase its attempts to disrupt us. For the next two years we were subjected to continuous, well orchestrated demonstrations and, on occasions, physical violence. At the main civic presentations it became second nature to assess the venue for the points of entry that the subversives would use to gain access to the halls, and after six months we were always accompanied by plain clothes Special Investigation Branch (SIB) and members of the RAF's HQ Provost and Special Security organization (HQP&SS). Not only did we receive a degree of protection and warning from these two bodies but they were able to track the nationwide movement of the principal subversives and pinpoint the printing sources of the anti-government literature that was inevitably distributed at the meetings.

I had always insisted to the Air Force Board that I would never utilize the 'No Comment' response to hostile questions and it was my belief that my very strong and well researched responses from the stage swung most audiences onto our side when under attack from the floor. At times, however, matters got out of hand, such as when sixty members of the Young Communist Party slipped through a rear entrance at our venue in Edinburgh and I was knocked to the floor by rampaging protesters before the police could corner and eventually evict them. The audience of 300 people watched in amazement but when quiet eventually ensued and I walked on to the stage to continue I received the biggest cheer and applause of our entire tour.

An even more violent reception awaited us in Hull when more than 100 CND protesters were waiting for us outside the hall where they kept on repeating a playlet depicting the dropping and effect of neutron bombs from cruise missiles. This was conducted against a backdrop of caricature air marshals shooting mutating survivors who were attempting to enter the air marshals' private nuclear shelter. The air was heavy with smoke from exploding thunder flashes and a continuous countdown of the four-minute warning we could expect to receive prior to the arrival of Soviet missiles. Bedlam reigned in the hall but by challenging them to put their points which I promised to answer (and did) we eventually gained control and the majority of the 400-person audience gave us a wonderful tribute at the end.

Much more sinister was the treatment we received in Cardiff where, for the only time, we had to pull out of our presentation. The SIB received information that the Right to Work Party (a left wing organization that had disrupted the Tory's Annual Conference) were intending to physically smash up the venue and attack the team just after the start of the presentation. Leaving the RAF logo on the screen we were smuggled away from the venue to our hotel and the police then moved in to detain some ringleaders, apologize on our behalf, and disperse the audience: scary stuff. Not all the events were so dramatic and in our first year of operation we drove more than 40,000 miles, spending five days of every working week away from home and, in the words of VCAS, 'Contributing significantly to the reasoned debate on defence in the UK and making a telling case for the RAF and the deployment of air power in NATO's resistance to Warsaw Pact aggression.'

I had fully expected to hand the team over at the end of the first year's operation but VCAS had other ideas. He explained that he wished to make use of my experience and proven track record to lead the RAFPT through its second year and to introduce two new members. It was with great regret that I said farewell to David and Jane but was not disappointed with their two splendid replacements, Squadron Leader David Hayward (a Victor pilot) and Flight Lieutenant Helen Randall (an Administrative/Secretarial Officer). They picked up the reins very quickly, updated the script and presentation in the light of comments from MOD, and became word perfect by the time we hit the road in September.

The RAFPT restarted its operation at the beginning of September with all the expected anti-RAF and anti-government demonstrations to which we had now become used, although for the new team members it was rather a shock. I did manage a little personal manipulation by doing a big civic presentation at Canterbury which enabled me to collect Dad and Auntie Nor and put them in the front row next to the Mayor: it gave me such a thrill to see their eyes shining as I performed in front of them and to see the Mayor taking particular trouble with them. As a couple they never ever sought the limelight but deserved so much for all that they did for others, and at last I was able to repay some of my debt to them.

As we moved into the New Year I was given the biggest shock and boost of my life when the Air Secretary phoned me to let me know that I was to hand over the RAFPT in May so that I could do my refresher flying prior to taking command of RAF Lyneham in November. As an ex-fighter pilot with only one tour of air transport experience I could hardly believe that I had been selected for such a prize appointment in competition with so many officers who had spent all their lives in the Transport Force. Terry was stunned by the news and for weeks we seemed to do nothing but talk about how we, and I do stress we, were going to handle the challenges of such an exciting and demanding tour. The children were thrilled but it did harden our decision to send Madeleine to boarding school prior to my taking up the appointment.

In the short term we had to completely revise our plans for 1981, as I would be handing over the RAFPT on 24 April and reporting to No. 6 Flying Training School at RAF Finningley, near Doncaster in Yorkshire, to commence my refresher flying training. I did reflect that this was completing a strange little circle as No. 6 FTS was of course the designation of the Flying Training School at RAF Tern Hill where I had first started my flying career; it was now the RAF's navigation school but it did house the Jetstream, which was used for refresher multi-engine flying.

It was, however, with many butterflies in my tummy, that I packed my bags, kissed Terry and Madeleine 'goodbye' and set forth in the trusty Triumph up the Great North Road for Finningley.

Chapter 15

Support, Save, Supply

Peace is best secured by those who use their strength justly and who show they have no intention of submitting to injustice

Sophocles, 433 BC

G roup Captain (later AVM) Tony Woodford grinned at me across the cockpit of Jetstream XX500 on 3 June 1981 as we flew over tranquil Yorkshire countryside, because we had bucked the system by insisting that we should go solo on type. For refresher students on the Multi-Engine Training Squadron this was not allowed but we had decided to flex our muscles and our rank carried the day.

I had known Tony at Staff College and he, like me, was returning to a flying appointment. In his case it was to become Station Commander at RAF St Mawgan where Nimrod maritime patrol aircraft were based and again, like me, he had been off flying for long enough to need refresher flying. Both of us had agreed that we did not need the twenty hours of flying on a type that we had never flown before, would never fly again and which was completely dissimilar to the operational aircraft that we would command. It was all to no avail, however, because nobody was prepared to bend the regulations to set precedents so there we were having a two-week 'jolly'.

The Jetstream was a pleasant, agile aircraft with modern technology so Tony and I determined to enjoy ourselves as well as getting as much practice as possible on instrument and procedural flying. The course ended with us both regaining our instrument flying ratings and completing a return flight to Gatow, Berlin. With eerie memories of my last refresher flight to Berlin in the Varsity when Terry was in hospital and I got caught by fog, I checked the Met forecast but the conditions were benign and I was home in Pirbright as planned on 11 June.

On 29 June I drove along the familiar road from Wootten Bassett to RAF Lyneham (Motto: Support, Save, Supply) and once again, wonderfully reassuringly, a Hercules thundered past me on its descent to landing. I stayed in the VIP suite in the Officers' Mess during my time on Hercules refresher and it was extraordinary to walk through the doors and, as though the last five years had not passed, come up against Flight Lieutenant Eric Heaton (one of my navigators on 24 Sqn) who, without any hesitation, said, 'Hi Boss. Good to see you back.'

I was home and it felt good.

Before assuming command I had to undertake the full refresher course and, although I truly did believe it to be unnecessary, it did enable me to reacquaint myself with the whole operation at Lyneham and establish contact with all those who would be working with me during the next two years. It also gave me the chance to be in at the start of a new phase in Hercules operations: the introduction of female aircrew. It had been decided that women could transfer from the strategic air transport fleet to operate as Air Load Masters and I selected Master Air Loadmaster Joy MacArthur to be part of my crew so that I could see if there were going to be problems. I was also delighted to have Squadron Leader John Stappard designated as my instructor because, not only was he an old friend of mine, going back to Vampire days, but he was to my mind one of the best Hercules pilots and instructors.

With no home distractions the ground school phase of No. 77 Hercules Course passed without any alarms and with a lowest mark of 95% in any of the six exams I was able to hold my head up as the top student which did, I felt, give me some kudos as the Station Commander designate. Going through the ground school was just like visiting an old friend and this was reinforced on 4 September when I climbed up into the cockpit of XV302 and settled myself into the left-hand seat whilst breathing deeply that familiar mixture of oil, fuel, leather and metal that defines the Hercules. There is no other smell like it and with one's hands falling naturally onto the controls it just did not seem as though I had ever had a break from the aircraft. John did not touch the controls once during our flight and on a cloudless, hot sunny day it was an unsurpassed pleasure to rediscover all the old familiar landmarks and realize yet again what a gloriously beautiful country we are privileged to call our own. All too soon we were turning in at the white cottage on the Wootten Bassett road, rolling wings level at 400ft and easing the power off to kiss the wheels onto the tarmac: the feeling was bliss and John amused me by turning to me and saying: 'Not bad Boss – what are you after – my job?'

Coffees in the crew room and a get-together of the whole crew enabled us to start that moulding process that is important for whole crew operation and I was impressed with the way Joy had integrated into the team. Certainly in the flying and operations side nothing seemed to have changed but this was not true in the operation of the station as a whole.

During my absence the Air Transport Force had been subject to a severe cost-cutting exercise and the very reason that I was doing my conversion at Lyneham was evidence of this. Treasury pressure had resulted in Strike Command deciding to meet its requirement by closing the Conversion Unit at Thorney Island and the 2nd Line Servicing at RAF Colerne, near Bath, and squeezing both organizations into Lyneham. This resulted in an immediate saving on real estate and the loss of two group captain posts with all the associated support infrastructure. From my point of view the Station Commander's job had been tripled with no real increase in support staff to handle personnel strength of more than 3,500 individuals and sixty-one Hercules, which made it the biggest base in the RAF, with a budget in 1981 terms of more than £110 million. The AOC, AVM (later Air Marshal Sir Donald) Hall and his Senior Air Staff Officer (SASO), Air Commodore (later AVM) Derek Bryant, left me in no doubt that there were continuing concerns about one group captain commanding such a large base and that my job was to ensure that it worked, with my personal flying being a bonus and limited to twelve hours per month; little did they know!

I went solo after the mandatory three flights and the next two months passed very rapidly with a mixture of flying and flight simulator work interspersed with briefings and visits designed to bring Station Commanders designate up to speed. Of particular interest to me as the designated carrier of SAS and SBS was a two day visit to the SAS base at Hereford where I was taken through all the elements of SAS operations and introduced to their hierarchy. Of 'terrifying' interest was their use of me as a live guinea pig to demonstrate hostage rescue in first of all an aircraft, and later in a building: the sound of real bullets flying around certainly sharpens one's attention and I needed no prompting when told to remain absolutely still throughout the exercise.

Suddenly the course was over and with Terry joining me on Friday 6 November I took over command from my good friend Group Captain (later Air Commodore) Joe Hardstaff. It was a seamless transition with a very low key ceremony, eased by the fact that I had been on the base for nearly five months and knew all the principal personalities. Despite this it was an extraordinary experience to shake hands with Joe and following his departure from the office to sit behind the big desk with its magnificent view across the main dispersal and to realize that you had personal responsibility for every aspect of its operation and that every single person of the 3,500 residents on the base would turn to you for guidance and leadership. I can remember sitting there waiting for the phone to ring and to be faced with the first problem and piece of decision making. It was almost a relief when my secretary Beth Spurway (wife of Flight Lieutenant Brian Spurway) buzzed to let me know that Wing Commander Daphne Veitch-Wilson, the OC Personnel Management Squadron, wished to see me and I was about to get my term of office started – what I was not prepared for and what no amount of Staff College training could encompass, was the subject.

'Now,' said Daphne. 'We've got a problem with airman x who has been held by the Bath police on an attempted murder charge of the school girl who was working in that brothel in Calne .....'

And all this after Joe Hardstaff had assured me that there were no nasties hidden under stones – I could have thumped him! Let me just say that this was not untypical of the extraordinary range of personnel incidents that cross the desk of a station commander. It became clear that the flying and operations are easy and uncomplicated in comparison with the myriad of people, administration and engineering problems that require resolution, demand the application of sound common sense, and the ability to make decisions and not sit on the fence.

The winters of 1981/82 and 1982/83 were two of the worst in living memory and I had only just got my feet under the table when the snows struck. Of primary concern was the airfield and keeping it open and operable but the human element was vital with exposure and accident an ever present risk. Using a combination of chemicals and physical clearance devices, such as snow ploughs and blowers, we managed to keep Lyneham open without a moment of closure during both the winters when even the main London airports had closed.

As a station we were fortunate to have Princess Anne as our Honorary Air Commodore: each principal member of the Royal Family has accepted this appointment in respect of one RAF Station and we were a natural for the Princess because of the nearby location of her home at Gatcombe Park and her use of the airfield whenever she used a fixed wing aircraft in pursuance of her duties. During my time in command she used the base two or three times every month and on one occasion each year spent a day looking round the base and meeting 'her' people. She took a great interest in the station, knew intimately what was going on and made sure that everyone knew how privileged she felt in holding the appointment and how interested she was. As a result of the interaction I did get to know her well and very much enjoyed the bi-annual tea and cakes session that I had with her in her home where she received me, poured the tea and served the cakes whilst quizzing me on all that had happened since her last update. This relationship between the Princess and the station was always good but became even more so as a result of the Falklands War.

All of this was in the future however, as we battled through the winter and I began to make my impression on the station. Getting to know people, how they ticked, which ones could be trusted, and what their capacities and capabilities were, became my immediate goal. With thirteen wing commanders, sixty-eight squadron leaders, and 400 officers and 900 members of the Sergeants' Mess it was a tall order but the Christmas period helped enormously because Terry and I were invited to the Christmas party of every element and this, whilst exhausting, meant that we really did get to meet people in a relaxed environment. It culminated with the Christmas Lunch in the Airmen's Dining Hall when I led the team of officers serving the lunch to all the airmen and airwomen who were on base that day, followed by a noisy get-together in the Officers' Mess and my then returning in a very bedraggled state to the Station Commander's residence, where Terry had been patiently waiting with the children for our own Christmas meal. The residence that we had taken over from Joe was one of the least prepossessing in the Service, as it was hardly more than an enlarged wing commander's quarter but it did have an extended dining room, a large garden and the unique feature of a small lake with about fifty ducks of various sorts. Rather like the ravens in the Tower of London, legend had it that if the ducks deserted the base then Lyneham would close, so Terry and I had the dubious distinction of being mother and father to the assorted brood and having to feed them every day on leftover bread from the Airmen's Mess.

The bread was brought to us by my driver Helen who was to become one of my most faithful friends and with whom we keep regular contact to this day. Devoted to reading novels she never complained about the extraordinary waiting that my job imposed on her and she never ever let me down throughout the whole of my tour. During the tour she fell in love with one of the technicians in Engineering Wing and she and Jonathan Frame married in Nottingham at a ceremony to which Terry and I were invited. To my shock she approached me after the wedding service and requested that I make the main speech at the reception. As the only people that we knew were Helen and Jonathan I was taken aback but before I could comment Terry had accepted on my behalf and after a meal that turned to ashes in my mouth I ad-libbed desperately for ten minutes. Yet again a situation that my staff courses had failed to cover!

January, February and March passed without incident and enabled me to consolidate my aircraft-handling skills and really get to grips with the station, the personalities, and the practices, and start imposing my own character on its operation. This time was invaluable in preparing me for taking on the biggest challenge of my life that occurred with very little warning but with the chance to spread my wings and make real decisions without interference or guidance from the higher echelons of the RAF.

Signs of trouble in the South Atlantic started on 19 March when some Argentinean scrap metal merchants hoisted Argentina's flag on South Georgia. I did, however, start to take real notice when we received a secret briefing that the Argentinean fleet was at sea, apparently en route to the Falkland Islands. Even a cursory look at an atlas showed that if we did get involved in a shooting war the only UK base which could come into the reckoning would be Ascension Island and there was no doubt that the Hercules would immediately become involved as we would be the main means of supply. I called a meeting of my wing commanders and, off my own bat, I instructed OC Engineering Wing to start bringing as many aircraft as possible up to full operating standard and, after consultation with SASO, started bringing as many aircraft back to the UK as could be managed. I also despatched an aircraft to Ascension Island (which we already used as a route stage airfield) with aircrew squadron leaders, one engineer squadron leader and a flight lieutenant mover, with instructions to prepare a draft for Hercules intensive staging and to make first grab at accommodation on the island. How this move paid off was evident when I was told on 2 April, when the Argentineans invaded the Falklands, to set up a slip pattern to carry high priority freight to Ascension staging through Gibraltar and Dakar in Senegal. We were, in effect, up and running and by 5 April, when the surface fleet sailed from Portsmouth, I was already sending eight aircraft a day down this route.

From then on for the next three months I concentrated on raising operational levels at Lyneham to heights they had never reached before as we nearly tripled our flying effort without receiving any extra engineering support, although I was allowed to claw back aircrew that had recently left the station but were still current on type. I brought Terry into the loop so that she understood what the demands were and she gave me the most fantastic support because she took all the domestic and social load on her own shoulders and impressed on me that I was to spend any time I needed on the base and that home life was of no priority until the war was won.

With this sort of backing I embarked on the most fulfilling phase of my career because there really were no rules and I was given carte blanche to fulfil the Prime Minister's dictum to 'Win the War'. I found the process exciting, demanding in the extreme, and physically and emotionally very draining. My own background suddenly came into play when we had to turn my aircraft into air-to-air refuelling aircraft so that we would have the range to air-drop supplies to the surface fleet when they reached the Falklands. None of the Hercules crews had ever performed air-to-air refuelling and had, therefore, to be trained in a real hurry to do this. And who better to devise their training programme than myself, as I was the only pilot current on type who had any experience of this strange art. I devised a four-trip conversion programme and placed it in the hands of Squadron Leader Peter Bedford (the son of the famous test pilot, Bill Bedford) who was OC the air-drop training squadron. The first Hercules with a receiving probe on it arrived at Lyneham on 5 May and we graduated trained crews as fast as slots with Victor tankers could be arranged.

Leaving Peter to get on with this I became embroiled with my next task of turning six of my aircraft into tankers so that my Hercules' could refuel from an aircraft with a similar performance. This became possible because SASO acquired a stock of Andover aircraft long-range tanks which we could plumb into the cargo hold and in conjunction with Hose Drum Units fitted into the rear of the aircraft, this would give us a tanker configuration. With that underway and crews selected to train as tanker providers I embarked on my most ambitious private venture.

My friend from Canberra days, John Ambler, was at Farnborough and had briefed me when I visited him on the night vision goggle (NVGs) trials that he was supervising using adapted Jaguar aircraft. When the Falklands War started it struck me that we would be asked to insert SAS forces and that the use of NVGs would give us a huge advantage for covert operations. I went to see John and, before anyone else could stake a claim, he signed over to me three of his helmets fitted with NVGs and I took them back to Lyneham and locked them in my safe. I then contacted SASO, told him what I had done and had a meeting with him to determine the way ahead. Derek Bryant needed no encouragement and set up a formal trial using the findings of John's trial at Farnborough. We quickly modified three of my Hercules' and started training my Special Forces crews on the use of the NVGs: they are now part of the standard operating procedures of the Special Forces crews.

I saw very little of my family during the period of the war but I did still have to carry out the normal duties of a station commander. Amongst these was participating in the local mayoral change-over ceremonies which occur at the beginning of May. As the station had the Freedom of Calne, Chippenham, Wootton Bassett, and Swindon, this meant taking part with Terry in four ceremonial events. What surprised and delighted me was that, at each of these as I entered the hall in my full dress uniform, the entire congregation stood and applauded me as the representative of the armed forces that they were unequivocally supporting in the Falklands War. On each occasion it was so spontaneous and heartfelt that I felt my eyes pricking and was almost overcome by an inordinate sense of pride for those I represented.

I made the round trip to Ascension twice during the war but was forbidden by the AOC to make the air refuelled trip down to the Falklands because he impressed on me that my job was to run the show and not to take part in the detail. The trips to Ascension were, for me, absolutely essential because I not only experienced every aspect of the operation that I was running but it enabled me to see and be seen at the sharp end. I never have believed that a good commander can run things entirely from his office because, in the RAF, his credibility depends upon being seen to be able to do the tasks he demands of others. My participation also enabled me to take a little bit of pressure off the squadrons because, as a B category captain, I was able to use crew members with the lowest categories who otherwise might not have been able to undertake the tasks. Everywhere I went I was impressed by the fantastic spirit of the air and ground crews who were prepared to work any hours to get the job done and revelled in the freedom they were given to make their own decisions and to cut corners where necessary.

The war finished on 14 June but we then commenced a phase of supporting the deployed troops in the Falklands by instituting the Air Bridge operation in which we flew 26-hour round trip missions dropping down to air-drop supplies to the troops and then climbing back to altitude for the return; all trips required two air-to-air refuellings on the way down and one on the return. The airlift during the war turned out to be the biggest since the Berlin airlift of 1948/49 with the Hercules' carrying more than 7,000 tons of freight, including 114 vehicles, 22 helicopters and nearly 6,000 troops. My engineers worked 54,000 man-hours over and above their planned duty time and the flying effort was extraordinary. The normal station task was 2,800 hours per month but in April we stepped that up to 5,000 hours, in May it was 7,000 hours and in June 6,000 hours. And all of that without any substantial reinforcement of personnel whilst still being required to satisfy any number of MOD-sponsored tasks that were unconnected with the Falklands War. I was delighted to see that my logbook recorded that I did twenty hours flying in April, forty in May and fifty in June but my biggest surprise was the telephone call from the AOC to let me know that I had been awarded the CBE (Commander of the Most Excellent Order of the British Empire) for my efforts during the war. Terry and the family were thrilled but I felt immensely humbled because I knew that the award belonged to the station as a whole. I went on to the station PA system and let them know about the award and my feelings and then went to every section of the station to thank them collectively for all their efforts and to ensure that every single member of Lyneham knew how proud I was of them.

The tempo at Lyneham was sustained as we set up the airbridge to the Falklands and were tasked to perform many operations that had been suspended because of the war. It came as a surprise, therefore, when Don Hall called me to say that he had checked my records and, having noted that I had not had leave or a holiday since starting my refresher flying at Lyneham in June 1981, he was ordering me to take a two-week break from the beginning of August. As we had no real notice we were at a loss as to what to do when Terry called Keith and Judy Webster and asked if we could use their empty house on the Isle of Man. They were only too happy to have their home occupied and we drove up to Liverpool for the ferry on 1 August and returned on 13 August.

The holiday was very different from anything that we had done before and the weather was variable to say the least. We did, however, visit most parts of the island and Guy drove the race of his life in a doctored race car on the Onchon Speedway near Douglas. We walked extensively on the lovely hills which ran up behind the Websters' home and were left with some wonderful memories of the beautiful scenery, triple rainbows, and scores of pairs of hares' ears outlined on the skyline as they always kept very wary watch on our progress. We ate delicious Queenie scallops and had only one real drama when, having climbed to the top of the Great Wheel of Laxey (the biggest water wheel in Europe), Terry and Madeleine lost their nerve and refused to descend the open spiral staircase of the support tower. With Guy taunting his sister I had to edge the two ladies down and then separate the children at the bottom when, the moment her feet touched ground, Madeleine flew at her brother like a dervish trying to scratch his eyes out. This was compounded when, still being distracted by their squabbling in the back seat, I reversed into the side of a vehicle in the car park and ended up at the police station. We resolved to stay on terra firma for the rest of the holiday.

With the children taken back to their boarding schools we were quickly back into the frantic activity of running Lyneham, relieved only during one weekend in October when the telephone in our married quarter did not ring once and we had the most relaxed couple of days of our tour. On the Monday I was besieged by my wing commanders, enquiring why none of their many calls had been answered: the answer lay with Smudge the rabbit who had chewed through all the telephone wires in the house leaving me in glorious isolation – clever rabbit!

The Christmas season with all its many parties was quickly upon us and made us realize that our tour was already halfway through. We all welcomed in the New Year in great style at the Officers' Mess, and I then flew down to Dakar and Ascension to take some gifts of drink to my detachments there and to wish them all a very happy Christmas and New Year and to thank them for their efforts away from home. The reception that I received was really heart-warming and reinforced that marvellous feeling of being part of a close family and valued by the members as its head. The Hercules was an extraordinary aircraft in the way it was able to adapt to so many tasks but it was also extraordinary in that it seemed to draw people to it and enable them to bond and identify with it as part of its family. Of the many aircraft that I've flown this was more pronounced with the Hercules than any other: I've been prouder to have flown others and enjoyed letting other people know of my exploits in them, but the Hercules has always been very special to me.

Changes were occurring for us on the domestic scene because we had decided that we needed to move to a larger house with less land to look after. Our home at Pirbright was becoming a nightmare because we could not find a reliable gardener to look after the grounds and it was a continuing battle for Terry to drive down there and try to control it. We decided that while we had the advantage of being housed in a married quarter we should put the house on the market and, if it sold, we could take our time finding somewhere else. Matters were then taken out of our hands when we received a cash offer at our asking price of £48,000 and found ourselves suddenly cash-rich but homeless. After a couple of abortive offers we chanced upon our current home in Purley quite by accident.

We spent a weekend with Gerry Crumbie at his home in Croydon and after looking at the property pages of his local newspaper saw several desirable houses that were just within our price range. He agreed that it would be fun to snoop round them and we looked at half a dozen but kept coming back to the first house that we had seen in Purley Bury Close: it just looked right, had potential and was ideally located for commuting to London and the MOD. I left it to Terry to negotiate and after she had agreed a price of £78,500 she then conducted the whole of the purchase process without any input from me: contracts were signed on 5 January 1983 and completion took place on 14 January. Happy though we had been at Pirbright, our new home was to prove to be everything that we had hoped for. We would not, of course, move to Purley until the end of my tour in November 1983 but it did enable us to decorate and furnish the house at leisure, and it became a large Wendy House for Terry to play with.

Our eyes were taken off the ball slightly by a request from Buckingham Palace for me to appear there on 8 February for the investiture by the Queen. There was a flurry of excitement amongst the ladies at Lyneham as they all chipped in with their ideas about Terry's clothing for the occasion and we also had to make arrangements for the children to be absent from school. We collected Madeleine but Guy made his own way to London by train and we met him at Charing Cross station before proceeding to the Palace. He looked immaculate in a dark suit; Madeleine wore a burgundy dress with a very smart new white raincoat and Terry was perfection in a tailored mauve tweed suit and matching hat. They were ushered to a front row seat in the presentation chamber and I was whisked off for the briefing. It was a very special day reserved solely for those being honoured for the Falklands War and it was quite emotional to see several recipients receive their bravery awards whilst still suffering from their wounds, including amputations.

When called upon to receive my CBE from the Queen I was delighted when she spoke very personally about the part that Lyneham had played in the war and how proud I must be of all the men and women on the station. I was also surprised at how small she was and at how much I had to bend forward for her to slip my neck decoration over my head. As I turned away after receiving the Order I could see Terry and the two children grinning like things possessed and knew that it was a moment that we would treasure for ever. After the ritual of the photo-taking on the steps of the Palace in the inner courtyard we all repaired to the RAF Club where we met Gerry Crumbie and received the effusive congratulations of all the staff and club members. Celebratory drinks, a sumptuous lunch, and relaxing tea and coffee in the Cowdray room were followed by a short tour of the Club for the children's benefit before we all had to say our goodbyes and return to the real world. It had been a perfect day with all the family participating and each one being able to store special memories from it.

Back at Lyneham I set up a special flight for myself because the US Forces had just made the airfield at Beirut in the Lebanon safe for operation following the Israeli occupation and the civil war. We were required to start supporting our troops who were participating in the peace-keeping process and I determined to do the first flight in. As I was also introducing a policy of taking my ground wing commanders on overseas flights so that they could see at first hand what Hercules operations were all about, I took with me Wing Commander Peter Canning who was my OC Administrative Wing despite his unease at going into a combat zone. When we arrived at Beirut we were escorted to our parking bay by two armed helicopters flying ahead and behind us, and could see tanks patrolling the airfield perimeter. We shut down next to a Lebanese Airways Boeing 707 which was riddled with bullet holes and had its rudder hanging off. When we went into the control tower we saw an arcing line of bullet holes curving up the stairwell: Peter looked even more uneasy! As the aircraft was going to take two hours to turn round, the major in charge of the detachment invited us to accompany him in his Land Rover for a tour of the so called 'Green Line' which separated the warring factions: in the hour that this tour took we saw only two buildings that were untouched by shell fire or bullets and drove past the notorious soccer ground that had been used as a killing field for Lebanese militants. Despite the large British flag flying bravely above our vehicle I must admit to feeling very vulnerable and it was a real relief to pass through the US Forces guarding the airfield and fire up our trusty Hercules for the return to Akrotiri and thence to Lyneham. It was hard to reconcile the peace and tranquillity of the Wiltshire countryside with what we had just seen and made us realize yet again how fortunate we were to live in Britain.

On my return I was told that Lyneham had been designated as the station which HRH The Princess Margaret would visit for her annual visit to the RAF and the countdown started for 13 April. Royal visits in the RAF are planned as precision events with RAF protocol determining how the visit will take place after looking over the station's proposal. We had four dress rehearsals prior to her arrival but these could not take account of the mischievous way in which she behaved during the day when she repeatedly asked for things that were not on the programme. The response of my team was magnificent and her requests were met on every occasion whilst little smiles began to appear on her face and at the end she thanked me very warmly for a most enjoyable day and followed it up with a lovely letter.

Her visit acted as a nice dress rehearsal for a very exacting AOC's Inspection after which Terry and I embarked on a real adventure because I had bid for and been granted two 'indulgence' tickets on a BCal air trooping aircraft to Hong Kong. I had used my contacts to reserve accommodation in the Ghurkha Officers' Mess, at the Gun Club Barracks for the first two weeks of May and, with the aircraft tickets costing only £20 each, we had enough reserves of cash to be able to really enjoy ourselves in the colony.

A car met us at Kai Tak Airport and whisked us to the Officers' Mess, which was situated in about fifty acres of beautifully preserved parkland with the Ghurkha officers living in their own Mess and their white British officers living in their own sumptuous Mess, in which we had been allocated a VIP suite at local messing rates of about £2 per day. The next two weeks were almost like a honeymoon as we rose late, had three servants looking after our needs and wandered around the colony without a care in the world. We used the Star Ferry to cross from Kowloon to Hong Kong Island and travelled to Victoria Peak by cable car to dine by candlelight overlooking the city below. Hong Kong is a magical sight by night with the city shimmering in its multitude of different lights and boats plying the waterway under starlit cloudless skies. On some nights we ate on the floating restaurants and took advantage of the C-in-C's kind offer to spend a day touring on his launch, bathing in the warm waters of secluded bays and eating at the fish restaurants alongside the fish farms that supplied them. And then we indulged in shopping as we bought bargain priced clothes and a new Akai VCR at half the UK price: I even took Terry to the crockery shop where I had bought all our Chinese tableware and the old Chinaman affected to recognize me. In the evenings we would wander the streets and absorb the vibrant atmosphere of Hong Kong at play and eat wonderful tasting dishes from the pavement sellers whilst during the day we would often repair to the gardens surrounding the Officers' Mess swimming pool and quaff ginger beer between lazy immersions in the water.

Our idyllic break came to a sudden end when the Movements Officer telephoned us to say that a very large troop rotation meant that there would be no indulgence passages for the next fortnight and that the ball was firmly in my court. I was suddenly put in a hard position because Lyneham was to undergo a TACEVAL (Tactical Evaluation) one week after our scheduled return and I could not afford to jeopardize my return. Accordingly I had to buy a full-price ticket on a British Airways flight to get back on my scheduled date but Terry dug her toes in and refused to come with me because the Officers' Mess was happy to accommodate her for as long as she liked at marginal cost. In her words: 'If you have to go and play soldiers it is up to you but I'm staying here on holiday until I get an indulgence flight.' She eventually returned after an extra ten days holiday and having avoided my involvement with the TACEVAL.

The TACEVAL itself went magnificently, with the station receiving the highest ratings that any air transport base had achieved and I stood down all but essential personnel for a two-day break. To achieve such a level of combat preparedness after a year of gruelling nonstop operations connected with the Falklands War was amazing and the morale of the station was absolutely terrific. Once again I tried to visit every section to ensure that they understood just how good they were and how very proud I was of them: it was a wonderful feeling.

Two months of fairly straightforward operations followed which enabled me to undertake some welcome route flying and 'taste' the atmosphere on the various squadrons. By flying with routine crews and briefing in the Squadron Headquarters it enabled me to get a true feeling of how the squadrons were being run, what were their standards, and also open myself up to gripes and general banter. It was for me an essential part of understanding the station and tweaking the tiller where necessary.

With only three months left of my tour I set up a trip to the Falkland Islands so that I could at last see the place that had affected my life so dramatically. Little did I realize in the light of what was to happen to me that I really need not have troubled! As it was I flew the old familiar route down to Dakar and Ascension on 17 and 18 August before setting off on the eleven-hour flight to the Falklands with Flight Lieutenant Terry Locke on 19 August. When I got there I was welcomed by my very dear friend Mike Graydon who was doing his three month stint as Station Commander RAF Stanley. He devoted all his time to looking after me and showed me every aspect of the base and its operations as well as introducing me to the Commander British Forces Falkland Islands and all the Headquarters' staff. More importantly he set me up for a re-supply flight to our forces in South Georgia on 21 August with Flight Lieutenant Harland as Captain. I completed an eight-hour trip in XV213 to drop supplies into Cumberland Bay where they were recovered by the troops who were stationed in the British Antarctic Survey buildings on King Edward Cove right alongside the abandoned whaling station at Grytviken, which had been the location for the start of the war.

We had to wear full immersion suits and lifejackets and for the drop itself we had to don 'bone domes'. We came in from the sea at 800ft and dropping speed over the entrance to Cumberland Bay, and after the drop had to apply full power and start climbing as hard as we could to counter the very strong downdraft and sink caused by the freezing temperatures and anabatic winds over the glaciers which faced us. It was not at all easy and we had to make four runs because the drop zone in the Bay was so short. The army were delighted with the drop, particularly as a large bundle of mail was included, and we departed with the whole contingent waving enthusiastically to us. Interestingly the flight brought home a telling fact, and that was that my neck was aching very badly from coping with the weight of the bone dome and reminded me that the doctors had not after all made a mistake when restricting me to non-ejection seat/bone dome aircraft.

Although I was not to realize it at the time this flight was to almost mark the end of my flying career because after it I was only to do one more sortie in September before hanging up my goggles. This was a very busy little flight to RAF Gutersloh and RAF Aldergrove, rotating troops between Germany and Northern Ireland with Flight Lieutenant Singh as my co-pilot. As we brought XV189 to rest in the parking bay outside my office on 13 September and stepped out to find the faithful

Helen waiting at the foot of the steps with my staff car I had no idea that my twenty-eight-year flying career with its 5,000 hours of flying had finished. It was just another uneventful flight on a routine day but never again would I settle into the captain's seat having signed for one of Her Majesty's aircraft and climb skywards with all the excitement and zestful enjoyment that it always occasioned. Perhaps it often creeps up on pilots like this but I had always imagined that I would know when it was to be my final flight and that there would be some ceremony attached to it. In a way, on reflection, I have felt cheated because my flying career finished without even a whimper and it was surely more significant than that.

However, the station claimed me with an extremely hectic schedule and my diary shows every day filled with events in the local community, with councils, RAF organizations and preparations for yet another TACEVAL as well as my required presence at the arrival and departure of Princess Anne and also Prince Charles and Princess Diana. The reason for this was that RAF Kemble had closed and all fixed-wing flights involving Prince Charles now had to take place from Lyneham. Much to the interest of the whole station and not least Terry, who secreted herself in the VIP reception room overlooking the pan, we now had regular contact with the Prince and Princess and what a luminous character she was. Both of them were very relaxed and chatty with me and all the team who looked after them, and she always looked glamorous and had a radiant personality. I feel privileged to have known them under such relaxed circumstances and those meetings are a very special memory.

Quite suddenly the end of the tour was upon us and amidst a flurry of parades, presentations, dinner nights, and emotional farewells I was handing over the black baton of command to Group Captain (later Air Marshal Sir John) Cheshire. We moved house to Purley on 10 November with my handing over the residence and the ducks on 17 November. I was dined out in the Officers' Mess on 18 November with an earlier visit to Gatcombe Park where Princess Anne spoke to me for an hour about the station and all that we had achieved during the last two years.

My Station Commander tour had been an unforgettable and hugely fulfilling period but it was now time to look forward and I felt very privileged to have been selected to attend the one-year postgraduate course at the Royal College of Defence Studies, for it meant that the RAF was looking to promote me further.

Chapter 16

Belgrave Square Bonanza

The art of war is of vital importance to the State, which can on no account be neglected.

Sun Tzu, 490 BC

The role of the Royal College of Defence Studies (RCDS) was 'to prepare selected officials of the UK and certain other countries for high responsibilities in the direction and management of defence, security and other related areas of public policy'.

Behind these fine words was the unspoken policy of the RAF that it selected only those officers with the potential for advancement to two-star rank (Air Vice-Marshal) to attend the course: it was, therefore, a huge vote of confidence by the top brass and a cause for great rejoicing by those selected.

There was no argument that the RCDS was the most prestigious institution of its kind in the world, bringing together eighty high fliers from every corner of the globe for a year-long postgraduate international relations and security course. It was Churchill's vision that led to what was then known as the Imperial Defence College in 1927 (renamed the RCDS in 1970) and it has remained an institution with ready and privileged access to leading international academics, statesmen, government officials and captains of industry to ensure intellectual and professional development of the highest quality. The status of the course was also enhanced by its location in Seaford House, Belgrave Square, London.

It was, therefore, with some trepidation that I passed through the hallowed portals to be enveloped in the din of eighty people renewing acquaintanceships or greeting newcomers. I knew all the other nine RAF members on the course but the first person I walked into (literally) was Air Commodore Ian (Westy) Westmore of the Royal Australian Air Force, who I had last seen in 1968 at Nellis AFB where he was flying the F-111 with me. What a reunion we had and how it brought home just how unified our defence forces were and how small the world was.

In addition to myself the RAF element consisted of:

Air Commodore Mike Alcock (later Air Chief Marshal Sir)
Air Commodore John Calnan (later Air Vice-Marshal)
Group Captain Paul Clark (later Air Vice-Marshal)
Group Captain Mike Graydon (later Air Chief Marshal Sir)
Group Captain Win Harris (later Air Marshal Sir)
Group Captain Terry MacIntyre
Group Captain Tony McCreery (later Air Commodore)
Group Captain John Thomson (later Air Chief Marshal Sir)
Group Captain Tony Woodford (later Air Vice-Marshal)

The Commandant of the College was General Sir Michael Gow and he was assisted by four senior members of the Directing Staff: Rear Admiral Baxter, Major General Airy, Mr Byatt, and Air Vice-Marshal Barry Newton, whom I had known as a fellow QFI at the RAF College Cranwell in 1960.

There were three terms, as in any UK educational establishment, but in September the course broke into eight groups of ten students, each to undertake overseas tours for the whole month. The purpose of the first term was to examine the general setting in which the defence policies of Britain and the West were formulated and executed. The second term studied the causes for conflict and tension. The last term studied the West's defensive posture and NATO strategy and sought, by innovative thinking, to formulate possible improvements. In addition, each student was required to produce an original paper of 10,000 words on any defence or security issue.

We also broke out from the academic side of things on the course to put some flesh on the defence bones by making visits to the Royal Navy (where we put to sea in ships), the Army (where we drove tanks) and the RAF (where everyone got airborne and I sampled the boredom of a long flight in a Nimrod and rejoiced that I had ended up on Hercules). The social aspects continued to attract as we had river dances on the Thames with jazz bands playing in the bows, formal mess kit dinners at the home of the Honourable Artillery Company and at the Royal Naval College at Greenwich, a magnificent cocktail party in the penthouse of New Zealand House, games nights at the college, and a never-ending series of informal parties and dinners.

The most exciting phase of the course was, however, the overseas tour. Arrangements were made to visit the most important countries in each of the areas designated and to meet the most influential people in those places as well as visiting organizations and elements of their armed forces so that we could assess the strength, weaknesses, fault lines and potential trouble spots. I was delighted to learn that I was to be part of the group to visit the Middle East because this was the area that was seen as most likely to spawn the conflicts of the future.

We left the UK on 8 September for Cyprus where we were met by the Commander of the British Forces, Major General Sir Desmond Langley and the AOC, Air Commodore Ray Offord, before dispersing to Flagstaff House and Air House where we would be accommodated for our four days' stay. Although I was very familiar with Cyprus this time it was fascinating because we were given special access to view the United Nations Force in Cyprus (UNFICYP) operations, to move freely along the 'green line' separating the Greek and Turkish Armed Forces, and view the whole Greek side of the island from helicopters. On the army side of things we were hosted by Lieutenant Colonel Ian Mackay-Dick, the CO of 2nd Battalion the Scots Guards, and I was enthralled to see the magnificent painting by Terence Cuneo hanging in their Mess showing the Scots Guards in the Falklands War storming the Argentine position on top of Mount Tumbledown with a bayonet charge: the atmosphere created by the painting was electric and you could smell the adrenalin of the Scots Guards and the fear of the Argentines.

We then flew to the United Arab Emirates and were entertained at the highest level in Abu Dhabi and Dubai; but in Sharjah there was a particular highlight. We were given a personal audience by the Sheikh and then entertained to lunch in his personal dining room in the Royal Palace which was decorated with reproduction Louis Quinze furniture. The strawberries for our dessert had, I was informed by the Sheikh's brother, been flown in that morning from Spain in one of the Sheikh's personal planes just for our lunch: unbelievable wealth ostentatiously displayed.

On 18 September we flew to Israel by the circuitous route of Doha to Bahrain, Bahrain to Larnaca, and Larnaca to Tel Aviv, thus avoiding direct contact between Israel and any of the 'antagonistic' Arab countries. Thus started an intriguing and immensely fulfilling eight days. We were given extraordinary access to the Israeli Defence Forces including a morning spent with General Levy, the Chief of its General Staff, and the most senior politicians including Yitzhak Rabin, who was Minister of Defence. We spent a night in Kibbutz Kafka Blum at the foot of the Golan Heights, toured the Israeli positions on the Golan, visited units of the Israeli Army, Navy and Air Force and laid a wreath at the Yad Vashem, the Jewish holocaust memorial.

Touring the country extensively as we did, the organizers ensured that we had time to visit all the major sites in the Holy Land including Christ's birth place in Bethlehem, his home in Nazareth, Galilee, and every significant spot in Jerusalem: as our day off occurred during our stay in Jerusalem I was able to separate from the group and spend a day in quiet contemplation in places which have so much significance in my faith. It was sobering, helpful, important and hugely satisfying, although it threw up many paradoxes and raised as many questions as answers. What I do know is that it refreshed my faith and the Bible stories have had more meaning for me since.

We visited Egypt next and with all my father's stories about his time in Cairo, Alexandria and along the Nile, fresh in my mind it was with a sense of real anticipation that we touched down at Cairo airport. We stayed at the Sheraton Hotel and had a very grand reception at the embassy, hosted by the Ambassador Sir Michael Weir. Although we visited elements of the Egyptian Armed Forces the highlights of our tour were undoubtedly the opportunities to view the antiquities of the country and to wander through the bazaars and streets of the city. Of much more significance, however, was the unbelievable privilege of being granted a forty-minute closed-door meeting with the President. President Mubarak greeted us personally and waved away his advisors saying: 'I am a fighter pilot. These men are my brothers in arms and I do not need advice or help when I wish to speak to them.'

With much protesting they withdrew and after closing the doors behind them the President proceeded to talk with us as openly and freely as if he were a member of the RCDS Course and we were engaged in a seminar discussion. We covered everything from the problems of education, poverty, relations with Israel, and the way ahead for the country. He seemed to have a grasp of every detail, seemed very aware of the real problems and the increased difficulty of raising standards and trying to alleviate poverty without destroying the country's fragile balance. He was so very impressive and won over every member of our group.

Memories of Egypt will always, of course, be influenced by the visual aspects of the country. We were awed by the pyramids at Giza; intrigued by the step pyramid at Saqqara and the underground burial chambers of the sacred bulls; fascinated and charmed by a trip on the Nile in a felucca, followed by a fish meal at a riverside restaurant where we ate outside under palm trees with fairy lamps swaying gently all around us and a magnificent panoply of stars above; enchanted by the desert and the extraordinary vivid green strip of wonderful vegetation that flanks the Nile; and bewitched by Alexandria and its lovely harbour.

All too soon in some ways, we were on an aircraft to Amman and yet another reception by an ambassador; this time Sir Alan Urwick. We spent the first part of the tour based in Amman and were privileged to have an hour with HRH The Crown Prince Faisal. He had just published a book called *Peace in the Middle East* and it was fascinating to hear his views as an Arab leader and to try and dovetail them with those of his fellow leader President Mubarak. It was very clear that neither the Jordanians or Egyptians had any serious designs on attacking Israel and it was thus of interest to contrast this with the monotonously repeated claims of the Israelis that they needed such a huge investment in arms because of the direct threat posed by their Arab neighbours. Before we left for the south of the country we paid a salutary visit to a Palestinian refugee camp in the Bekaa Valley. These camps increased in number after the Arab-Israeli hostilities in June 1967 and when we visited there were nearly 700,000 refugees resident in the sixty-one camps. It was the first such camp that I had ever visited and it really did bring one up short to see the mud brick two-room shelters which housed whole families, and the hopeless situation with no future that faced the hundreds of thousands of people who spent endless days relying on the goodwill of others to just exist. We were brought up short when, at a meeting with the refugee leaders, the British members of the group were angrily denounced as the race that had caused their problems because of the way we fled Palestine in 1948, leaving all our weapons for the Israelis' use against the Palestinians.

It was in a rather sombre mood that we drove south to Aqaba to see the defensive arrangements in this important port. The road trip gave us a real feel for the conditions in which Lawrence of Arabia operated and enabled us to pay an afternoon visit to the rose-red Nabataean city of Petra. The Petra complex is administered by the Jordanian Army and we were met by a brigadier and driven in Jeeps through the narrow defile, or siq, flanked by towering cliffs that is the only approach to the 2,000-year-old city. Our breath was taken away by the sudden view of Petra's most spectacular monument, the Khaznah or Treasury, which confronted us without warning as we rounded the last bend in the siq.

We spent three days at Aqaba which had its own beach running into the Gulf of Aqaba and from which we could see the sister Israeli city Eilat on the other side of the barbed wire boundary. The city is a massive port complex and an important supply base and delivery point for the thousands of trucks that shuttle all the way up as far as Iraq; a country with which Jordan has always had a difficult and uneasy relationship.

We returned to the UK on 8 October with minds bursting with ideas and endeavoured to put these across to the rest of the college, who were themselves presenting their findings on the regions they had visited. With hindsight our findings were reasonably prescient in that we believed that the Soviet Union was showing all the signs of overstretch, financial pressure, and internal political dissent that could cause its break-up; that China was the truly awakening giant of the world and that the Middle East would continue to be a flash point with the Palestinians and their terrorist organizations bringing increasing pressure on the State of Israel, with the potential for full scale uprising but without the direct involvement of the Arab countries.

On a personal basis, all of us began looking to our futures post RCDS. The Air Secretary began speaking to us individually and in the middle of November I was told that it was intended that I would be promoted to Air Commodore and sent to the Falkland Islands for the whole of 1985 as the Deputy Commander of British Forces and Chief of Staff to the Commander. Excited as I was at the news I was not at all certain that, if asked, it would be wise for Terry to accompany me: the conditions in the Islands were primitive and I could not see what role Terry would play. I made these points to the Air Secretary and was told in no uncertain terms that my promotion was dependent upon being accompanied because my wife and the wife of the Commander were considered essential bridges between the military and the local civilian community.

My position was completely undermined, however, when Terry took it upon herself to telephone the Air Secretary's representative, Group Captain John Preston, and tell him that she was looking forward to accompanying me and could not understand the reluctance on my part. She effectively signed and sealed the deal and, when she told me, I let her know that she might as well take over running my career from now on and I would just get on with the mechanics of the job! Her action did, however, clear our minds and the rest of the course passed in a blur as we mentally prepared for our year in the Falklands. We decided that we would have a grand Christmas bash and organized for the whole family to come to us. It was a wonderful period as we gave the festivities a Falklands' theme and Terry and I dressed up as penguins and recited Falkland rhymes that we had made up, with all the food being called after Falkland items. We also did a skit with me appearing in air commodore's uniform and performing a take-off of a 'modern Major-General'.

There was, of course, an air of sadness with the knowledge that we would not be seeing each other for about a year and when the time came for everyone to depart for their own homes there were more than a few tears. We had a very special farewell evening with the children when, after asking them what they would like to do, we took them to see the new film *Ghostbusters* at the Odeon, Leicester Square and then had a slap-up steak dinner with anything they wished to order, including wine.

The next day (4 January 1985) I drove to Brize Norton and departed on a VC-10 for my old stopping points at Dakar and Ascension.

Our South Atlantic adventure had started.

Chapter 17

Falkland Islands Odyssey

There could be real peace only if everyone was satisfied. That means that there is not often real peace.

Paul Valery, 1931

The past year rolled away as I settled into the captain's seat of the Hercules and did a four-hour stint at the controls whilst the captain dozed happily on the crew bunk. He did, however, diffidently suggest that he undertook the air-to-air refuelling and the landing at RAF Stanley at the end of the twelve-hour flight. I had no difficulty with this although the aircraft felt as responsive as ever in my hands and I itched to do the whole thing myself.

A nice little touch occurred as we ran in to the Islands when two Harriers appeared and took up station on our wing tips with a cheery 'Welcome to the Falklands Sir' from the pilots. Upon coming to rest alongside the tiny Air Traffic Control tower I embarked to a warm handshake from my new boss, Major General Peter de la Billière and a peck on the cheek from his wife Bridget. I was popped into their Range Rover and driven over rough crushed stone roads, which gave way to paved surfaces as we entered Port Stanley, to their home in Britannia House and a refreshing cup of tea. Peter left me in no doubt as to how welcome I was because the upper hierarchical structure of the British Forces, with seven officers of the equivalent rank of colonel having direct access to him, was a mess. I immediately displaced and replaced the colonel Chief of Staff and the group captain Air Commander: the remaining five officers reported directly to me, leaving Peter free to act in his proper capacity as Commander. After a pretty detailed talk I was driven to Lookout Camp on the hill overlooking the town, where I was to lodge in a temporary building until Terry's arrival, when we would move into a Falkland Island wrinkly tin-roofed local house.

My belongings were laid out in my half of the Portakabin-style building (which I shared with a lieutenant colonel) and after cleaning my teeth I stretched out on my bed and reflected on my new life. My thoughts turned immediately to home and Terry with the children because I was missing them already. We had held a family discussion group in December to work through the problems because, with Terry joining me in February, we were faced with leaving our home empty and the children on their own. The latter problem was partly resolved by their boarding school attendance and Carole and Ralph, Dad and Auntie Nor volunteering to look after them at half-terms, but the big breakthrough was the MOD's agreement to fly them down to us for the Easter and Summer holidays. We also arranged for the bank to allow Guy, now 18, to have access to our current account and gave him permission to use the home as his own whenever he wished.

My reverie was broken by a knock on the door and the appearance of an army driver with the keys to my 'staff car'. Staff car was a misnomer because no car could cope with the Falklands, where the only paved roads were those of Port Stanley, and I had been allocated a captured Argentine Mercedes four-wheel drive 'Land Rover' lookalike: this proved to be a fabulous vehicle and, in my opinion, superior to the Land Rover. I was thrilled to see the glistening Silver Star on the bumper as I was later when I drove to the helipad to fly in my personal Gazelle helicopter which also sported a general's star.

I had to hit the ground running because Lord Trefgarne, who was the Armed Forces Minister, was visiting the Islands and Peter decided that I should accompany him so that I would get the feel of the various units. He allocated me one week to familiarize myself in this way and he then required me to assume the full responsibilities of his Chief of Staff and Deputy Commander of all the British Forces on the Islands. The working hours were interesting because the Islands were manned on a two shift system with each shift lasting twelve hours and with only one 'rest' day per week; so a seventy-two-hour week. It was done in order to reduce by a third the manning that would have resulted from a normal eight-hour working day. This had been deemed acceptable for troops undertaking the scheduled four-month detachment, but no account had been taken of those of us who were posted to the Islands for the whole year and we had to work to the same intensity, which in the end proved very draining. Only three of us came into this category: Peter, myself and Colonel Peter Jones (the Assistant Chief of Staff Logistics), who was also accompanied.

The weather in January was very hot and dry because it was in the middle of the Falklands' summer, the only problem was that everywhere had become very dusty and this dust was blown into the air by the strong winds which are a feature of the summer. As a result one of my first actions was, strangely, to badger the MOD for increased supplies of sun cream for the troops, who were becoming sunburned in the field.

I spent some time at the house we had been allocated trying to tame the 'hayfield' that was the garden and which had resulted from the house being unoccupied for two years. My work came to a sudden halt when my shears locked onto an unexploded clip of 7.62mm ammunition. Calling in some of the engineers we discovered hand grenades and mortars in addition to more ammunition, as the garden had clearly been an Argentine position: the one benefit to me was that in clearing it the grass had to be cut for me. I had to do all this sort of work myself as well as cleaning out my own Portakabin because the minimum manning levels meant that Peter was the only person in the theatre with personal staff.

Sir Rex Hunt and his wife Mavis invited me to dinner and I found him warm, welcoming, and extremely friendly. I was, as was Terry later, to be a regular guest at Government House and formed a real friendship with them both. It was, however, with Peter and Bridget that really strong bonds developed because not only did we get on so well but I knew that Peter trusted me and it gave me enormous confidence to be asked to get on with things without him constantly looking over my shoulder. In fact he used my presence in the Headquarters to get out into the field and make regular and extensive visits to all the many units. The restriction on our movements was that Peter and I were the only individuals allowed to authorize the use of live fire and, as it was considered a real risk that the Argentines might launch a surprise raid, one of us always had to be physically within four minutes of the fire-controlling operations room in the Headquarters; ergo only one of us could be away from the Headquarters.

He did agree, however, to my temporary absence so that I could undertake the most exciting of my familiarization visits. Although all the Naval, Army and Air assets in the theatre came under our command and control there was one exception: the nuclear submarine that was on the Falklands' station. This was always controlled from Fleet Headquarters at Northwood in Middlesex, as it was a strategic and not a tactical asset, but I still needed to know just what its capabilities were in case we needed to use them. Accordingly I made arrangements to spend three days aboard her and took off from Stanley in a Royal Navy Sea King helicopter. We flew towards Argentina and then hovered over the transfer point for about ten minutes until I saw a dark shape materializing under the surface. It was just like every war movie I had ever seen, as this enormous monster suddenly surged out of the water, but I had little time to admire it before I was pushed out of the helicopter door on my strop and lowered swiftly to the streaming fore deck, where two burly sailors bundled me down the hatch. With the classic 'Dive, Dive, Dive' ringing in my ears I was just able to shake the Captain's hand before he thrust the handles of the periscope at me and pushed my head down to the eye pieces so that I could witness the eerie sight of the water swishing over the fore deck and then coming up to and engulfing the scope. For three marvellous days I shared the lives of the crew of the nuclear attack submarine HMS *Swiftsure* and was shown the practice operation of all her weapon systems as well as all her operational capabilities. Very few non-submariners ever get the chance to see the inside of a nuclear submarine let alone go to sea in one, and it was yet another extraordinary experience to log into my life's book. All too soon the submarine tilted sharply upwards and I had to don my immersion suit and climb the ladder into the sail for my winch out and return to the Falklands. Before I left the Captain presented me with some superb photos of the submarine and of my being winched down to her from the Sea King: these now adorn my study.

As January ended I used my spare time to smarten up the house at 8 Ross Road West because Terry was scheduled to arrive on 5 February. She had an epic journey down because her Tristar had an engine failure at Dakar, which entailed an unscheduled stopover with 150 paratroopers in temperatures of more than 90°F and no change of clothing from the wool suit and leather boots that she had needed for the English winter. She sweltered in the heat and was not best pleased when she went in to the hotel for her evening meal only to find that the ravenous paratroopers had eaten all the food! Hungry and disillusioned, she had to wait for a snack on the repaired Tristar next day en route to Ascension Island, where she transferred to the SS *Uganda* for the voyage to the Falklands. Even this was eventful as they ran into a fierce storm and, when one engine failed, started to drift towards the South American coast with the passengers all having to be strapped into their bunks. When she did arrive and the ship was anchored safely in the outer harbour I flew out to her in my Gazelle and, after a stupendous welcome and reunion plus a couple of drinks with Captain Dennis Scott-Musson, flew her on a quick sightseeing trip of the Stanley area so that she could see our new home from the air; we landed right by the house.

The house itself was a bit of a shock to her even though it was reasonably substantial by Falklands' standards, with its four large bedrooms, interesting corridors and a very large kitchen, lounge and dining room. We had also inherited an extraordinary cat called Gypsy who played football, stood on her hind legs and boxed, ran up your back without warning, and sucked people's sweaters and beards. She was the most wonderful pet and it was with the greatest regret that we left her to my successor on our return to the UK. After unpacking our crates, hanging up our pictures, and discovering that I had civilian clothes to supplement the combat kit that I had worn continuously since my arrival, it really did seem that life was on the up.

Terry was rather overwhelmed with the hospitality extended to her and we had an evening event on every day for the whole two weeks following her arrival, including receptions on board the warships of the Task Force. As one of the only English ladies on the Islands (and the only pretty one with lovely legs) she was in great demand by all the units who pleaded with me to let her attend the functions and, 'please let her wear a skirt, Sir!' She quickly learned to make her arrival in boots and slacks carrying her high heels and skirt in a bag in order to make the appropriate clothing change in the CO's room or cabin. How the boys loved having Terry attend their units and you could sense the morale lifting with every visit. It is worth recording that never ever was there an inappropriate comment or action: they just loved having an attractive lady in their midst who took the trouble to dress for them and to talk to them.

Terry became, as the MOD had hoped, very involved with the local community and was responsible for bringing the locals into a much more favourable relationship with the military. She was out nearly every day mixing with the local people of Stanley and, with the allocation of an old Land Rover to her and Bridget, became actively involved in local affairs, including the hospital and school. On our one day off per week we explored the Islands and took advantage of the organized 'Battlefield Tours' to visit all the sites of the major battles such as Mount Longdon, where 200 paratroopers of 3 Para had routed 1,000 Argentines and, for his part in it, Sergeant Ian McKay was awarded a VC posthumously. To walk on a recent battlefield is an extraordinary experience as the detritus of war is everywhere, from shell cases to abandoned personal effects such as beer cans, tubes of toothpaste, combs, boots, gloves and so on. It suddenly becomes very personal and immensely sad and, as we always had as a guide someone who had taken part in the battle, you were able to experience the event in a very real way. It was eerie to be told by the guide for example how he had crouched behind the very rock where you were standing and shot two Argentines just 15yds away: the goose bumps really did raise themselves on your skin.

Our social life was more hectic than on any other tour of mine in the RAF because we set ourselves the task of entertaining all the officers of all three Services and, with them rotating every four months, this became a mammoth task. The reward of it, however, was the marvellously genuine appreciation because, for some, it would be the only time during their four-month tour that they could spend time in a real home with a family. We made our bath available on request, because all units used showers and, once again, it would be their only chance to have a soak in a hot bath. We also put up senior officers when they visited from the UK and could not be accommodated at Britannia House; such visits invariably resulted in our laying on a dinner for them and I came to know some very senior officers of all three Services very well indeed. We were also entertained by the units and Terry became very adept at scrambling into my Gazelle helicopter for the flight to these centres because the distances were usually great and there were no roads at all outside Port Stanley. In this way she visited places such as Goose Green, Pebble Island and San Carlos Water, and came to share with me a deep understanding of the islands, their inhabitants, the terrain and the huge difficulty our forces had faced in fighting the war.

With myself now firmly entrenched Peter did not only take to visiting the units in the field but took the opportunity to return to the UK on several occasions for briefings and liaisons. This gave me a great thrill because I assumed total command and control of all forces and I could never really get over having battalion commanders, full captains in charge of the Task Force as well as my full colonel staff officers, deferring to me and requiring direction and, on occasions, guidance. It had seemed natural in the narrower context of the RAF where I was very confident in my specialization, but to have senior officers in dark blue and brown accept my position and to seem to have no difficulty in accepting my decisions was quite different.

The only real tussle of wills that I had was with the Commander of the Task Force on one occasion. Quite dramatically one night the Argentines opened fire on some Korean fishing boats that were fishing in Argentine territorial waters just outside the 150 mile Falkland Islands Protection Zone (FIPZ) that we had imposed. They started screaming over the radio that they were under attack and needed our armed help to stop the Argentine hostilities. My Task Force Commander (with my approval) made all speed towards them but he disagreed with my order to remain within the FIPZ as he wanted to sort out the Argentines. I was convinced that they were engineering the incident to lure us out and to do something which could become a huge international incident. I ordered him not to go beyond the FIPZ and we had a very interesting exchange on the scrambler before he accepted my instructions and it was never spoken about again. Most fortunately by the time the Task Force reached the edge of the FIPZ the incident was over, with the Korean vessels being sailed under escort to an Argentine port. As a 'thank you' for holding the fort in his absences Peter agreed that I should do the next troop inspection in South Georgia and take Terry down with me on the RFA *Reliant*: a container ship that had been converted to carry a squadron of RN Sea King helicopters.

Before that, however, we went on a Battlefield Tour of Mount Harriet, where 42 Commando RM saw off the 4th Regiment of the Argentine Army. It was a unique fight in that it was the only one (except Goose Green, where they could not get away) in which we captured the officers because the Royal Marines attacked from the rear of the position having gone through an 'impenetrable' minefield and the Argentine officers had no way of leaving their troops. We also attended a Mothering Day service in our Portakabin-style church and one could sense the sadness of the chaps who were, of course, all without their families and afterwards all cornered Terry, who seemed to act as a substitute family for them. Terry was then invited to join the Harbour Master on his visit to a Russian mother ship to inspect their compliance with Falkland regulations. Having accepted with alacrity she was shaken rigid when she was told that she would have to jump from the side of the Harbour Master's tug onto the climbing net hanging from the Russian boat and then climb up to the deck. Gutsy as ever, she did it and then ended up drinking whisky and eating cake with the captain. So entranced was he with the lovely 'English lady' that the very next day he sent us 30kgs of frozen squid in three large boxes of 10kgs each. We gave two away but then dined on squid for months served in every way known to man: only two squid escaped our attention, as these were stolen by Gypsy, who secreted them under her blanket in her box and chewed on them furtively until the smell eventually alerted us to their presence.

On 20 March we donned our immersion suits and descended the ladder of the Port Stanley pier into a rigid raider for the trip out to the RFA *Reliant* and onward to South Georgia. Terry had spent a lot of time making herself look pretty for her forthcoming meeting with the sailors and it was a shock therefore when, as we went over the bar at the harbour entrance, a huge wave went right over us and she emerged looking like a drowned rodent. By the time we had been soaked by another dozen waves she had given up caring but we were then appalled to find that the only way to board the *Reliant* was by climbing a 30ft rope ladder which we could only get on to by flinging ourselves from our little boat, which was careering up and down in a 10ft swell. How we did it I will never know but we eventually dragged ourselves over the rail to be met by the usual cacophony of piping before squelching our way to our cabin.

The *Reliant* was a big ship at 16,000 tons and extremely well fitted out for the small crew. We did, however, have to cope with two conflicting swells and, despite being fitted with stabilizers; she rolled from 25° one way to 25° the other for the whole two-day passage. The

Captain, Dick Thorn, had generously given us the use of his cabin, in which there was a large double bed. So severe was the rolling, however, that Terry made me sleep in his single bunk because I nearly crushed her every time the ship rolled. Dick treated us as family, took us over all parts of his ship and let us join him on the bridge whenever we wished. Terry was in her element as the only lady on board and lapped up the compliments of the young RN helicopter crews, all of whom had travelled south with her on the *Uganda*, and with whom she was already great friends. We ate like kings with beautifully prepared meals and, of course, made extensive use of the bar, which provided the evening entertainment.

The journey took us two-and-a-half days and, as we arrived at 0200 hours, were sound asleep when *Reliant* anchored in Cumberland Bay East. We awoke to an impenetrable fog and it was mid-morning before a small rubberized boat tied up alongside and I made the exciting descent by rope ladder to the welcoming arms of the two soldiers deputed to get me ashore. After an eerie journey through the dense fog, we suddenly bumped against the jetty and the major commanding the Royal Welch Fusiliers detachment of forty-five men hauled me onto the landing stage and escorted me to the British Antarctic Survey building at King Edward Point, where they were accommodated. After a very business-like briefing and the opportunity to meet every member of the detachment, the fog suddenly lifted and with *Reliant* revealed in all her glory, it was safe for Terry to be brought ashore and join me for lunch, a chance to meet all the soldiers, and then to be taken on a tour of the local area.

The surrounding scenery was staggeringly beautiful and even more impressive than I remembered from my air delivery flight in 1983, as range after range of mountains and glaciers (162 in all on South Georgia) towered above one in all directions save that of the seafront. Every now and then you could hear the crash of ice calving from the face of one of the glaciers, but apart from that there was an almost ghostly silence. And the ghosts were everywhere, from the explorer Shackleton's grave to the rusting hulks of the old whalers and the collapsed buildings of the abandoned whaling station at Grytviken. We then took ourselves off for a walk through Grytviken where one could see all the artefacts, such as harpoons, which had just been thrown down or left when the last whalers were suddenly withdrawn. We reached the Penguin River and were enchanted by a King and a Gentoo penguin that waddled up to us as we sat, and carried out a long and involved conversation with us. When we started to walk back they were undeterred and accompanied us for about 200yds until they bade us farewell by an immense chattering whilst standing still with their flippers touching until we disappeared around a bend. We saw huge elephant seals and fur seals that barked at us, and all provided an indelible memory of our visit.

This was as nothing, however, to the next day when I was flown to St Andrew's Bay and allowed to spend an hour in the bay in the company of 500,000 King penguins as well as Gentoos and elephant seals. Most of them I suppose had never seen a human being before and one had to keep reminding oneself that they were completely wild and that the elephant seals were potentially dangerous, because, once the helicopter had left, they all crowded around to investigate me and the photos that I took of this gathering are absolutely amazing. I returned to the Army HQ to meet Terry and in the afternoon a Royal Marine sergeant took us on a three-mile climb up to the top of the 2,000ft high Mount Hodges glacier, where we could look down onto the tiny shape of the *Reliant* and obtain magnificent views all over the bay and the surrounding glaciers. We left a token offering at a 'break out' cabin where some of the tins dated back to Shackleton's time and were museum pieces in their own right. After a last lingering look at the breathtaking scenery we embarked on a hilarious yet exciting scree-run descent to Grytviken, which made me fear for our sanity and our lives before arriving breathless, bruised, and in hysterical laughter at the bottom. Our final act was to attend a very simple yet intensely moving evening service in the Grytviken Church, which is the only restored and habitable building in the town: it was restored by successive detachments of our troops. As darkness closed in the unaccompanied voices of the Welsh troops were so beautiful that you could feel the hair rise on your neck, and it was a religious experience such as I have never experienced. Reluctantly we said our goodbyes and after a flat two-day return sea trip we disembarked at Port Stanley and the strange world of the Falklands.

The next major event was the arrival of the children on 6 April on an airbridge Hercules and it was an incredible feeling to see their faces at the portholes of the aircraft as she shut down and then to have them run down the steps, across the tarmac and fling themselves into our arms: all the months dropped away and the reunion was overwhelmingly joyous. The flight had not been uneventful because the crew knew them both from their time at Lyneham and allowed them to come up on the flight deck, watch the air-to-air refuellings and, as I found out much later, allowed them into the pilots' seats to try their hand at flying. The complication for Madeleine was that she was the only female on board and there were sixty paratroopers amongst the passengers, who watched her every movement with great interest. The result was a twelve-hour flight for her with no visit to the Elsan toilet at the rear of the aircraft: an extended visit to the toilet in the air traffic control tower at Stanley was her first priority after landing!

We celebrated Easter as a family at a service in our 'Portakabin' church and I then took a day off so that we could take the children sightseeing in my Mercedes. We drove south for about five miles along the new road that was being built to link Port Stanley with the military airfield that was under construction at Mount Pleasant, and then hiked for one-and-a-half hours across rough ground, peat pastures, stone runs and streams to a place called 'The Lagoon', where there was a Gentoo penguin colony. We spent an amusing hour creeping up on them, photographing them and being just generally amused by their antics, for they are hilarious to watch. Guy almost touched one that was asleep but it woke up just in the nick of time and bolted for the water as though it had seen a monster. The long walk back occasioned a lot of moaning but we all agreed that it had been worth it.

The next night we all went to an Army Air Corps barbecue and self-generated revue and evening's entertainment and the next night to a big cocktail party at Britannia House, where Madeleine met Prince Andrew, who was the helicopter pilot on HMS *Brazen*, (his helicopter was known as the 'Brazen Bitch') but insisted that she was not overly impressed with him! The following day we all went on a Battlefield Tour of Mount Tumbledown, which the Scots Guards took after a ferocious firefight ending with a bayonet charge to clear the Argentines from the mountain top. We had a Scots Guardsman who had taken part in the assault as our guide and Madeleine and Terry became very quiet as he described, and then showed us the spot, where he had bayoneted an Argentine. As elsewhere the detritus of war was everywhere and you kept on reflecting on the dreadful waste that is always the result of going to war: leaders and politicians have a great deal to answer for and rarely, if ever, put their own lives on the line. Perhaps a compulsory spell in the front line for everyone making the decisions would sharpen their minds as to the need for conflict.

As 21 April was the Queen's birthday it was the occasion for the first airing of my No. 1 dress air commodore's outfit, as the Falklands celebrated Her Majesty's birthday in some style. The Governor and General Sir Peter took the salute at a march past headed by the regimental band of the Royal Welch Fusiliers in their scarlet uniforms and featuring representatives of all the contingents in the Falklands. A 21-gun salute was fired by the Falkland Islands Defence Force (the equivalent of the Home Guard) during which Terry jumped visibly as each volley was fired and complained to Peter that her nerves were in shreds. The weather was so perfect that, after attending the obligatory drinks party at Government House, we changed into summer gear and caught one of the harbour ferry boats for the thirty-minute cruise across the harbour to Navy Point. We then had a one-and-a-half hour stroll over the crags of Wireless Ridge before returning on the ferry for tea and my birthday cake. Not too many people get to celebrate their birthdays in the Falklands and it had been a wonderful day in every respect with all my family around me: quite extraordinary when one considered that it was all taking place 8,000 miles away from home.

The 26 April was, however, such a sad day as we had to let the children return to the UK. Guy put a brave face on it but poor Madeleine just crumpled up before boarding the Hercules and clung to Terry, sobbing her eyes out. Luckily I knew the crew and they promised me that they would put them both on the flight deck after the take-off and give Madeleine lots of TLC on the return flight. The last thing we saw were two little hands waving at us from the portholes near the crew entrance door, and I then had to cope with a wife who crumpled up on me and sobbed her eyes out: life can be so exciting and yet so cruel.

My biggest management task since my arrival had been to coordinate the civil and military activity involved with the building of the new airfield at Mount Pleasant (MPA) and the construction of the road linking Port Stanley with MPA. I had driven the army element quite mercilessly and had caused ructions by my handling of a situation when the civilians downed tools after discovering live munitions and mines in the ground where they were working. Despite being taken off the Christmas card lists of the people I offended, my solutions worked and, with days to spare, the projects were completed in time for the first Tristar to land on its proving flight on 1 May, with two of our Phantoms clinging to its wing tips as escorts. The work force surged across the concrete apron in front of the hangar, cheering and shouting in an atmosphere of absolute euphoria after which a huge drinks party developed in the hanger. It was a time milestone and gave us real confidence that the formal opening on 12 May would be a success.

As it was, 12 May dawned bright and clear and it was the easiest decision of my life to give the go-ahead for the Tristar to make the inaugural trip and for the parade and reception to take place on the tarmac outside the hanger. All the VIPs arrived on the Tristar and the landing took place to the second, once again with a Phantom escort, and Prince Andrew and Michael Heseltine led the ceremonial with great aplomb. The royal luncheon was superb and I then acted as the personal guide to Prince Andrew for his tour of the new facility: he was full of fun and to the huge delight of the workforce wise-cracked his way at every stopping point. With MPA now open, the number of weekly Hercules flights was reduced to four supplemented by two jet flights. The scandal here, however, was that for the first six months they would be British Airways 747s rather than RAF Tristars because Lord King, as Chairman of BA, put the squeeze on the British

Government, using the threat of withdrawal of support for the RAF's ex-BA Tristars as the means.

Our best news, however, was from Guy, to let us know that he had been given unconditional entry to the Central School for Art and Design near Kingsway in London for a three-year Industrial Design degree course starting on 23 September. He had worked extremely hard to compile his portfolio of paintings and drawings and on his visit to the Falklands had spent many hours sketching the local wrecks and landscapes. From his letter he had a good interview, they were impressed with his portfolio, and he did well at his IQ and other tests. From our point of view it was splendid that, as it was a London College, he could stay at home during the course and travel on a daily basis. As one always worries about one's children it was an enormous relief to hear that he was set to embark on a tertiary education course that could give him training that would suit him for the real world, as well as giving him a degree qualification.

The navy entertained us well at the end of May as we went to a formal dinner on HMS *Avenger* (a type-21 frigate) with beautiful food and fine wines. It was, however, slightly spoiled because of the hangover I had acquired from my much less formal party given the previous night on board HM Submarine *Opportune* (a diesel electric 'O' boat). It was absolutely hilarious and Terry and I were amazed at just how many people could be crammed into a submarine. A young officer who had recently qualified in submarines was presented with his 'dolphins' which he had to retrieve from a glass of neat rum by tilting it back and drinking it until they slipped into his mouth. He was one of several to pass out and a young Hercules co-pilot called Paul Oborn (a New Zealander who went on to become the Station Commander at RAF Lyneham) cracked his head open when leaping into the air doing a haka. All in all it was a riot and part of the reason why we enjoyed ourselves so much during this strange tour.

Terry was delighted when an unexpected knock on the door revealed Wing Commander Tony Bagnell (now Air Chief Marshal Sir Tony) the CO of No. 23 Phantom Squadron, with a truck bearing the squadron's piano. She had been learning to play the piano during 1984 but had to stop in the Falklands because of the lack of an instrument. The Harrier Squadron had 'liberated' a piano for their crew room but upon their return to the UK it had become ownerless and Tony had very thoughtfully remembered Terry's need. She installed it in the dining room and, despite one or two wonky keys, played away quite happily on it for the rest of the tour.

I could hear her thumping away as I left home on 3 June for two days aboard a Falkland Islands Patrol Vessel (FIPV). There were three FIPVs in the Islands and all were ex-North Sea oil supply ships purchased by the navy for patrolling the inshore waters of the Falklands. With three officers and a dozen men they carried seven royal marines as a fighting/rescue patrol and did survey work as well as putting the marines ashore at spots around the coast to see if there had been any Argentine incursions. They also performed liaison duties and I went ashore with them to strike up relationships with the Islanders, which involved many cups of tea and scones and resulted in an enormous amount of goodwill.

We celebrated our twenty-second wedding anniversary with home-made cards and I gave Terry a little model penguin as a permanent reminder of our time in the South Atlantic. The big event, however, was the third anniversary celebration of Liberation Day on 14 June when all the Islanders go to extreme lengths to celebrate the signing of the ceasefire. Blizzard conditions prevailed during the early morning but had luckily stopped by the time I came to lay the RAF wreath at the Memorial. I shivered throughout the whole ceremony but half a dozen drinks at Government House in front of a blazing peat fire soon restored a feeling of wellbeing.

On 26 June the worst incident of my tour occurred when a Hercules and an RN Sea King from the *Reliant* collided, killing all of the helicopter's four occupants. The Hercules was on a routine patrol around the Island at about 1,000ft AMSL in patchy cloud, using its weather radar to plot the positions of fishing vessels when the Sea King was launched and ascended straight into the path of the Hercules. The Hercules captain told me that he saw nothing prior to the enormous crash, which sheared off the outer 12ft of his port wing and its complete aileron as well as stopping the outer port engine. Luckily I was in the operations room when it happened and took immediate control. The Hercules was barely controllable with only rudder, elevators, and starboard aileron working which meant that it could only turn with difficulty. I managed to get him lined up with the runway at MPA and ordered all contractors off it after clearing their equipment and breathed a huge sigh of relief when he somehow managed to land safely. I then had to get on with the distressing job of trying to recover the bodies of the RN crewmen and personally oversaw the off-loading of the bodies in the body bags from the rescue helicopter to the morgue. I then set up the Board of Inquiry whilst trying to calm the recriminations between the RAF and the RN.

It was a tragic affair and, as the senior airman in the theatre, I kept on mentally revisiting it to see where the mistakes had been and if I could have done something to avoid it. As so often happens, it resulted from a whole series of small decisions, none of which should have caused problems but, by accident, misfortune and sheer timing, came together with fatal results.

As all this was going on we were involved in saying 'goodbye' to Peter who was due to depart on 19 July. Before he left he authorized me to have a weekend off (my only one during my tour!) during which he would remain on call at the Headquarters. This was very thoughtful because he knew that I would not be able to go away with the new Commander fresh in post.

We decided to spend the weekend at Pebble Island, which is on the north coast of West Falklands and which had been the location of the Pucara aircraft that the SAS had blown up so spectacularly in the war. We were flown by helicopter to the settlement and stayed with Ray Evans, who was the manager. He served us huge slabs of mutton complete with yellow fat for our meals, which made us blanche but the hospitality was tremendous. One peculiarity was that he controlled the generator for the whole settlement so that when he switched it off we were all plunged into blackness whether we were undressed or ready for bed or not. We explored the island and found a complete whale's skeleton on one of the beaches, from which we took a selection of vertebrae as souvenirs. We also saw the memorial to HMS *Coventry* as she was sunk just off the coast, and visited the airfield site where all the wrecked and burnt out Pucaras were littered. We also walked a great deal and it really did help us to recharge our batteries and prepared us for the strain of bidding Peter farewell and welcoming in the new Commander, Air Vice-Marshal Kip Kemball (later Air Marshal Sir John).

Immediately preceding this was a visit by C-in-C Fleet, Admiral Sir Nicholas Hunt, and Air Chief Marshal Sir David Craig (later MRAF Lord Craig) who was C-in-C Strike Command. They both wanted to talk with Peter about the changeover of Commander British Forces and also to probe into the mid-air collision. Sir David stayed with us, whilst Sir Nicholas stayed at Britannia House, and proved to be a marvellous guest and a superb guest of honour at a dinner party that Terry gave. It was also the first time that I had met Group Captain Peter Squire, who was his Personal Staff Officer and later became the RAF's Chief of Air Staff in the rank of Air Chief Marshal. He had commanded the Harrier squadron during the Falklands war and it was fascinating to hear him recount his bombing runs on Argentine targets.

Madeleine arrived for her summer holidays having travelled all the way in the first class section of the BA Jumbo and been treated like a VIP, with as much to eat and drink as she wished. She was growing up so fast and looked so very nice when she got off the aircraft with her modern short-cut hairstyle. She amazed us by deciding not to laze around but get stuck into things and obtained a job at the Public Works Department of the Government, doing general filing, record keeping, simple typing, and general 'dogsbody' duties. She worked five days per week (mornings only) for £1.60 per hour and I added £1 for every £5 that she earned, so that she could accumulate a respectable amount for her labours.

Matters became complicated because at the precise time of the handover of command of CBF, Mr John Stanley MP, who was the Minister for the Armed Forces, insisted on paying a one-week visit to the Islands. Peter would not allow Kip to get involved with the visit and I was deputed to escort him everywhere personally. In the event, despite demanding many changes to the programme, the visit went off splendidly and we seemed to get along pretty well. I was, in fact, rather pleased when I received a long handwritten letter of thanks from him two weeks later, enclosing a collection of very good photos of us taken during his tour.

His tour programme was hectic and wide ranging and is worth detailing as it reveals the diverse nature of the forces in the theatre. After briefing in the Headquarters we flew by helicopter to MPA for a three-hour tour of the new airfield facility before driving down the nine-kilometre road to Mare Harbour, where the new port was being constructed. We then embarked on the Falkland Islands Protection Vessel HMS *Guardian* and sailed out to sea to perform a gunnery firing exercise against flares suspended from parachutes. We then sailed south, round Lafonia and up Falkland Sound to San Carlos Water. We transferred to HMS *Diligence*, the RN engineering repair ship, in time for breakfast and, after a tour of the ship, flew by helicopter all the way down the Sound to Fox Bay where we refuelled en route to the radar site at Mount Alice. We then flew to the other West Falkland radar site of Byron Heights, where we had lunch before flying to the north of Jason Island where we landed on HMS *Reliant* for a one-hour tour before being transferred to the frigate HMS *Danae*. After another tour we witnessed more night shooting and a demonstration of all the other weapon systems before turning in. The next day we flew to Fox Bay where we spent an hour in the field with the Light Infantry doing battle manoeuvres, before visiting a woollen mill owned by the Cockwells, as an example of one of the new industries on which the future of the Falklands depended. Then into the helicopter again, across the Sound to Kelly's Garden, where the Chinooks were based, to see how they interacted with the Light Infantry, who were providing the Quick Reaction Force. After lunch we flew to Blue Beach cemetery, where all the British dead were buried, to lay a wreath and then across the water at San Carlos to visit the Scots Guards home-made memorial in the deserted refrigeration plant at Ajax Bay, before flying all the way to Port Stanley to inspect the Army Air Corps helicopter base. Then a visit to the Light Infantry HQ outside the town before staying overnight with the Royal Engineers. The next day featured a three-hour tour of RAF Stanley and a visit to a Rapier missile site before meetings with local people. The last day was spent in discussion with the civilian councillors and local government before they took him on their own tour. His return to the UK the next day left me exhausted!

Once he departed, however, it was time for me to get together with Kip and get him fully up to speed and to straighten out all the aspects of his new directives for the theatre. Every commander brings something new to the position and, although I had known Kip from the time when we were QFIs together at Cranwell, I knew that it would not be as easy as with Peter as CBF because he had left all the air matters to me and this, I knew, Kip would not do.

Quite cleverly Kip killed two birds with one stone by suggesting that Terry and I flew north to Ascension Island with Madeleine when she returned to school on 6 September. It was a very kind gesture to give us a break after eight months, during which I had only had one weekend off. But it also gave him a full week when I would not be in theatre, to establish himself fully in command.

Our trip did not start in the most auspicious way because the journey along the new road to MPA turned into a nightmare. It started to blizzard as we set off from Stanley and at the exact halfway point a tyre blew out. It took me twenty minutes to change the tyre whilst Terry and Madeleine sheltered inside from the howling snowstorm. The incident left me soaked to the skin and exhausted but I was really fussed over by the crew and flight crew on the journey north. There were only six of us in first class and it was almost like a private flight. On arrival we were given the most tremendous welcome by Group Captain Alan Bowman and Alison his wife, who were determined to repay the hospitality we had shown him when they had visited the Falklands. They drove us to our hutted accommodation by the Officers' Mess in the foothills of Green Mountain and shared drinks with us until we indicated that we needed to get our heads down. Madeleine would continue on home in the Jumbo after we had left, but until then she had the Bowmans' 15-year-old daughter for company and we reminisced about her and the way she was growing up before sleep overcame us.

After breakfast we lazed in the shade of a bougainvillea until it was time to go to a Battle-of-Britain cocktail party which was held outside the Mess on the terraces overlooking the swimming pool in a very un-Falkland-like temperature of 80°F. That evening we relaxed with a film on the video in the Mess followed by drinks with the Hercules crews at the terrace bar. I knew them all and it felt so good to still be called 'boss' by them.

We had been given a Cortina staff car for our stay and so we drove down to the Bowmans at their lovely house in the capital of

Georgetown before going to the opening of the Ascension Historical Society Museum, where champagne was served. At 1400 hours we went to the pier and were transferred by a little boat called the *Red Pepper* to a launch called the *Fairy Lady* owned by a South African, who took us tuna fishing. We fished by trawling and I caught a 10lb Jack which turned out to be the only catch of the day, to my immense satisfaction. It was marvellous just to be cruising along under the hot sun with dolphins gambolling all around us in the bright blue sea and the volcanic shape of Ascension Island thrusting up into the sky as a backdrop. That evening we had a formal dinner at the Bowmans' sitting outside on their large terrace under the vines. The next day was a beach day spent on white sands, which are not really sands but crushed shells, with highly dangerous waves, because if one gets knocked over by a riptide it is almost impossible to stand up or regain one's footing, and drowning becomes a real possibility. That night was spent playing bridge in the Exiles Club, which is a colonial-style club with a decaying air that was straight out of Graham Green or Somerset Maugham. The next day we drove up Green Mountain and walked all the way round a level path near the top that had been built so that the Royal Marines could keep a lookout for French ships sailing south to rescue Napoleon from St Helena. The views were breathtaking and after a visit to the farm, from which the islanders obtained all their fresh produce, we continued our descent to take tea with the Administrator and his wife at the Residency, which is half way up the mountain. Green Mountain is quite extraordinary because it changes from volcanic ash at the bottom to lush vegetation at the top, with thick grass and thickets of bamboo; all resulting from the almost permanent cloud and mist caused by the prevailing moist winds from the south east. Another evening of bridge was followed up by a beach day and plenty of fishing, during which someone else caught a 45lb tuna and a 30lb Wahoo: me, nothing. On the last evening we had dinner at the US base which is used for satellite tracking and communications, and enjoyed steaks, shellfish, and salads such as we had not eaten since our time in the States. The next day we caught the Jumbo south after farewells with Madeleine who would stay with the Bowmans until the Jumbo returned to the UK. Our holidays were over and it was time to return to the reality of the Falklands.

Upon my return I was told that my tour in the Falklands was to be curtailed because it was seen as undesirable to have two airmen in the top two positions and I was, therefore, to be replaced by a Brigadier Brownson at the end of October. I was to be posted to the RAF Personnel Management Centre at RAF Innsworth near Gloucester as the Deputy Air Secretary and Director of Personnel (Policy and Plans). The Air Secretary was an Air Vice-Marshal who controlled all the postings, appointments, promotions, manning and personnel policy of the RAF and my appointment was a one-and-a-half star slot because I was primus inter pares of five air commodores and ran the show in his absence.

The only obvious drawback to the job was that, as it was at Gloucester, I would commute at weekends so that Terry could move back into our house in Purley. There was a certain interest for Dad in the posting because his last tour in the air force had been at RAF Barnwood, looking after airmen records, and the bulk of my staff would be working out of the same satellite site at Barnwood: I would in effect be commanding the very unit at which he had worked and this gave him a real buzz.

With the news about our return to the UK a sudden nostalgia began to creep into our thoughts as well as some sadness. Gypsy gave us such a rapturous welcome as we walked through the door that we became quite choked up at the thought of leaving her in a month's time. It was also sad to sit back and look out of our windows at the waters of the harbour with the petrels swooping and gliding along the shoreline and realize that we would soon not be seeing them again.

In the meantime we were back in harness with us having dinner on HMS *Amazon* and RFA Sir Geraint and a visit from Air Marshal Sir John Sutton to discuss the Force levels required for the future in the Falklands. Heseltine had given us a clear directive that for presentational reasons he wished us to reduce below the 1,950 number of actual Falkland Islanders, so that we were seen not to outnumber them. On a slightly lighter note we had a sheep (called 'Sheep') introduced into our family because she had grazed her owner's garden to exhaustion and ours was in a very lush condition: it suited us to have her 'cut' ours and solved her owner's feeding problems. Gypsy could not believe her luck at having a playmate and spent all her time darting at her and then running up her back: poor Sheep looked very confused, but seemed quite content to have it happen.

Leaving Gypsy to play with Sheep, Terry and I hitched a lift on an RAF Sea King that was doing a surveillance trip to the south and got the crew to drop us off on Sea Lion Islands for the day. The islands are twenty miles south of the most southern part of East Falklands and we were able to spend three hours all by ourselves walking and looking at the wildlife. With most of the creatures not having seen humans before they were quite fearless and we could go right up to the elephant seals to photograph them. The cows were having their babies and there were scores of black furred pups all bleating for milk and turning their huge liquid eyes on us whilst their mothers growled and the bulls reared up and bellowed. At the same time the ferocious Cara Caras (buzzards) were strutting all around us within touching distance and the sweetest little tussock birds quite literally hopped through our legs. There were thousands of Gentoo penguins as well as numerous but fewer Magellans, who had cleverly made their nests under the huge tussock grass clumps and eyed us curiously from the security of their burrows. It was a wonderful last outing prior to our return and left us with indelible memories of this distant remnant of our empire.

On the last night, with all our crates packed and gone, we sat outside the empty bungalow with Gypsy on our laps and reflected on all that we had experienced. We were not sorry to be leaving but knew that we would miss many things that were uniquely Falklands and one of those stretched above us from horizon to horizon – the Milky Way. Untainted and unobscured by pollution, the band of stars were as white and thick as if they had been painted by a brush, and all of them shone steadily because of the clear air; not a twinkle in sight. It was a sight to treasure and a fitting finale to our Falklands odyssey.

Chapter 18

Personnel Matters

The pen is mightier than the sword
Lord Bulwer-Lytton, Richelieu 1839

On 17 November I reported for duty at the RAF's Personnel Management Centre at RAF Innsworth near Gloucester, after having driven there the previous night and taken occupation of the suite in the Officers' Mess that would be my home for the next three years. Terry and I had decided that it was important for her to live in our own home and become 'Mum' to Guy and Madeleine again whilst I would commute home at weekends.

The job at Innsworth was exacting with very long hours but as it was not an operational appointment there was no weekend working and our lives would have a stability in that sense. It would also enable me to work without family distraction during the week and allow Terry to take up employment again as she felt a strong desire to re-establish herself as a person in her own right. For far too long she had been forced to act as 'the wife of' in my support so as to enable me to fulfil myself in my career as well as assuming the command appointments that required a wife's input

I knew all the senior personalities at RAF Innsworth and considered all to be my friends, although not close ones. Apart from acting as the deputy to the Air Secretary my day-to-day activities involved formulating the policy and plans for all the personnel aspects of the RAF and providing a personnel and costing statement on any action or activity of the Service, such as closure of a station, introduction of new equipment, reorganization of the RAF, or straight cost-cutting resulting from reduction in force size. I also produced the overall requirement for numbers of officers and airmen to meet the stated policy of the RAF, and included in this were recruiting targets, promotions and redundancies. The details of these policies were then passed to my fellow air commodores who were tasked with their implementation.

Commuting every weekend was extremely tiring, so Terry decided to come to Innsworth once a month and stay overnight in the Mess with me for the weekend. It not only helped take a little weight off me for the travelling but enabled us to have some real quality time together and to explore the beautiful Cotswold countryside. We used to have the Mess to ourselves and it was almost like being the owners of a very large and luxurious country mansion. We planned a different trip and set of visits for each occasion and these weekends together became mini holidays in which we relaxed, discussed family issues at leisure and without interruption, and rediscovered each other.

I also started writing original papers dealing with such things as the introduction of female pilots and navigators into the RAF, the complete disestablishment of trades such as carpenters and physiotherapists, the revision of all officer branch structures, investigation into poor retention of officer aircrew, and the effect of large scale drawing down of RAF strengths. The latter sprang from the Air Secretary requiring me to front up for the Personnel Department on all finance and long-term costing matters and also to undertake the Secretary of State's (Heseltine's) demands for a ten per cent year-on-year reduction in departmental spending. This resulted in my having regular periods in London at the Ministry of Defence participating in lengthy committee meetings, as the future spending and shape and size of the RAF was determined. I found the experience depressing because there rarely seemed to be long-term visions, but constant disagreements and bickering as each of the three Services, and within them the individual departments, sought to protect their favoured projects. The result, it seemed to me, was a dog's breakfast, often lacking coherence and always in danger of being dismantled by the Treasury and civil servants, who seemed to lack any understanding of the type of fighting forces required by the government to undertake its policies.

I had long since ceased writing a weekly letter to Dad and Auntie Nor, but I made a point of calling him on the phone every weekend and having a cheery and lively exchange with him. At the end of October, however, when I called him he sounded morose and uninterested in anything I had to say. His whole attitude disturbed me and I asked to speak to Auntie Nor to find out what was going on. Her response was alarming because she said that his whole nature appeared to have changed quite suddenly and that he was behaving in a most unpredictable fashion.

So concerned were we that we drove down to Chestfield the very next weekend and were truly alarmed at the way he behaved, as he appeared listless, morose, and uninterested in anything at all. I took him at once to his GP and thus started a nightmare which culminated in his death early in the coming year. I was able to take time off from work so that I could drive him to the Kent and Canterbury Hospital and be with him during the taking of x-rays and the consultant's interviews. The diagnosis was clear as he was riddled with lung and chest cancer, and tumours on his brain were causing his personality changes: he did not have long to live.

We spent as much time as we could with him, but he slipped quietly away on 2 February. I dropped everything, handed over to my deputy and drove straight to Chestfield Road where Terry had joined Carole and Ralph who had spent the weekend there but stayed on when they realized that he was deteriorating so badly.

I spent some time alone with Dad who in death had lost the strained and bothered look that had been so noticeable during the last month. I said my prayers and reflected deeply on all that he had done in his long life and the care and love that had been so much a feature of his relationship with me. I got through that night by immersing myself in the paperwork and actions that always result from the death of a parent, but there was an added feature with Dad's death which Carole highlighted when she said: 'You realize that we are now orphans!'

The pressures of work helped to soften Dad's loss because I was required to make weekly visits to London to handle the financial impact of the many cuts and changes to the personnel structure of the RAF. I was also involved in preparing the original drafts proposing the opening up of all aircrew positions to females, the checking of RAF candidates for HIV/AIDS, and new retention measures for pilots because of the worrying increased outflow to civilian airlines.

There was also, however, happiness as we all joined in the celebrations for Guy's twenty-first birthday party with the whole family gathering in Purley for the weekend of 2/3 May. Terry organized a fantastic spread and I produced enough champagne to float him happily into the great river of life post-twenty-one. Everyone was very generous and for once he looked truly relaxed, happy and comfortable, with no sign of his usual self-restraint.

Terry continued her once-per-month visits to Gloucester and this enabled her to bring Madeleine and her friend Spink down on 26 June to attend a magnificent Summer Ball in the Mess. Terry looked lovely but Madeleine looked quite ravishing and very grown-up in her ball gown and was the centre of attention for many of the young bachelor officers. The two girls really did enjoy themselves and it is occasions like this that make one, as a parent, feel very proud and convinced that all one's efforts have been worthwhile.

As the year began to come to an end I started the heartbreaking ritual of having Christmas as we had always had it, but without Dad. Carole and Ralph came to us on Christmas Eve and I suppose we did have a happy time, but I wanted to cry every time I saw Auntie in her chair on the other side of the lounge fire, but with the matching chair empty. Terry produced a magnificent Christmas Day meal and there was a lot of laughter but the toast to absent friends and our departed parents did cause some real tears. Auntie said that she felt Dad's death more keenly then at any other time and it was a very sad little old lady that we returned to Chestfield.

However, 1988 started with a bang with the Air Secretary telling me formally that I was to be promoted on 20 June to the rank of Air Vice-Marshal in order to take over as the Senior Directing Staff (Air) at the Royal College of Defence Studies. My immediate feeling was, strangely, not one of exultation at the news but of relief that I was going to soon be leaving Gloucester and be able to live with my family at Purley. I had not the slightest trepidation about being able to do the job because I knew and loved the work within the RCDS. I decided not to phone Terry but to give her the news when I drove home that weekend because I wanted to savour the whole experience of her reaction and to be able to immediately get involved in the inevitable planning and speculating. In the event I could not have made a better decision and that weekend was a blur of celebration and speculation.

It also came at an appropriate moment because Terry and I were suddenly faced with the news that Guy had applied to join the RAF and would be going to the Officer and Aircrew Selection Centre at RAF Biggin Hill on 5 March to undergo the selection process. He knew that I would try to deter him from trying to follow in my footsteps and had, accordingly, gone to a recruiting office without a word to us. I drove him across to Biggin Hill and, with all sincerity and from the bottom of my heart, wished him all success. When I picked him up four days later he was on top of the world because he was convinced that he had done well and this hope proved well founded when he was informed that he had indeed been selected for aircrew training. The only disappointment was that as there were so few pilot vacancies he had had to accept training as a navigator: he would report to the RAF College at Cranwell on 6 October. We were really very proud of his achievement and despite Terry's concerns about the danger involved (a typical Mum's fears that did not appear to be ameliorated by the fact that she was married to a pilot herself) were rather thrilled that he had chosen to follow in his Dad's footsteps.

My working life seemed to drag at Gloucester as I, literally, ticked off the days remaining until my move. Madeleine seemed to thrive at school during her final year and turned in a marvellous performance in the school production of the *Diary of Anne Frank,* in which she played the pregnant Niep. Terry reckoned that it was as realistic a performance as anyone could give and wonderful training for when she did eventually become pregnant!

The mind-numbing car commuting had been getting to me and I decided to make a change to my car when I came across a new sports car that Toyota were introducing. The MR2 was a pure two-seater with very racy lines and appealed to me in the way that my MG and Triumphs had. I justified it on the safety aspects of acceleration and powerful braking system which would get me out of any dicey situation that could occur on the winding A40, and traded in the Corolla for my fun machine. Almost immediately we gave it an opportunity to flex its muscles when Mike Graydon invited us to spend four days with him at his mansion in Belgium where he was serving a one-star appointment at NATO's military headquarters, SHAPE, located at Mons. Terry and I went across on the ferry on 7 April and I nudged the car along at more than 100mph on the Belgian motorway. Mike and Liz treated us royally and we went to parties at the Mess and in private homes as well as being taken on conducted tours of the battlefield and museum of Waterloo and, of course, Brussels, where we ate ourselves to a standstill on mussels at Vincennes. The MR2 was much admired and proved to be as much fun to drive as I had hoped. Once again we let her stretch her legs on the return to Dunkirk with Terry behind the wheel and, much to my chagrin, she refused to surrender the keys at Ramsgate and insisted on doing the drive home to Purley.

June brought with it our special celebration of our Silver Wedding anniversary and a decision to not have a family get-together but to go abroad. Terry had long hankered to revisit Cyprus where she had spent a happy part of her childhood and which she had envied me for visiting on so many occasions since our marriage. Accordingly, we left the UK on 12 June for Limassol and hired a car so that we could tour the island with the most nostalgic visit being to Berengeria where Terry had been to school; the establishment was still there and as far as she could see was unchanged from her time in the late 1950s. As I knew the Station Commander at RAF Akrotiri I was able to give her a VIP tour of the base, down Tom Collins drinks with her in the Mess, and swim and sunbathe at Cape Gata beach. The night of our anniversary we spent in the hotel because there was a special Cypriot entertainment evening with a lavish meal and the management providing us with free champagne for our special occasion. We danced until the early hours and spent a marvellously quiet time on the patio overlooking the sea, reflecting on all that had happened to us in the twenty-five years of our marriage. Yes, there had been some lows, and the car crash had reshaped our lives, but at the same time had strengthened us as a couple. The highs, however, were too numerous to list and the wonder and glory of our two children put everything else into perspective. We had been lucky beyond all measure and we returned home on 20 June with light hearts and the excitement of knowing that I was to start the next phase of my career in the rank of Air Vice-Marshal the very next day.

Chapter 19

Winding Down

By good fortune in the game of military snakes and ladders, I found myself a general

Viscount Slim, 1959

Opening the familiar front door of Seaford House in Belgrave Square and stepping inside rolled back time as if the years since my attendance at the college had been but a dream, and I settled into my role as the senior airman at the college as though I was slipping on an old familiar well-loved coat.

I was to take ten members with me on a tour starting in Finland on 11 September and visiting France and Germany before going behind the Iron Curtain to Czechoslovakia and Hungary. With three countries that I had never visited and with two of them being members of the Warsaw Pact, I had a keen sense of anticipation as we lifted off from Heathrow for Helsinki in the luxury of the first-class seating. Three hours later I was being embraced by Colonel Perrti Nykanen, my very dear friend from my own 1984 RDCS Course: a clear indication of the valuable networking resulting from RDCS Course attendance.

Our six days in Finland included the usual mix of military, civil, industrial, and political visits spiced with overwhelming social hospitality and some memorable events. My first surprise, however, was how flat and watery Finland was, as we used Russian-built MIL helicopters to travel everywhere over endless lake systems interspersed with massive forests. After one such flight we landed in the Arctic circle at Rovanieimi where, magically, we were whisked to Santa's Workshop and had a lengthy session with the great man himself before being allowed to pat his reindeer. It was surreal to see the CIA member of the course shaking Santa's hand and promising to be good for the rest of the year!

We arrived in Paris on 16 September and were then taken under the wings of the Ambassador, Sir Ewen Fergusson for a heavyweight series of presentations and discussions. It was almost a relief to climb aboard the TGV train at the Gare de Lyon for the five-hour trip to Marseilles and a very relaxing visit to the French Navy at Toulon. This was followed by a superb trip to Nimes where General de Brigade Pinceuin gloried in displaying the virtues of his 6th Light Armoured Division. I nearly came to grief when my leather-shod feet slipped on the sleek steel upper works of a tank, only to be caught in the arms of a giant French Foreign Legion soldier who, with a huge grin on his face and in the softest of Irish accents, said: "Twould not be in the best interest for Anglo-Irish relations to let the general fall flat on his arse!'

What an impressive outfit was the 6th LAD and their precision, professionalism and pride left a lasting impression on us all, as did the beautiful environment of the lovely city of Nimes with its many Roman remains.

It was a complete culture shock to arrive in Bonn for the German stage of the tour on 23 September, but a Rhine cruise to Koblenz softened the welter of presentations and visits that concluded with a flight to Munich, courtesy of the Luftwaffe. We left Munich on 30 September for the train ride to Prague. Innocent though this seemed, it set the scene for a very ugly confrontation the next day when we met about a dozen hatchet-faced Czech generals. Lieutenant General Brychta launched into a tirade in which he stated that it was insensitive of us to arrive by train from Munich on the fiftieth anniversary (to the day) of the signing by Chamberlain of the infamous piece of paper with Adolf Hitler, that condemned Czechoslovakia to the Nazi rule and what was I, as an English general, going to do about it? I could sense the Ambassador inching away from me until I became an isolated figure trying to respond to the proposal that I should immediately get my government to revoke the past and make a public apology. With no help from anyone I played every card that I could until the situation ended in a stalemate but with the assurance that as military men we should not be drawn into political minefields and that we were essentially brothers in arms. For the next four days I worked furiously at establishing this accord and on our departure I was locked in stifling bear hugs by my new 'friends' who pledged lasting friendship and a new relationship between us.

After an overnight stay in Bratislava to view a collective farm we travelled by coach to Budapest for five fascinating days before our return to the UK. Hungary was so very different to Czechoslovakia as the hardline communists of the latter were replaced by more relaxed cosmopolitan individuals who gave me every indication that they would not be averse to a move away from their Russian masters. We were even allowed to converse with Hungarian soldiers, though from their wide eyed responses it appeared that they regarded us as some sort of dangerous alien species.

The visits to these two Warsaw Pact countries made a great impression on me because they are beautiful lands with generous, friendly people who were struggling with an imposed centralized system and creed that was stifling them. I longed to see them break free and reported, on my return, that Hungary was giving all the indications that, given the right circumstances, she would not be averse to change. Little did I realize how soon that change would be. Upon our return the rest of the RCDS term passed in a flash with my mind being taken off things with the news that Guy would be starting his Initial Officer Training at the RAF College at Cranwell on 6 November. When the time came and we said our au revoirs to him it brought back so many memories of my own departure thirty-four years before and amidst our own sadness there was also a sense of pride that he had decided on a similar career to mine and climbed the first rung. It was in a turmoil of emotion that we saw him start on his new journey.

The course ended in a flurry of parties and emotional farewells before the college closed down and we welcomed Guy home on 18 December for his Christmas break: he had clearly done well, was enjoying meeting the demands of his course, and looking forward to the start of his flying career. I picked up Auntie Nor on 23 December, Carole and Ralph arrived on Christmas Eve and we all went to St Mary's Church for the midnight mass prior to a wonderful Christmas Day with a magnificent lunch and a mountain of presents. The year had ended on a high note and we looked forward with anticipation to 1989.

1989

A hubbub greeted me upon my arrival at Seaford House on 9 January 1989 with the eighty new members milling around in the reception hall. I established contact with all the RAF members and then had my first meeting of the seminar group that I would be looking after for the year. I was determined to stamp my own personality on the course and Terry and I gave three buffet luncheons in the first month to entertain all the air force and seminar members with their wives. With the breakthrough established we enjoyed the happiest of relations with all of them for the rest of the course.

Guy was continuing to receive good reports from Cranwell and in anticipation of his graduation at the end of March I pulled some strings so that I could act as the Reviewing Officer for the occasion. The day of the graduation for No. 115 Initial Officer Training Course dawned warm and cloudless and under azure skies I tried to give a Command

Performance for the particular benefit of my son. Terry looked lovely and stood out from all the other ladies as she was escorted to the special seat behind the dais, where I could see her as I arrived just as four Jet Provosts flew over in box formation. The parade was impeccable and I nearly choked with pride as I came face to face with Guy during my inspection: he looked so very smart and mature and responded to me with no sign of emotion whilst I knew that I was grinning like a Cheshire cat. Terry felt tears running down her cheeks as he marched past us whilst I took the salute, and I nearly cracked up during my peroration from the dais. An unexpected surprise was the low-level fly-past of a Hercules in my honour at the conclusion of the parade and it signalled the end of a perfect day. Sometimes in life you can have events which are so perfect in their constitution and composition that you are reassured that your life's work has been all so very worthwhile: and 30 March 1989 was just such a day.

Guy spent some time with us before reporting for the start of his navigator training at RAF Finningley, near Doncaster (where I had carried out my Jetstream refresher). His mood was one of exhilaration and anxiety as he confessed that he didn't know how he would cope with the academics and was uncertain as to how he would like operational flying.

In September we departed on the overseas tours with my taking ten members to South Asia. We left on 10 September for Delhi where we were met by the Defence Attaché before being hosted at the reception cocktail party by the High Commissioner, Sir David Goodall. The two weeks that we spent in India were a very clever mix of professional, social, and tourist activity, so that we could see all arms of the Indian armed forces at work, but at locations that enabled us to visit the major tourist attractions. Thus we travelled by train to Agra to spend time with their Parachute Brigade but also to visit the breathtaking Taj Mahal, which I found more staggeringly beautiful than pictures could ever portray.

We travelled to Jodhpur to view the Indian air defences but, whilst staying at the luxurious Maharajah's Umaid Bhawan Palace, now a hotel, I succumbed to a stomach bug and became so ill that it was feared that I might have amoebic dysentery. Confined to my room the tour group had to leave me and I rejoined them three days later in New Delhi feeling very much the worse for wear.

Then it was on to Kashmir for two of the most heavenly days of my life, during which we stayed on a huge houseboat at Srinagar on Dal Lake. Exquisitely decorated and built of fragrant cedar planks, Mother India left an indelible impression as I watched the sun set over the placid lake from my lounger on the aft deck with a scotch and soda in my hand. Medicinal of course! Our purpose for the visit was to liaise with the Indian troops guarding their side of the Line of Control that splits this divided country and we all came away with the feeling that only a full scale war could change things. One unexpected delight, however, was exposure to the local papier mâché industry, for which the area is famous and I came away laden with the exquisite objects which now decorate many of the rooms in our house.

We were soon to receive a counter briefing to all that we had experienced when we crossed into Pakistan for three days of briefing and discussion at Islamabad. The Ambassador (Pakistan had not at this time been readmitted to the Commonwealth), Mr Barrington, escorted us for a one-hour session with the President and he and all the Service Chiefs gave us very detailed reasons for their side of the dispute with India: there seemed to be very little room for manoeuvre. After visiting Lahore we moved on to Peshawar where the Commanding General took us in convoy up the Khyber Pass to the frontier with Afghanistan. I found it very hard to believe that I was travelling up this famous pass where there was constant evidence of the previous occupation by British troops. The forts were very obvious but more evocative were the regimental insignia carved into the rock faces and the lonely burial grounds. I was treated with enormous respect and following lunch at the Afghan Rifles Officers' Mess the troops, dressed in full ceremonial costume, performed a stirring martial dance and then presented me with two ceremonial Pathan knives with 6in blades.

We arrived in Colombo, Sri Lanka, on 2 October to find that there was a curfew in place with roadblocks everywhere because of some recent Tamil Tiger atrocities. We were provided with military protection and were flown everywhere so that there was no chance of ambushing. The Sri Lankan forces were small but well organized and with a constant running guerrilla war against the Tigers were fully stretched. They could not have been more hospitable and it was with some regret that we said our goodbyes on 6 October for our flight home. Another memorable tour packed full of new experiences.

An even more memorable experience was just around the corner, however, when we left the UK for the RCDS visit to NATO in the Northern and Central Region. After our time spent in Norway we were joined by our wives in Berlin on 23 November to be greeted by the momentous news that the East Germans had opened all the crossing points between East and West Berlin and the Berlin Wall (as the physical divider of the city) was an object of history. We were all loaded into a coach and, with barely a check, cruised through the Allied Checkpoint Charlie and toured East Berlin without hindrance. Although we had been through the Wall before, the atmosphere this time was electric and you could see East Berliners pouring through the checkpoints in their thousands and staggering back, laden with consumables. The memory that stands out above all others, however, is that of a never-ceasing chipping noise as hundreds of people knocked chunks out of the Wall as souvenirs: I have my own piece of Wall in my rolltop desk, and some very atmospheric photos of Terry standing with her back to the graffiti-covered Wall. After three days of revisiting the sights of the city and going to the opera and a concert we flew home with some of the most vivid memories of actually being part of an event of historical significance.

Of less historic importance but, perhaps, with greater emotional impact was our trip north to attend the wedding of Terry's friend Mandy to Richard Sutton at St Andrew's Church, Aysgarth in Yorkshire on 16 December. We were allowed to stay for the weekend in the VIP suite of the Officers' Mess at RAF Leeming, which enabled us to roll back twenty-six years and revisit the scenes of our courtship and our first little home in Bedale. We looked over my old room in the Mess, visited Terry's butcher Mr Megson, our flat in Bedale, the Leeming Garth Motel where I proposed to her, and all the various parts of the station where we had both worked. Lastly we visited St Gregory's Church and spent some time praying and quietly thinking about all those people who had been part of our lives and so enriched it over the years.

1990
The RAF contingent on the 1990 RCDS Course was a very strong one and included some old friends like Tony Bagnell, John Day, Mike Donaldson and Tim Thorn, as well as some rising stars that I had not met before such as Rocky Goodall, Dick Best, Peter Eustace, Mike Smart, Peter Mackey and Richard Fletcher. A good, friendly and hard-working bunch they all went on to make their mark in the Service and I considered them the best group that I had looked after.

The course proceeded in its own measured and enjoyable pattern but life was made far more interesting because Terry and I had been participating in a night-school course since the previous September to qualify us for yachting certificates. This was all part of our plan to buy a yacht following my retirement and to spend part of the year sailing in overseas waters. We undertook a course which would qualify us for our skipper or competent crew certificates and in April we went to Gosport for a week's practical sailing under the auspices of the RAF Sailing Association. We had a marvellous week on a 34ft Contessa-class yacht called *Flarepath* under the supervision of Squadron Leader Hall. Terry was the only lady with five males and, apart from disliking the cold, enjoyed herself immensely. We ran through the full gamut of yacht operation with each person having an examination on the last day. We kept to the Solent but berthed in a different port every night from Port Solent, Yarmouth, Newtown, Shamrock Quay, Cowes, Lymington, Bucklers Hard and Hamble, and had one very adventurous night-sailing experience. We logged 100 miles of sailing in winds up to Force 7 and consumed more liquor than was decent. *Flarepath* was a boat that handled beautifully and it was with some regret that we said goodbye and returned home on 19 April to the humdrum existence of Purley. There was something quite magical about holding a straining tiller with one side of the boat awash and the feeling of slicing through the water before ordering and executing a precise tacking manoeuvre. Terry's waterborne skills were excellent and she agreed that it would be fun to own a boat but we must sail it somewhere warm!

A concentrated period of lectures preceded our departure on the RCDS overseas tours but we were able to fit in a visit to the SBAC Air Show at Farnborough on 5 September. I called in a few favours and set up the day for Uncle Bill in such a way as to repay him for all the magnificent entertainment he had given me at the Air Shows over so many years when he was fronting for GEC on their stand and caravan. We lunched splendidly at the RAF Farnborough Officers' Mess and then, after taking in all the static displays, were entertained by the Superintendent of RAE Farnborough in his President's enclosure on the north side of the runway. The beauty of this was that the aircraft in the flying display passed almost overhead as they were kept on the opposite side of the runway from the public, and the impression and sound was breathtaking. We returned home exhausted but happy and on the following day, before he returned home, Uncle Bill held us enthralled by telling us about all his wartime experiences, including his being shot down in his Blenheim and his five years as a POW in Germany. Reluctantly we let him go and two days later I set off in charge of a ten-man group visiting Latin America. Little did I realize that I would never see him again.

Our first leg on the tour was the long haul from London to Maiquetia Airport for our week's stay in Caracas, Venezuela. Upon arrival HM Ambassador, Mr Giles Fitzherbert entertained us to a lavish cocktail party where I was introduced to the Minister of Defence, Vicealmirante Hector Toro and the Inspector General of the Armed Forces, General Edwardo Jiminez. I got on famously with them both and this was to pay dividends later when the General made personal arrangements for us to be taken on a Venezuelan Air Force aircraft to view the Angel Falls. The sight of this waterfall, the highest in the world at 3,000ft, was unforgettable, as the solid jet of water cascading from the top of the plateau gradually atomized into a fine spray before reaching the pool at the bottom. The falls are one of the most spectacular sights in the world but are inaccessible and can only be viewed by tourists from the air after a flight lasting for an hour: we were more than fortunate to be given the chance.

Our week in Venezuela was the usual mix of meetings, discussions, dinners, and cocktail parties but the highlight was a day spent in the jungle on the border with Columbia. On arrival at Guerrero Air Base the general commanding the area escorted us to a river which forms the border and went on patrol with us as we assessed the army's ability to control the kidnappers and drug runners that infest the area. Suitably impressed after a very operational sortie we repaired to a jungle clearing where the general and I had the first slices from an ox that was turning slowly on a spit over a glowing fire: after we had been served all the rest of the troops fell on the carcase and a magnificent barbecue party ensued.

Also impressive was the emphasis on the Venezuelan oil industry in Lake Maracaibo and in Zubia State, which is vital to the United States who obtain twenty per cent of their needs from it. Even more intriguing was our visit to the Guri Dam on the Orinoco, which is the largest hydro-electric dam in the world (and is guarded by missile batteries), and a detailed brief on the massive coal tar deposits in the Orinoco which stretch all the way to Trinidad and Tobago. If a way can be found to extract and process it commercially the deposits could yield an unbelievable amount of oil.

With some reluctance we bade farewell to Venezuela and moved on to Mexico where the highlight on the cultural side was a visit to the archaeological site at Teojuacán to view the Inca civilization and to be suitably awed by the sacrificial aspects of their lives and the magnificence of the buildings that remain. We were also suitably awed by a visit to the Heroic Military Academy, where all the officers of their three Services are trained, because the size of the academy is astounding. I was, therefore, totally surprised by the request of the Commandant to speak to all the cadets once he had put all 4,500 of them on parade and had to extemporize wildly whilst our Ambassador, Mr Michael Simpson-Orlebar, smiled gently at my discomfort.

Our next port of call was Chile where we were looked after most attentively by the Ambassador, Mr Richard Nielson. After comprehensive meetings with the heads of all the government departments we made a trip to Valparaiso to spend time with the navy, a visit to the El Teniente Copper Mine (high in the Andes with condors gliding overhead) and a marvellous visit to the El Diablo vineyard. We were, therefore, in good shape to make the most sensitive of our visits to our former antagonist, Argentina.

Very well aware of the potential for problems as I was the first senior military man to visit the country since the war (and they had been briefed on my part in it and also that I had been Deputy Commander of British Forces in the Falklands for a year), I was overwhelmed by the courtesy, friendliness, and very positive intent to re-establish relationships between our two countries. I was left in no doubt that they wished to 'recover' Las Malvinas but they were intent on not letting this be an insurmountable problem to re-establishing good relations. I responded by laying a wreath on their memorial to their war dead and ensuring that the media reported my comments on the bravery of the Argentines involved. We spent most of our time in the vicinity of Buenos Aires and despite all the intensive discussions, presentations, visits and meetings, the thing that the group talked about most was the fact that we sat next to Eric Clapton on a visit to a tango show and actually spoke to the great man.

All our fascinating tour was, however, put firmly into perspective for me on my return to the UK when Terry met me with the news that Uncle Bill had died and the funeral had been held for my return on the very next day at Ashingdon in Essex. He had suffered a massive stroke and died instantly as he fell to the floor of his home in Ashingdon. The funeral service was a moving memorial to a great man and I chose to wear full uniform as a tribute to his service to our country in time of war and the long five years that he spent as a prisoner of war. Another very important person had disappeared from my life but I knew that I would never forget the impact he had had on me or his enduring friendship.

A very special event was planned for 9 November when I was to be one of the guests of honour at the fiftieth anniversary dinner of RAF Lyneham. The dinner was magnificent and the occasion memorable for having nine past Station Commanders present, who were all able to wallow in nostalgic recollection of their time in command. I stayed overnight with my friend Wing Commander Peter Bedford but awoke in the early hours with agonizing abdominal pains and, after a visit from the Station Medical Officer, was taken by ambulance to the nearby RAF hospital at Wroughton were I was misdiagnosed as suffering from gallstones. The delay incurred as a result of this misdiagnosis nearly killed me because my appendix had burst and I was in fact suffering from peritonitis. The group captain consultant realized immediately what had happened when he came on duty and performed emergency surgery to save me. In this he was successful but repeated complications (all resulting from the delayed surgery) kept me in hospital for a month and caused me to shed 3st in weight. Terry brought me home in the week before Christmas with my weight below 10st and a feeling that I had lost all my strength and, most surprisingly for me, an almost complete lack of will to do anything for myself to aid my recovery.

1991

As I entered my last full year of Royal Air Force service I discussed my future with Group Captain John Preston, who managed the affairs of all air rank officers and, to my disappointment, was told that there were no plans for my promotion. The 3-star slots for the next year had already been determined and, although I was a strong contender, unless something unplanned happened, I was expected to serve out my career in a 2-star position. It was agreed, therefore, that I should remain at RCDS.

With my mind cleared and my health on the upturn I turned my full attention to the new course. I did, however, suddenly feel my age when I realized that I did not know on a personal basis any of the ten RAF members on the course. Five of them I knew by reputation but not a single one had I met before: such is the rate of change and advancement in the Service.

In April my peritonitis wound suffered a hernia when my insides tried to become my outsides. The doctors were not unduly alarmed because my whole wound had opened up and there was, therefore, no danger of strangulation, but arranged for an early return to the RAF hospital at Wroughton for a repair job. I was driven there by staff car on 23 April and the same surgeon opened me up, sorted matters out and sewed me up on 24 April. After two days on a morphine drip I had two days convalescing in the hospital and was then allowed home on 29 April: I never looked back because, as my surgeon said, 'you have the constitution of an ox'.

My wound healed well and I was, therefore, in good shape by the beginning of September when I gathered my brood of ten members at Heathrow for our flight to Washington to start our five-week RCDS tour of Canada, the United States and Barbados.

We started by flying to Washington DC for a day spent with our Ambassador, Sir Robin Renwick, and the Head of the British Defence Staff, Air Vice-Marshal Peter Dodworth. Peter was an old friend of mine and he ensured that we had excellent briefings to prepare us for our tours of Canada and the United States because, after spending nine days in Canada moving from east to west, we would be entering the States at Seattle and not revisiting Washington until the end of the tour.

We stayed at the impressive Chateau Laurier Hotel in Ottawa whilst meeting the most influential members of the Canadian government and the heads of their armed forces. Ottawa is a lovely city but could not touch the scenic aspects of Quebec which we visited next, so that we could experience and question the 'francophone' aspects of Canada. We spent all our time in the company of French-speaking Canadians including the Secretaire-General du Secretariat aux Affairs Intergovernmentales Canadienes, before being given a reception by '2e

Bataillon Royal 22e Regiment'. We were left in no doubt that the Province regarded itself as different and quite capable of standing by itself.

Quite different was the atmosphere at Edmonton, which is an industrial city, but the memories of my time as OC 24 squadron came flooding back when the military part of our visit included the Canadian Forces Base at Edmonton, where my sister Hercules squadron was still based. Disappointingly for me all my friends had moved on but I was given a very special welcome by the current Officer Commanding.

After a visit to Vancouver we started a whistle-stop tour of the United States. We were suddenly drawn into the most up-to-date aspects of military might by making our first visit in the States to the Submarine Base Bangor, where Admiral Marsh took us under his wing before handing us over to Captain Woodman who, very proudly, gave us a three-hour tour of his nuclear Poseidon-equipped missile delivery submarine the USS *Alabama*. Unarguably the most awesome and powerful weapon system in the world, we were all stunned by its size and complexity, and the eerie feeling of walking between the huge tubes containing the missiles was unlike anything I had ever experienced before. With considerable reluctance I left (clutching my *Alabama* captain's baseball cap) for an afternoon spent with Boeing at their Seattle plant, watching the manufacture of 747 and 777 aircraft, (memories of my visit to the plant with Air Chief Marshal Sir Neil Wheeler intruded).

We had two days at the Californian capital of Sacramento for intensive briefings on the State Legislature and Executive before being hosted by the California National Guard so that we could see what an effective force they are and how they interact with the regular forces. We moved from State to Federal aspects when we next went to Omaha, Nebraska for time at HQ Strategic Air Command, where Lieutenant General Leo Smith, the Vice C-in-C SAC, revealed the awesome power of the air-delivered might of the US and the extraordinary command, communication and control of the Command.

It was rather a relief to fly to New Orleans for a weekend break, where I had arranged for Bill Fisher to meet us and stay in the same Monte Leone Hotel, in Rue Royal. He joined us for breakfast at Brennan's which developed into a noisy party and kept going, as he showed us all the delights of the French Quarter. We spent the evening at various jazz clubs and said our goodbyes in an alcohol-fuelled haze of bonhomie prior to departing for MacDill AFB and our visit to HQ Central Command and HQ US Special Operations Command. In the light of what has happened in the Gulf and Afghanistan our visit could not have been better timed because we touched on nearly all the elements that have since been involved. After visiting Martin Marietta on 1 October we flew north to New York, where we took in the UN, Police Operations, Wall Street and inner city regeneration before heading south to Washington, where we had a visit to the Pentagon, hosted by Admiral Jeremiah, the Vice Chairman of the Joint Chiefs of Staff before the icing on the cake – a half-day visit to the Central Intelligence Agency at Langley. Seven Agency officers, all wearing their RCDS ties, gave us a really warm welcome and we then were given remarkable access to the operations, planning and communications aspects of the CIA: the members of my group were all very quiet after the visit, as we had been given a great deal to think about and were very aware of the privilege that had been extended to us.

It was rather an anticlimax to fly down to Barbados, but after a few gin slings at the Hilton in Bridgetown the world seemed a much better place. Quite naturally my ex-RCDS colleague, Brigadier Rudi Lewis, looked after us in his capacity as Chief of Staff of the Barbados Defence Force. He ensured that our visit was informative and hugely enjoyable so that we could take away the fondest memories of this small island. Dame Nita Barrow, the Governor General, met us and spent considerable time putting the Caribbean into a clear perspective as well as warning us of the dangers of the island as a drug distribution staging post into Europe: hence the presence in the island of a British Advisory Team. Rudi took us on a full tour of Barbados and we enjoyed a marvellous lunch and briefing about the old sugar plantations at the beautifully preserved plantation house of St Nicholas Abbey. Our final day was spent at Paynes Bay, where Commander Mick Humphreys had his home with its garden running down to the beach. We barbecued, drank, swam and sunbathed; it was this memory that stayed with us back in the UK on 11 October, long after the intense discussions on missile technology and Martin Marietta had been forgotten!

The rest of the course passed in a flash although we did have a memorable visit to AFNORTH, at Oslo, Evenes, and Bodo after the standard NATO visit in Brussels. The edge did, however, seem to be rather blunted with the collapse of communism and there was a feeling everywhere of people trying to reinvent themselves and re-establish their positions as necessary for the future.

I was very touched when, on 25 November, I was taken to the RAF Club by the RAF members of the course and given a formal 'lunching-out', with the presentation of a whisky decanter and a solid silver plaque inscribed 'AVM Clive Evans. From the 1991 RCDS Light Blue'. The lunch was delicious, the wines carefully selected, and the words in tribute apparently heartfelt. I was made to feel very special and the event turned out to be more significant then I had imagined because it was the only event that was to mark my retirement from the Service.

In fact the end of my RAF Service was a complete anticlimax because my replacement arrived at the college at the beginning of 1992 and, as I was told in no uncertain terms that it would not be politic for me to hang around, I arranged to go to Catterick for February and March on a computer course. At the end of this I was given accrued leave up to my retirement date of 21 April and, upon reaching this date, received a formal letter from the Secretary of State for Defence 'Having it in command from Her Majesty the Queen to convey to you on leaving the Active list of the Royal Air Force her thanks for your long and valuable service'.

Rather strangely I did quite literally drift into retirement and it has always remained with me as a rather odd way to have ended my service career which had occupied, at thirty-seven-and-a-half years, slightly more than half of the whole time that the RAF had been in existence. I was, therefore, particularly grateful for the thoughtfulness of the members of the 1991 RCDS who had given me my only 'farewell'.

I woke on 21 April surrounded by cards and presents from the family who had certainly not forgotten me and wondered what retirement had in store for me.

Chapter 20

Days of Wine and Roses

Old soldiers never die; they only fade away
Anonymous

I really need not have had any concerns because my retired life turned out to be nearly as varied and interesting as my time in the RAF. I did, quite deliberately, put all flying behind me but continued my Service relationship by chairing Retired Officer Selection Boards for the MOD and also becoming, for ten years, one of the Commissioners of the Duke of York's Royal Military School at Dover. I also, with my friend Gerry Crumbie, became involved in a commercial IT venture called Merlin Aviation, became the Representative Deputy Lieutenant for the Borough of Sutton, and agreed to act as the President of the Surrey Wing of the Air Training Corps.

I joined Rotary, which enabled me to enjoy not only the company and aspirations of fellow Rotarians but to indulge in a considerable amount of sailing whilst acting as crew on yachts owned by them. I took up golf and, after two council-run art courses, regained my latent interest in watercolour painting. Any spare moments became occupied by dog walking because Guy had given me a surprise retirement present in the form of an elegant black Lurcher (Skygee) who became my inseparable companion and the most faithful of friends.

I was also called back to full Service duty in 1993 and 1994 when asked to lead RCDS tour parties on the overseas tours to the Far East (Japan, Korea, Hong Kong, and Singapore) then lastly to Sub-Saharan Africa (Tanzania, Zimbabwe, South Africa, and Namibia).

On the domestic front our children got married and our grandchildren arrived. The pace of life changed and family affairs gradually replaced the more active and demanding professional activities, with the grandchildren occupying more of our time as they grew and developed.

Life does mellow as one ages but the zest for life remains and the great beauty of retirement is that one can shape it as one chooses. And, as I sit in my study surrounded by the memorabilia and photographs of myself and Terry from our RAF years, I realize just how incredibly lucky I have been.

I was born at a time when I can remember the demands caused by a global war and the deprivations that followed, but also the determination of our country to re-establish itself. I grew up fully aware of the threat posed by Russia and the Warsaw Pact and felt that I was playing a full part in restraining the advance of communism by doing something that I found more exciting and enjoyable than I could have believed: indeed flying for me was an intrinsic and necessary part of my life.

By good fortune I met and married a lovely girl who turned into a perfect mother and, as a wife, motivated me to realize my potential. And everywhere I met and found friends who enriched my life.

Has anyone, ever, been so lucky!

Index